THE
KING'S
SMUGGLER

THE
KING'S
SMUGGLER

Jane Whorwood
Secret Agent to Charles I

JOHN FOX

For Glen, Karl, Mark, Daniel,
With Ellen and Osian
Our 'Secret Islanders'

First published 2010

The History Press
The Mill, Brimscombe Port
Stroud, Gloucestershire, GL5 2QG
www.thehistorypress.co.uk

British Library Cataloguing in Publication Data.
A catalogue record for this book is available from the British Library.

ISBN 978 0 7524 5001 8

Typesetting and origination by The History Press
Printed in India by Aegean Offset Printers, New Delhi

Contents

List of Illustrations

Preface and Acknowledgements

My wife and family have put up with Jane Whorwood and Holton's 'secret island' for years. In fact, Holton Park's landscape, evocative and barely chronicled, prompted the search which became this book. The editors of the *Oxford Dictionary of National Biography* trusted me with their new article, *Jane Whorwood*, in 2009. Stephanie Jenkins, Kevin Heritage and Nigel Philips enthused me about the Whorwoods, whose former home, Holton Park, now 'Wheatley Park', hosts a comprehensive school. It enriches their teaching of history. Marian Brown of St Bartholomew's church, Holton, and Julia Dobson of Holton village, 'history whisperers', encouraged me quietly. Caroline Dalton's hoard of local wills and Kay Hay's midlands discoveries have been unofficial archives, while professional staff – ever cheerful at the Bodleian; thoughtful at Lambeth Palace – have helped greatly. These include Guildhall Library, British Library, London School of Economics, The National Archive at Kew, National Archives of Scotland, Royal Library at Windsor Castle, municipal and county archives in Westminster, Kingston, Windsor, Oxfordshire, Kent, Surrey, Dover Cinque Ports, Newport IoW and the English and Scottish National Portrait Galleries. Christie's auction house also chimed in. I cannot hope to comb the tens of thousands of seventeenth-century wills held in TNA, Kew, let alone those in Edinburgh, but the several hundred which I have explored threw up many unexpected clues to Jane Whorwood's life. No book is a final word. I hope this one is presented humbly enough to welcome finds and revisions, and that the reading is as enjoyable as the search has been. Simon Hamlet and the editorial staff at The History Press have been patient with my afterthoughts and additions.

John Prest, fellow Vetelegan and Balliol historian, read my manuscript, claiming with typical modesty to represent only 'the mythical general reader'. Allan Dell shared his ancestor, William Dell; Emma Clarke-Bolton of Sarah Eastel Locations guided me through the maze which is English Heritage; Robin Harcourt Williams and Victoria Perry on behalf of the Marquess of Salisbury were hospitably efficient; Rosalind Marshall gave freely of her expertise on the Hamiltons and, with Bruce Royan, kindly secured me access to the *Virtual Hamilton Palace* research project; Mark Bateson of Canterbury Cathedral, Sarah Poynting of Keele University, Malcolm Gaskill of the University of East Anglia, Martin Maw of OUP and my numismatist friends from the Ashmolean (Heberden) Coin Room patiently fielded my sometimes gormless questions; Antony Green, anthropologist and former pupil, 'combed out' red hair for me; Tim Wilson, Curator of Western Art at the Ashmolean, and Philippa Glanville, formerly Curator of Metalwork, Plate and Jewellery at the Victoria and Albert Museum, pondered at really generous length the significance of plate and jewels inventoried at Holton Park in 1684; Tony Lynas Grey of Oxford University Dept of Astrophysics quite literally shed moonlight on the king's letter of 3 May 1648. The curators of Carisbrooke Castle Museum and the owners of Passenham Manor welcomed us warmly; Maureen Jakob has familiarised our family with Hampton Court Palace across half a century, and is thanked with love. Kevin Heritage produced the genealogies. Andrew Kinnier introduced me both to Cromwell's Sydney Sussex College and James Maxwell's Inns of Court. Martin Roberts, a valued colleague of many years and a historian of repute, quietly and tangibly encouraged my history 'hinterland'. I thank him warmly for this – and much else.

The book's shortcomings and mistakes are mine, as are its idiosyncrasies. I use [parentheses] to clarify opaque period writing. I replace 'civil war' with 'the War' and 'Wartime': even contemporaries thought that 'civil' was inappropriate to describe the brutalising of the community. I cite 'Mrs' in full, to remind that 'Mistress' was stronger than the muttered abbreviation of today, and indicated rank; 'Mr' (Master) was also stronger, but its full form is dead beyond reviving. John Taylor the Water Poet, whose biographer calls him 'a genial companion', has been adopted as company through the book, lightening up Wartime Oxford, romanticising the Thame at Wheatley Bridge, enjoying beer and oysters on the Medway, and kissing the king's hand at Carisbrooke. Wartime was not all sombre and Taylor made contemporaries laugh, like the pub landlord he was. Finally, in Chapter 6, I have dared to reconstruct from evidence, for the first time, the overlooked Cromwell family wedding in the Whorwood house at Holton. It marked the first anniversary of Naseby and allowed the commanders of the new-modelled Army an occasion to 'leap and smile' when the War seemed to be over. Oxford was about to surrender, and Naseby had been pivotal in the victory. The wedding by the new Parliamentarian rite was a cameo of national issues. It was also a dramatic Whorwood event in which the Whorwoods, Jane and mother-in-law Lady Ursula, the recusant's daughter, were completely silent participants. If only for that, it deserves its airing here.

John Fox

Abbreviations

APC	Acts of the Privy Council
CCAM	Calendar of the Committee for the Advance of Money
CCC	Calendar of the Committee for Compounding (and Sequestration)
CSP	Calendar of State Papers
HER	English Historical Review
HCJ	House of Commons Journal
HLJ	House of Lords Journal
HMC	Historical Manuscripts Commission (Reports)
LSE	London School of Economics
Ms(s)	Manuscript(s)
NAS	National Archives of Scotland
ODNB	Oxford Dictionary of National Biography ('New' DNB)
PROB	Probate
RPCS	Records of the Privy Council of Scotland
SP	State Papers
TNA	The National Archive (formerly PRO, Public Record Office)

Timeline

1647–8	Agreement at Newcastle on Scots war expenses; Charles handed into English custody; travels via Holdenby to Hampton Court; Army subdues London; Charles flees to Isle of Wight after Army threats
1648	King on Wight, November 1647 – November 1648; four failed escape attempts, naval mutiny, county uprisings; Scots invasion by the Hamiltons defeated at Preston; Royalists surrender Colchester; end of 'second civil war'; Parliament negotiates with Charles, August – November; Army arrest him
1649	Charles I executed; monarchy and House of Lords abolished; Commonwealth (Republic) declared; Army take war into Ireland and Scotland
1651	Prince Charles and Hamilton invade England from Scotland ('third civil war'); defeated at Worcester, September; Jane Whorwood returns to Holton
1657	Jane leaves home permanently; Brome junior drowns
1658	Cromwell dies and is succeeded by son Richard, briefly and reluctantly
1659	Jane obtains judicial separation and alimony from Brome
1660	Charles II invited to return in a 'Restoration' of monarchy
1661	Brome Whorwood MP for Oxford City, over three Parliaments, 1661–81
1684	Brome Whorwood dies, April; Jane Whorwood dies, September. Buried at Holton
1688–9	Flight of James II; William of Orange and Mary (née Stuart) offered Crown

RYDER-MAXWELL GENEALOGY

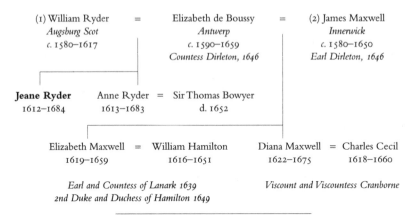

(1) William Ryder   =   Elizabeth de Boussy   =   (2) James Maxwell
Augsburg Scot   *Antwerp*   *Innerwick*
c. 1580–1617   *c.* 1590–1659   *c.* 1580–1650
       Countess Dirleton, 1646   *Earl Dirleton, 1646*

Jeane Ryder   Anne Ryder = Sir Thomas Bowyer
1612–1684   1613–1683   d. 1652

Elizabeth Maxwell = William Hamilton   Diana Maxwell = Charles Cecil
1619–1659   1616–1651   1622–1675   1618–1660

Earl and Countess of Lanark 1639   *Viscount and Viscountess Cranborne*
2nd Duke and Duchess of Hamilton 1649

BROME–WHORWOOD GENEALOGY

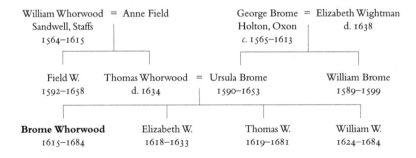

William Whorwood = Anne Field   George Brome = Elizabeth Wightman
Sandwell, Staffs   Holton, Oxon   d. 1638
1564–1615   *c.* 1565–1613

Field W.   Thomas Whorwood = Ursula Brome   William Brome
1592–1658   d. 1634   1590–1653   1589–1599

Brome Whorwood   Elizabeth W.   Thomas W.   William W.
1615–1684   1618–1633   1619–1681   1624–1684

WHORWOOD GENEALOGY

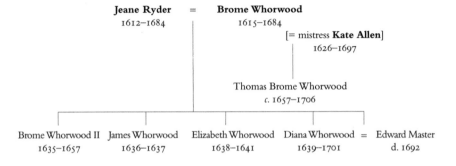

Jeane Ryder   =   **Brome Whorwood**
1612–1684   1615–1684
       [= mistress **Kate Allen**]
       1626–1697

       Thomas Brome Whorwood
       c. 1657–1706

Brome Whorwood II   James Whorwood   Elizabeth Whorwood   Diana Whorwood = Edward Master
1635–1657   1636–1637   1638–1641   1639–1701   d. 1692

1612–84:
Finding Jane Whorwood

A tall, well-fashioned and well-languaged gentlewoman, with a round visage and with pock holes in her face.
Derby House Committee, 1648

She was red haired, as her son Brome was, and was the most loyal person to King Charles I in his miseries of any woman in England.
Anthony Wood, Oxford, 1672

No known portrait exists of Jane Whorwood, but they remembered her height and figure, her fine speech and the flame-hair. Pockmarks spoiled a girl's marriage prospects, but they made her actions, not her complexion, her measure. Diana Maxwell, Jane's half-sister, sat for Lely, the court painter, and was celebrated for her looks, but they only remembered her greed. Jane's marriage broke up violently, publicly, and after three of her four children had died. No Whorwood staircase or great parlour would have hung her portrait, and given the tempo of her life she would hardly have sat still long enough to be painted. John Cleveland of the Oxford garrison wrote *To Prince Rupert*, a tribute to ideal beauty, male or female,

Such was the painter's brief for Venus' face,
Item, an eye from Jane, a lip from Grace.

All others named in his poem are real and Jane Whorwood was Cleveland's Wartime contemporary in Oxford. A Titian-haired Scot with green or hazel eyes, a painter's convention, turned heads in a small city; Anthony Wood and

Elias Ashmole also remembered her from there years later. Red hair was an obstacle in life, but it was memorable, like the pocks.

The failure of her cause helps explain Jane Whorwood's obscurity. Jane Lane succeeded in helping Charles Stuart II escape after his defeat at Worcester in 1651; she sat for Lely, had a pension from the king and a valuable jewel from Parliament. Flora McDonald was painted onto the popular mind (and shortbread tins) for assisting another Charles Stuart, self-styled 'III', to flee his failed uprising in 1746. Jane Whorwood, despite several attempts in 1648–9, failed to free her Charles Stuart I. There was nothing to celebrate, except her courage in the trying, and the occupational secrecy of a clandestine agent hid that, along with the rest of her service record. Conspirators were often hidden, even from each other. 'What other private agents the king had at London, I do not well know,' wrote John Barwick, clerical spy and secret correspondent with King Charles I: he knew fellow-conspirators only 'as it were through a lattice and enveloped in a mist'.

The Stuarts were always fugitives, Scottish, but aliens at home as much as in England, although they had ruled unruly Scotland for 200 years. South of the border they were married to queens from Denmark, France and Portugal, and ruled England for only eighty-five years (eleven of those from exile), little more than Jane Whorwood's lifespan. King James's mother, Mary of Scots, fled in and out of her own country; as a child James was carried in flight; Charles I fled London for Oxford, and Oxford for Newark, from where in defeat he was conveyed like a caged bird to Newcastle, then back to Hampton Court, from where supporters led him to the Isle of Wight. After a failed uprising, botched escape attempts and futile talks, the Army put him on trial.

Charles II, the fugitive king-in-waiting, returned in 1660, but not to the land he left. Parliament, Nonconformists, generals, the Irish and the Scots had discovered their strength. His brother, James II, fled the country with his successor a babe in arms, but Dutch William and his Stuart wife stepped to the throne by invitation and broke the direct Stuart line. Pretenders pretended, but the battle of Culloden in 1746 terminated the Stuart threat (if not the pretence) to the two kingdoms, now united. The last pretender, Cardinal 'Henry IX', styled himself humbly in Italy, *King of England by the Grace of God, but not by the Will of the People.* After the battle of the Nile, Nelson exchanged gifts with Henry, George III healed scars and finally moved on with a pension to the cardinal and Canova's monument to the pretenders in St Peter's, Rome.

The English War and Republic prompt many 'what if?' questions. What if the king had won, or abdicated? What if Richard Cromwell had been stronger? If Ireton had lived longer, would the English Republic have been 'the Consulate' not the Protectorate? Similarly, what if Jane Whorwood had freed Charles I? In the summer of 1648, as the king's escape committee grew weary of repeated failure and Jane emerged from a naval mutiny and county uprising on the Medway, the Marquess of Hertford wrote from London to

Jane's brother-in-law, William Hamilton, Earl of Lanark, in Edinburgh: 'Had the rest done their parts as carefully as Wharwood [*sic*], the king would have been at large.'[1]

Her mother's two marriages and her own wrapped her in family surnames like a fog. She was Ryder from her German-born Scots father. Her mother, born de Boussy in Antwerp, changed Ryder to Maxwell on remarriage. Jane married into the Staffordshire and Oxfordshire Whorwoods, spelled variously Whorewood (pronounced 'Horrud' in the nineteenth century), Horwood (as pronounced now), and Harwood. Jane was London-Scottish-Brabanter, and Scottish tradition recognised the maiden name after marriage. Her Ryder and Maxwell sisters took on more surnames – Hamilton, Cecil and Bowyer. To complicate further, her mother and stepfather were ennobled in 1646 as Earl and countess of Dirleton, on the Forth. While Jane was the quintessential Royalist and an Oxfordshire squire's wife, her red hair and given names 'Jeane' and 'Ginne', remind that she was more than nominally Scottish. Her Charing Cross home was in 'Little Edinburgh'; her father's will named her his 'bairn Jeane'; her service to Charles I was to a Scot in an English court bitterly resented as 'scottified'. Her younger sisters married aristocratic dynasts in both countries, and Jane named her daughters after them.

Jane left no will or last words, although some of her letters survive. She died in genteel poverty, possibly mentally damaged. No Whorwood ever mentioned her in a will; her three sisters predeceased her and ignored her, as did most of those who once conspired with her in the king's cause. Her mother, however, and members of the Hyde-Clarendon family, remembered her generously. The evidence for her early life at Whitehall is unusually focused because of the court roles of her parents, her stepfather, and her sisters' husbands. The site of her childhood home at the top western side of Whitehall is occupied (appropriately for 'Little Edinburgh') by the old Drummond Bank, now Royal Bank of Scotland. The nearby equestrian statue of Charles I marks the site of Charing Cross, Jane's waking landmark in life. Her first married home, Sandwell Park, Staffordshire, is now a golf course; her second at Holton Park, Oxfordshire, is campus to a university and a comprehensive school; her final decades were spent in Soho and Holborn. All her homes have gone, but at least the atmospheric moated site of Holton House survives as a hidden Oxfordshire gem.

Other buildings she knew still stand, if slightly modified: Carisbrooke Castle, Passenham Manor, Oxford's colleges, Hampton Court Palace and the Banqueting House, Whitehall, on which Rubens was working as Jane left home for married life in Oxford. Only a fraction remains of Holdenby House, 'pulled down [in 1649] two years after [the king's stay], among other royal houses, whereby the splendour of the kingdom was eclipsed'.[2] No record suggests Jane visited Scotland, but her father died after organising the royal visit there in 1617, and her stepfather hosted travelling kings at his

Innerwick mansion near the Forth. His castle at Dirleton is a tourist draw, but the Maxwell Aisle in Dirleton kirk lacks the ambitious marble monument Jane's mother planned for his tomb. Lambert and Monck took the castle with a token mortar salvo after Dunbar in 1650. The chamber where Maxwell died at Holyrood Palace disappeared in the rebuilding by Charles II, but the successor to his coal-fired lighthouse on the island of May in the Firth of Forth still guides ships and can be seen from Edinburgh and Dirleton.

Family life suffered more in the War than bereavement, destruction and confiscation. Insecurity reshaped morality, making for odd bedfellows and intense working relationships. Psychological and marital casualties surfaced afterwards. Whorwood, Milton and Gardiner marriages in the same small area of Oxfordshire were all casualties of the War. Cromwell, Milton and Oglander families were split in their loyalties. Of the Hammonds, Uncle Hammond was the king's chaplain, nephew Hammond his jailer, and another uncle his judge. The Royalist Whorwoods entertained the Puritan wedding of Bridget Cromwell and Henry Ireton, Cromwells and Whorwoods both blood cousins to the iconic John Hampden. The Committee of Both Houses (it exhausted several names) at Derby House which brokered intelligence on Jane's activities throughout 1648, included her brother-in-law Lord Cranborne. Another brother-in-law, the second Duke of Hamilton and the king's cousin, to whom Jane was close, died at Worcester after invading England in 1651. *When did you last see your father?* is a romantic cliché, but it reminds of the separation and insecurity of parents, siblings and children in civil war, which made contemporaries yearn for peace, or at least neutrality. *When did you last see your husband?* or much more aptly, *When did you last see your children?* could have been put to Jane Whorwood when she came out of imprisonment in 1651. Childcare is fundamental and Jane's mother-in-law gave legacies to her grandchildren which jar with the silence she accorded their mother.

Extraordinary public actions often command an unrecorded personal fee. Towards the end of her life 'poor Mistress Whorwood', as the bishop of London called her, was an embarrassment, bowed, if not quite broken, and poor. Her husband, MP for Oxford for twenty years and a threat to Charles II, hated her publicly. Jane in turn apologised to the king for his Whig disloyalty. By the end of her life the adventures of her younger years were irrelevant, forty years old, in their day a Wartime secret necessarily kept from co-conspirators and Parliamentarians, yet as forgettable as yesterday's news. This seventeenth-century secret agent survived England's civil war physically unscathed, only to be seriously injured afterwards by her manic husband. Failure, divorce and a Whig husband dulled her halo and prevented a legend.

Most of Jane's close collaborators predeceased her. Life and death rolled on. Rewards to others for service to the dynasty were generous, but thinly spread. Either she did not qualify for, or more likely she did not request, a reward. She was also a woman back in conventional peacetime, the roles and freedom reversed which the War had afforded her. Around her, old courtiers fell out, 'all at daggers drawn' as Pepys described them, in haste to reinvent and justify their contribution to the lost royal cause. None blew Jane's trumpet on her behalf, even former close colleagues. John Ashburnham died still fighting Clarendon's accusation that he had connived with Cromwell to trap the king on Wight. Henry Firebrace highlighted his liaising of intelligence and escapes for the king but, like Ashburnham, never mentioned Jane Whorwood (though he kept her letters). Silius Titus ('I have ten times ventured my life in His majesty's service when his affairs were desperate') was promoted, rewarded financially and entered Parliament. Thomas Herbert admitted Jane's role, then took pains to deny it before he died. Sir Purbeck Temple told the wildest tales, with Jane in the background and himself prominently heroic. Outside the restored *Prayer Book*, Charles I quickly became history as Restoration took over. Jane drew a veil over her activities. In the summer of 1684, just before she died, leading figures at court, including the Archbishop of Canterbury, began to quiz Sir William Dugdale about exactly who had been involved in those daring attempts to liberate the old king.

Dugdale, a chronicler, had tapped Firebrace and Herbert, Jane's fellow conspirators, for their memories, in order to document the attempts. The letters Firebrace and others preserved, all from 1648, are a small fraction of hundreds of secret messages, written, oral and hand-signalled, from the period.[3] No letters survive from Jane directly to the king out of nearly twenty she is known to have written to him in the last six months of 1648. Two have been saved in Charles's hand to Jane, from almost three dozen he is known to have written to her. Seven can still be read from her to Henry Firebrace, page of the bedchamber and coordinator of intelligence to the king between London and Wight, but they exchanged many more. A single letter, now in the Royal Library at Windsor Castle, from Jane (as 'Hellen') to William Hopkins of Newport for the king's eyes also, and two letters in the National Archives of Scotland, from her to her brother-in-law William Hamilton, Earl of Lanark, signed as '409', are all unquestionably in Jane's handwriting.

That any letters survive at all from the conspirators and the prisoner-king is remarkable, given the danger of writing and receiving them, their regular interception by Parliament, and their routine burning by recipients. The shredder had not been invented, but the Oxford garrison burned almost all its records before surrendering and Secretary Nicholas even *ordered* King Charles on Wight: 'For God's sake, burn them!' It is all the more remarkable that the two intimate letters from the king to Jane of July 1648 (we cannot judge whether they were the *most* intimate) should have been preserved at all, when more than fifty others between them were not. Somehow, either they passed from her (or her daughter's) possession to Firebrace and others, or they may have been left behind at Carisbrooke and cleared by friends like Firebrace after the king's arrest in Newport in November 1648. They would have made welcome black propaganda for Parliament, more explosive than the letters between king and queen captured after Naseby. Someone also risked treasuring them in the dangerous Republican years up to 1660. Their re-deciphering in 2006 was still able to spark prurient press interest in the martyr-king's private life.[4]

Tantalisingly, the ninety-five per cent of letters now lost between the king and Jane included an intriguing 'careful postscript' from Charles, and a 'wise long discourse' and a 'long memorial' from Jane. The surviving notes themselves (quality cartridge paper endures) are often minute, 4cm by 15cm folded into sixteen, small enough to be concealed in a shoe, the finger of a glove, or in the crack in a wainscot panel. Others to other couriers were hidden under the edge of a chamber carpet, or passed in the act of taking the king's hand to kiss. They are usually written in cipher, a common convention among letter writers to hide confidences. Jane's signet and stamp seals on the back of her letters range from simple crest to the marital impaling of Whorwood and Ryder. They may have been useful curios in a writing box, or decoration: Dorothy Osborne carried hers on a chatelaine belt; Queen Henrietta Maria hung her signet at her wrist.

Three of Jane's autograph signatures survive, in the 1647 papers of the Committee for the Advance of Money at Haberdashers Hall, and in Chancery papers from her judicial separation. She signed enciphered notes variously as 'N', '390', '409' and '715', and unciphered or part-ciphered notes as 'JW' or with the nom de plume 'Hellen'.

She was literate and fluent, 'well-languaged', and certainly well-connected. The Scottish Hamiltons were addressed by Charles I as 'cousins', the Cecils had been the English kingmakers, although Jane's brother-in-law was strictly a Parliamentarian. Her stepfather was Gentleman Usher of the Black Rod to the Lords, the king's herald in Parliament and house-jailer to grandees arrested by Parliament. As Usher also to the Order of the Garter, he organised the dazzling liturgy of chivalry around the king. His titles formalised his real use to the Crown as fixer and financier. Sir Robert Maxwell, Jane's uncle, was Serjeant-at-Arms to the Commons; her stepfather's cousin, John Maxwell, was Bishop of Ross, Laud's religious *provocateur* in Scotland. Two of her in-laws, Bowyer and Cecil, were Long Parliament members, as was her cousin, Sir Christopher Lewknor.

Jane's web of cousins, in-laws and contacts was wide and can be traced through wills, court cases, church registers, state papers and Heralds' visitations. Titles honorific to modern ears were power and influence in 1640, the Garter Star being the ultimate elevation. Garter ceremonial enhanced the surviving quasi-sacrament of coronation, whereby God 'ordained' the monarch; Order members, like Jane's brother-in-law Hamilton, had to wear the embroidered Star at all times, proclaiming the king's (and God's) favour and virtual presence. Jane's stepfather derived further public authority from his service to the Order. Family ties between ruling gentry often help make sense of an action or a relationship, as the aristocracy and gentry of the seventeenth century numbered about 100,000 atop a population pyramid of perhaps five million. Family was important beyond today's understanding of its claims. 'Kinship' and 'kinsman' included distant cousins and even people of the same name; 'family' included gentlefolk attendants, servants and tenants. Ann Manwood, Captain Maxwell and Jane Sharpe, all deployed by the Countess of Dirleton to monitor Jane's imploding marriage at Holton, were 'family'. If Mrs Cromwell and Lady Whorwood really did sit down after the Naseby wedding at Holton with the genealogy charts, which we know were in the house, they would have found extensive family in common.

The letters by which Jane is best known are not the only or even the main sources for her life. She shared the discomforts of garrison life at Oxford for four years with the king and court, with Sir Thomas Bendish, Sir Lewis Dyve, the Marquess of Hertford, Anthony Wood, Elias Ashmole, John Ashburnham and his gentleman John Browne, not to mention the fugitive merchants of the Levant and East India companies, commercial partners of her stepfather before they fled to Oxford. They invoked her name afterwards, as did William Lilly, the national astrologer who was himself a Parliamentarian agent. In 1651, when she was fined for 'applying herself to [corrupting]' the chairman of a parliamentary committee, the dossier recorded her name with six different spellings.[5] Astonishingly for 1647, a Royalist mocked the same committee by asking whether Jane Whorwood was its real '*Chairwoman*'. In 1659 she obtained a judicial separation from her husband on the grounds of his life-threatening violence. Her well-marshalled witnesses crushed any *riposte* his legal expertise might concoct. She had fled from home twice. Vivid, virtually scripted accounts of the violence, insults, and her husband's passion for a maidservant, are preserved in Lambeth Palace.[6] Repeatedly, after judicial separation in 1659, her husband withheld alimony; repeatedly she fought him for it, at the Bar of the Commons demanding Parliamentary privilege, appearing before Charles II three times and rejecting his judgement, distraining her husband's property by forced entry, and finally attempting to annul his will in the last months of her life. She literally went down fighting. Jane Whorwood played out her life on two levels, defending firstly her king, and then herself, and in the service of both no tactic or weapon was beneath her.

Piecing together the story of Jane Whorwood for the first time is like attempting to restore a shattered vase from pieces, fragments and slivers; some well known, others newly discovered, many missing, yet the sum restoration never recreates the tension or vibrancy of the intact original.[7] It merely indicates it. Her smuggling of nearly 800 kilos of gold to the king at Oxford has only now come to light; her missing years still tantalise; the received caricature of a passing royal mistress distorts perspective. However misplaced, her loyalty was genuine, courageous and acknowledged by those who knew her, including the king, who expected loyalists 'to forsake themselves' for him. She was ruthless in his cause, smuggling, embezzling and bribing; she was warm and reckless, in and out of season. Sadly, for the rest of her life she paid for it. When, in 1648, she described one dangerous urgent journey as 'like a Romance [*novella*]', she was war-weary, but had not yet had the full invoice for her adventures.

The front line wedding of Cromwell's daughter to General Ireton at the Whorwood home, Holton House, deserves closer investigation, even though the Whorwoods attending were silent witnesses. It was Cromwell's first attempt, however confused, at a political marriage alliance. In less than six years, his radical 'junior consul' took the English Revolution to the brink, and Cromwell with him. The wedding was among the first solemnised by the new Parliamentarian ritual, but with two parsons, a Royalist rector and a Parliamentarian minister officiating. It also marked the first anniversary of the crucial battle of Naseby. Thankfully, although surprisingly, Victorian genre painters failed to notice it. The Commonwealth took marriage out of church jurisdiction two centuries ahead of civil registration.

Given that Jane was Charles I's intelligence agent, financial conduit and escapologist, and allowing their 'brief encounter' in the summer of 1648, she has still had to be romanticised to make up for the lack of portrait. This freeze-frames her in 1648, ignoring her saddened old age. She becomes the disappearing rustle of a long skirt, a riding habit or a sea cloak; she is the Royalist in dashing, colourful company, like the boy in blue facing darkly dressed interrogators. She is never old, riding post-haste between Wight and London to warn the king, or waiting for him on board ship in the Medway mutiny. Jane was one of a small band of women ahead, at least of their *recorded* time, in performing what Clarendon called 'intrigues which at that time could be best managed and carried on by ladies'. She shared the spirit of the chatelaines of both sides defending their houses or sustaining the old religion in the absence of husbands, women who brought out what a servant described as Cromwell's 'feminine compassion towards distress'. Her War role, however, was not as poet, diarist or letter writer observing the War, nor as wife, mistress or colourful shadow to a warring male; she was directly involved, often *sola*, at risk, and answerable directly to the king's person. When this maverick returned home her marriage became her second 'war'.

Jane has been a useful joker, replacing lost cards. She is depicted at Holdenby in the king's early captivity, dropping a message behind an arras as she was body-searched, 'most likely Jane Whorwood'. She was, in fact, elsewhere at the time.[8] Her breaking through the king's escort to hug him on his way to execution so powerfully evokes Veronica comforting Christ that it has been relayed by several modern historians. Flame-hair and dark cloak against purifying white frost on the royal park is a vivid palette, but as unverifiable (and as moving) as the unscriptural Veronica herself. The women at Christ's tomb are also invoked, in 'Jane Whorwell [*sic*]', the mysterious lady who asked Sir Purbeck Temple to find Charles I's body. A study of seventeenth-century bank records recently attributed to 'Lady Jane Whorwood' a current account which clearly belonged to Lady Ursula Whorwood, her estranged mother-in-law.

Even a Jane Whorwood hoax has been perpetrated, Piltdown-style, to compromise historians.[9] *The Tendring Witchcraft Revelations* was a purported manuscript source which an MI5 cipher clerk confected in 1976. 'Richard Deacon' (Donald McCormick), wove together Jane Whorwood's activities in 1647–8 with those of William Lilly, the national astrologer. Lilly left notes of his clients in which Jane Whorwood does feature, but Deacon alleged that the two travelled together to Essex in 1647 to meet Matthew Hopkins the witch-finder. Hopkins, claimed Deacon, had known Whorwood since 1642 when he told her of his Huguenot family, the 'Hopequins'. The source also revealed that Hopkins was a double-agent, driven by money whether bartering intelligence or hunting witches, therefore ready to help Jane Whorwood and her Royalist friends.

The MI5 cryptographer was understandably attracted by enciphered correspondence between the king and his circle, including Jane, but cipher was a device long used by correspondents. Jane's red hair may have suggested the witch link to Deacon, but in 1648, more relevantly, it marked out a Scot. The real Jane Whorwood story has been shipwrecked on fictions and distortions, not to mention the narrows of moral rectitude: Cordell Firebrace in 1932 actually censored the original sources of the king's more earthy asides. Jane was a secret agent in royal service, ruthless and unscrupulous, spying, smuggling gold in bulk to the king's capital at Oxford and managing the king's attempted escapes. She brought him passing physical warmth and evidently 'applied herself' elsewhere for the cause, but it was not the sum of her story. Her fight for personal survival at home after the War proved to be as gripping as her Wartime adventure, and consistent with it.

In 1978 an American academic produced a by-product novel, *à la Cartland*. Jane Whorwood would have called it a romance and enjoyed it. *Sweete Jane* came from the opening words of a letter to her from the king in 1648. Like the Deacon hoax, the novel was to help fill the wall where a portrait might have hung. Distance-research from New York caused solecisms about the grandeur of Holton 'town', its 'castle', and the geography of Jane's England. Jane's emotional geography was even more graphic, as lover variously to the ambassador to Constantinople, to the lord mayor of London, to the governor of the Tower, and to King Charles himself. Had it all been true, Jane's husband might have been forgiven his fleeing abroad for the duration of the War and for distancing himself from her after it. However, the scholar novelist added an appendix listing allusions to Jane which other professionals may not have noticed.[10]

Nineteenth-century folk tradition around Jane's former home at Holton still remembers the family which gave the village in one lifetime its ration of excitement for the millennium. One tale runs of a boy killed by a wicked governess: in reality Jane's son did drown at sea in 1657, aged twenty-two, the year she fled from her husband and his mistress who had the title 'governness' at Holton House. Another tale told of Brome, Jane's husband, being summoned to London 'dead or alive' by angry royal command, and how he killed himself, but left an empty coffin to taunt the king – a great oak in Holton Park is still called the Brome Oak, supposedly linked to this suicide. In reality Brome died of a stroke in 1684 in London, four days before he was due to appear before Judge 'Bloody' Jeffreys for treasonous talk. Jeffreys demanded testimony on oath that Brome really was dead. Such traditions are rooted in the known local support for Jane against her violent husband before she fled Holton.[11]

Cromwell's name is strongly associated with Holton Park because of his daughter's marriage there. The Holton Cromwell portrait is now Oxford University's first official portrait of its former Chancellor. The *si-dit* Holton Cromwell Cup, a *Deckelbecker* made in Augsburg, said (but only in Victorian times) to have been Cromwell's gift to the house after the wedding, bears later hallmarks; a cherry tree and a green velvet saddle shared the same tradition. The four years of King Charles's Oxford 'head garrison' have been curiously neglected by historians and this biography only sketches them. Bastioned Oxford and its outer perimeter, which included Holton, lies at the heart of the Civil War narrative and of much of Jane Whorwood's activity. Oxford's fall, even if never quite the sack of Troy or the burning of Atlanta, was deeply symbolic.[12]

Holton House, Jane's married home, was levelled two centuries ago, 'because of ghosts' said local lore. Fragments remain, including an ancient black mulberry which still fruits: they planted such trees – deep-rooted and productive – to mark important weddings, and Jane did produce a male heir for the Whorwoods. Holton, a medieval pile, was pretentiously remodelled in 1600, and let, neglected, to tenants by 1785 when a direct turnpike road made Oxford more accessible. Local homes still sport panelling and fire surrounds from its demolition sale in 1804, one even named *Cromwell House* on the strength of a wardrobe door! The new owner of Holton Park in 1801, ironically the descendant of Colonel John Biscoe, a regicide, built his 'statement' house near the moated site with the proceeds from his West Indies plantations. When Thomas Carlyle visited the park in 1847, after the Rector of Holton told him of Bridget Cromwell's wedding there, he recorded its evocative atmosphere.[13] Victorian renovators obliterated Jane and Brome Whorwood's graves, and that of Brome's mistress, in Holton's tiny chancel, together with any stones which marked them.

The Civil War period is fertile with drama, one of the most harvested fields in English history, and the fate of Charles I still fascinates. Finding Jane Whorwood breaks new soil. Her story was largely lost with her burial in 1684 and the death of her last child in 1701; Diana, her daughter, was the final recipient of any stories her mother may have recounted. This review of the evidence, old and new, shows that Jane was no 'royal hanger on' as one modern history described her: she masterminded the king's two escape bids, and pressed for a third; she organised the main gold flow to his war chest at Oxford; she was the hub of his intelligence network in 1648. Others stole her credit in 1660 when she was too broken to speak up for herself. The feisty lady whom King Charles I called 'Sweete Jane Whorwood', and whom her husband called 'whore, bitch and jade', is, as Henry Firebrace's descendant suggested with classic understatement in 1932, 'a lady worthy of extended notice'.[14]

Notes

1. 'H' to Hamilton, 27 June 1648, Hamilton Papers, Camden Society, NS, 27, 1880, 224. Clearly an aristocrat was writing to his equal. Hertford's house at Netley was the forward base, near Wight, for conspirators in 1648. Jane and others travelled between Wight and London, often via Netley; John Ashburnham was at Netley, banned from the island, and messages were routed through there; Hertford who had also been in the Oxford garrison, knew Jane and her circle: see Chapter 9, note 20.

2. British Library, Harleian Ms 4704, f. 34, Memoirs of Sir Thomas Herbert.

3. The correspondence frequently refers to Jane Whorwood, but as one among many conspirators. It is summarised in Chapter 8, note 1, and integrated into the narrative of Chapters 8–10. In 1932 Cordell Firebrace published *Honest Harry*, about his ancestor Henry Firebrace's royal service. It is well argued, reproduces most of the letters in print, but it is dated: he was proud of his ancestor, he censored the king's earthier phrases and sometimes transcribed inaccurately.

4. *The Times*, 20 January 2007, reported that Dr Sarah Poynting of Keele University, while re-deciphering the king's letters to Jane, had discovered the ancient word 'swyving'. ('F--king,' Dr Poynting explained, 'is the only modern word which can convey it without being coy.') *The Times* commented: 'the re-decoding of this old love letter makes the Martyr king more like his son the Merry Monarch. Insiders at Court knew about Charles' mistress, but that was before the Freedom of Information Act.' *The Guardian*, 17 January 2007, carried the headline: 'Historian exposes secret sex life of Charles I.' Dr Poynting's research itself appeared more soberly as 'Deciphering the King: Charles I's Letters to Jane Whorwood', *The Seventeenth Century*, 21, 1 (2006), 128–40.

5. TNA SP 19, 162: 92–8, 103.

6. Lambeth Palace Archives: *Whorwood vs Whorwood*, Case 9938, 1672, including papers from the Chancery case 1658–9, and from the appeal hearing 1672–3.

7. *Victoria County History, Oxfordshire*, V, 172, accords Jane Whorwood seven lines. John Fox, 'Jane Whorwood', *ODNB*, 2009. In July 1646 Charles wrote to the queen, 'failings in friendship animate me to be firm to all those who will not forsake themselves, of which there were many in Oxford', Charles I in 1646, *Camden Series*, 1856, OS 63, 99.

8. Pauline Gregg, *King Charles I* (1981), 412. Jane was in London consulting Lilly the astrologer and corrupting a parliamentary committee when the suspects were remanded at Northampton; ibid., 443. Antonia Fraser, *The Weaker Vessel* (1984), 227; Alison Plowden, *Women All On Fire* (1984/2004 ed.), 181. Royalists found ready parallels with the first Good Friday, but no Scots Veronica. The intervention in St James's Park may be a later (? Victorian) device to gloss over a more cynical Parliamentarian newspaper story, see Chapter 10. Geoffrey Robertson, *The Tyrannicide Brief* (2005), 201 and n. 3, for 'Whorwell'; Linda Levy Peck, *Consuming Splendour* (2005), 257, names Countess Dirleton as an Abbott client, unaware that she was Jane's mother, while casting Jane's mother-in-law, Lady Ursula Whorwood, as Jane herself.

9. Richard Deacon, *Matthew Hopkins, Witchfinder General* (1976), 196. Deacon (real name Donald McCormick) died in 1998. He wrote on MI5, Jack the Ripper, microwave cookery and enciphered erotica. He claimed *The Tendring Witchcraft Revelations, Ms, 1725* was compiled 1645–50 by one C.S. Perryman. His 'citations' have not been used in this book. Matthew Gaskill in *Witchfinders* (2005), 283, 342, called it a 'clever hoax … an elaborate fantasy' and described it to this author as 'strange and rather disappointing, invented to add an element of espionage and intrigue to the story … the language is extremely odd. No historian has ever seen it.'

10. Virginia White Fitz, *Sweete Jane, Mistress of a Martyr King* (1988), 325–8 (Historical Notes). The author, who died in 2005, also published *Glorious Conspirator: the Secret Life of John Locke* (1990). She suggested that Cleveland's poem referred to Jane Whorwood's green eyes, fit for a red-haired Venus with Grace Bellaysis's shapely shoulders. After the king's execution, Parliament sold ten Venus paintings from the royal apartments; the Hamilton collection had just as many.

11. Cecil Earle Tyndale-Biscoe, *Tyndale-Biscoe of Kashmir* (1951), 18–19; Robert Stafford-Biscoe, *Tales From Jimmy, Memories of an Oxfordshire Village* (1963); Oxfordshire County Council Archive, *Holton Parish Box*, Par 135/17/JI/2 1859.

12. Frederick John Varley, *The Siege of Oxford* (1932); Frederick John Varley, *Supplement to the Siege of Oxford* (1935); Margaret Toynbee and Peter Young, *Strangers in Oxford, 1642–46* (1973); Rosemary and Tony Kelly, *A City at War: Oxford 1642–46* (1987); Nicholas Tyacke, ed., *History of Oxford University*, Vol. 4, Seventeenth Century (1997), 687–731; Ian Roy and Dietrich Reinhart, Chapter 4, Civil Wars.

13. After the second edition of *Oliver Cromwell's Letters and Speeches* (1846), Thomas Carlyle was informed by the Rector of Holton of the Cromwell wedding, *Carlyle Collected Letters*, Vol. 21, 77–8, 79, 21 and 24 October 1846. He visited Holton and included it in the third edition of *Letters and Speeches*, 1849, 200: 'Lady Whorwood ... rather in the royalist direction. Her strong moated house, very useful to Fairfax in those weeks, still stands conspicuous in that region, though now under new figure and ownership; drawbridge become fixed, deep ditch now dry, moated island changed into a flower garden; rebuilt in 1807.'

14. Cordell Firebrace, *Honest Harry* (1932), 50.

2

1612–19: *Jeane Ryder, 'Bairn' in a 'Scottified' Court*[1]

They beg our goods, our lands and our lives,
They whip our Nobles and lie with our Wives,
They pinch our gentry and send for our Benchers
They stab our Sergeants and Pistol our Fencers
Leave off, proud Scots, thus to undo us,
Lest we make you as poor as when you came to us.
John Chamberlain enclosed to Dudley Carleton, June 1612

Just north of Charing village green and its Eleanor Cross, where The Strand curved southwards to become King Street and Whitehall, stood the Royal Mews. It had once been the Royal Falconry, called a 'mew' from the moult (*mue*, Old French) of a bird of prey. Single-storey stables covered the modern site of Trafalgar Square and the National Gallery. A Gate of the Lions allowed entry to the complex, and its stone frontage curved round up a street named after the spurs made there for fighting cocks. Tudors and Stuarts spent hours in the saddle interweaving politics with the hunt and archaic mounted exercises, ritual chivalry to some and 'amourous foolery' to others. The royal horses gave Jeane Ryder's father his living as one of several overseers or surveyors of The Mews. By 1612, when Jeane was christened a stone-throw away in St Martin's, the falcons had long gone. The extensive Mews was an ageing but essential transport pool for the growing palace complex at Whitehall. It stabled about 130 horses (from an estimated fifteen breeds) for Crown and court officers' use, in an establishment divided into Great, Lower Green and Upper Back Mews. It was also a coach and wagon depot.

Falcons had needed less room than horses and the swelling court around Westminster put a premium on 'parking', 'garaging' and 'servicing' space for mounts and vehicles. As many as sixty horses at The Mews were for the king's exclusive use, and the hay barns, forges, exercise circuits, not to mention the tack, coach and riding school buildings of this great establishment, were essential to maintain them. They were washed and watered at a large pool at the centre of The Mews. Every royal servant had his livery, and in the stables alone, under the master of horse, clerk to the stables and seven surveyors, were lesser surveyors of the races and the hunt, a marshal of the farriers, a bitmaker, a packman, grooms, littermen, waggoners, saddlers, falconers and bow bearers. Prince Henry, heir to James I, had an equestrian complex of his own complete with surveyor's lodgings built within The Mews after 1605. His public persona was closely identified with horsemanship. When the king moved to other palaces or lodges – Oatlands, Nonsuch, Hampton Court – much of the transport pool moved with him.

Royal bird droppings also took up less space than royal horse manure. A waking experience for the Ryder baby's nostrils was the smell of The Mews dunghill on Cockspur Street. Its smell blended readily with that of the overburdened drains in a parish where new settlers, mainly Scots, vyed for accommodation close to the new Whitehall palace and the old St James's. Between 1612 and 1631, Jeane's first twenty years, the number of households paying the poor rate in St Martin's parish increased by 250 per cent, the bulk of it on the parish Landside towards St James's Park, away from the Thames. Revenue rose by 212 per cent and payments to the needy by 222 per cent. Living space expanded as timbered houses extended skywards or out into gardens, even in The Mews compound itself. West of the manure heap lay the Haymarket, which supplied the lofts and barns of The Mews, and ultimately the heap itself.[2]

The Stuart court had descended on London from Edinburgh nine years before Jeane's birth. (There, too, a haymarket stood close by the royal stables under Castle Rock.) A courier had hastened north with Queen Elizabeth's Boleyn ring for James VI of Scotland, a dying monarch's treasured possession to signal an undisputed succession. James I was proclaimed on the Tiltyard Green at Whitehall in 1603, exactly a century after a Tudor-Stuart marriage which had been intended to unite the two dynasties. Four decades later his son would be executed across the road at the new Banqueting House. Inevitably many English saw the Scots as invading, grasping barbarians, led by mere 'stewards' who had transformed a title into a dynastic name. They sprang, it was muttered, from a soil too poor to produce anything more useful than Scotsmen. James 'VI and I' never united the two kingdoms – the English Parliament resisted that – but he, his son and his two grandsons did rule them in tandem, one wearer of two crowns in separate courts, ruling through two distant Parliaments and two established churches whose bishops and presbyteries were mutually anathema. Kingdoms so disparate, yoked on such terms, were bound to war with each other.

Scotland provided land tracts from which retainers could assume titles and revenue. England provided a refuge from feuding clans and a money-bag from which to sweeten the loyal. Some aristocrats like the Hamiltons had titles from both kingdoms, but too few of them to bridge the ethnic divide in the way James I had hoped. In the end, the Stuarts lost touch so badly with their roots, that when, in 1644, a Scots army invaded to assist Parliament against him, Charles I eventually turned to them for safety, deluded that they were the lesser of two evils. They 'sold' him back to England, 'too much of a Scot for England, and too much of an Englishman for the Scots'.

At first the new King James from 'North Britain' gave office to his own at Westminster and Whitehall, then sensing local grievances attempted some fairer distribution. In 1603 the entire bedchamber staff of sixteen lords, gentlemen, grooms and pages, were Scots, the close 'cabinet' of influence around the king; but by 1622 half were English. At least, only half of the Privy Chamber staff of forty-eight were Scots appointments from the start and remained so. This 'narrowing of counsel' gave James some security after living in constant fear of assassination; it kept him in qualified touch with Scotland, but it also fuelled racial prejudice in London. Guy Fawkes warned that the two races were irreconcilable: 'Even were there one religion in England, nevertheless it will not be possible to reconcile these two races, as they are, for very long.' The venality, sexual laxity and extravagance of the new Scots court, claimed Sir Walter Raleigh, 'shine like rotten wood', and repeated scandal among royal favourites shaped that wood. An extravagant Danish queen added to the sense of an alien monarchy and her appetite for 'playing the child again' did not help. King James accused Parliament of turning financial issues into attacks on the Scots, while Lord Wentworth accused the Scots of 'drawing out of the cistern as fast as we could fill it'. James even coined an optimistically named *Unite* gold piece, yet his own country's coinage was suspect for its 'black metal' (copper) farthings and its formerly debased silver.[3]

When racial tension was high, the Scots found refuge from insults and violence in the 'royal' area round Charing Cross, The Mews, Whitehall Palace and the Scotland Yards. Scots ghetto succeeded Huguenot such, and Little Edinburgh flourished as had Petty France. The neighbourhood was home to better-placed Scots courtiers and close to the palaces, offering symbolic security to the more vulnerable. London prejudices were often revealed only later when the Stuarts could no longer retaliate, and when truth and myth could no longer be disentangled. Scotland, they sneered, was 'a dunghill, not a kingdom', Edinburgh a 'parish not a city'; the 'swarms who came after [James] sucked him of vast sums'; 'to be married to a Scots woman is to be married to a carcass in a stinking ditch'; 'their Sabbath is to preach in the morning and persecute in the afternoon', although 'the organ will find mercy because there is affinity between it and the bag-pipes'; 'a tree in Scotland is a show, like a horse in Venice'. Personal hygiene was a soft target, alien toilet routines leaving the Scots and their breath 'stinking and lousy'. Wars against the Scots were fuelled by such racism and Scotsmen could not win against the inconsistency of prejudice. James I was hated because of his mother's open Catholicism and his Danish wife's secret such, but he was also blamed for his country's Presbyterianism which rejected bishops and ritual as papist relics. Speech is a key indicator of ethnic origin: Shakespeare, it is argued, refrained from aping the Lowland Scots dialect in *Macbeth* as it was so sensitive an issue, and that his parable of Scotland could only be told in the guise of Hamlet's (and Queen Anne's) Denmark. When Milton defended the execution of Charles I he accused the Scottish Presbyterians of hypocrisy, 'juggling fiends [who] palter', precisely the description of the witches in *Macbeth*.[4]

The London street violence was as real as the insults, but more sporadic. In May 1612, when Jeane Ryder was still being suckled, 'James Maxwell, a sewer or gentleman usher, upon very small occasion plucked or pinched one James Harley, a gentleman of the Temple, by [a jewel in] his ear at the feasting of the Duke of Bouillon, that the blood flowed freely'. There was uproar among Harley's English lawyer colleagues and he 'called Maxwell to account for it by a challenge, [which] came to the king's notice'. The king reassured the injured party that he 'would not maintain any servant to do wrong' and heard the complaint himself. As word spread, 'the Scots pluck in their horns, absent themselves from plays and from the hither parts of town and keep close about Charing Cross; they find unruly youths apt to quarrel and ready to offer ill-measure'. The first attempt at reconciliation failed. In front of four lords and forty gentry, Maxwell 'offered satisfaction in words, but [refused to] kneel, whereupon they broke off abruptly'. Two weeks passed before Maxwell finally apologised in private before the king, Harley and four lords, with no others present, and 'because he could not read [English dialect], repeated a wordy satisfaction after the Earl of Northampton, and in saying [it] he asked forgiveness on his knees, which was accepted'. The Scots who had sought shelter by Charing Cross were not so reassured. 'It seems the Scots were bodily afraid for ... above 300 passed through Ware towards Scotland within 10 days.'[5]

Old scores were settled when feelings ran high. A court fencing-master 'was slain as he was drinking with some Scots, upon an old grudge of putting out an eye in [foil] play with him at Rycote [Oxon]'. At Croydon races that summer a Scot slapped the Earl of Montgomery's face, but the Earl did not retaliate for fear of a pitched battle between racially mixed spectators. The uproar which followed James Maxwell's attack on the English lawyer's ear stud cautioned the lesson of biding time, but time allowed resentment to fester and thirty years later it had not abated. Charles I, according to Clarendon, was 'always an immediate lover of the Scots nation, born there, educated by that people, betrayed by them, always having few English about him till he was king: the major number of his servants being still of that nation, who he thought could never fail him'. In Clarendon's eyes, not only were Scots courtiers a liability, but the royal cousins, the Hamiltons, failed Charles I more than any of them.

The rector of the royal parish of St Martin-in-the-Fields watched his parish grow in the two decades from Elizabeth's death in 1603 to the reign of Charles I. He had to enlarge the church and extend the burial ground by an acre, while parish housing proved insufficient for the influx of Scots, who reputedly were turning London 'from sticks into bricks'. Increasingly the church register listed Gallic clan names (including MacBeth) and the parson would not have found Jeane Ryder's red baby hair remarkable when he baptised her on 3 February 1612. In Queen Elizabeth's day red or fair hair in an English girl promised an attractive, lively woman; now it denoted a Scot, long before the language of 'melanocortin receptors' and 'phaeomelanin pigment'. The gene pool in Charing Street and surrounding Westminster was wider than in most places in England; elsewhere red hair still had associations with threatening aliens, among them Danes, Scots and witches. Jeane's registered name was latinised to *Janna*, appropriately for her cosmopolitan background. Her father, William, who probably bequeathed her the red hair, was Scottish but born in Augsburg, while her mother, Elizabeth de Boussy ('Bessie' to the world and 'Betsikins' to her husband), had come to London from Antwerp, born of a Portugese mother with Bohemian blue blood.[6]

Technically, both Jeane's parents were aliens: William as German-born and as a Scot, and Elizabeth as a Brabanter. Denization, the royal grant of citizenship in response to a parliamentary bill for the naturalisation of a named individual, was argued in Parliament with some of the emotion generated in modern immigration debates. 'William Ryder, the king's servant, born in Germany, and Elizabeth of Bonfyn, born in Antwerp and now his wife' were granted citizenship in May 1612, just months after Jeane's birth. It was never a foregone conclusion. James Maxwell, the ear stud pincher, also an alien but senior to Ryder, had his bill repeatedly refused by Parliament until 1622. At least the *post-nati*, those born after the accession of James to the English throne in 1603, automatically received dual English and Scots citizenship. The Ryder 'bairns', as their father called them in his will – Harris (*Henricus*), born in 1611, Jeane (*Janna*) in 1612, followed by Anne (*Anna*) baptised at All Souls, Kingston upon Thames, November 1613, where the family had a residence for attendance at Hampton Court – were all English *and* Scottish by birth.[7]

William Ryder's German, his organisational skills and his understanding of horses raised him to the rank of 'Principal Harbinger' among the seven over-seers who administered the Charing Mews. His role was to arrange journeys. Horses were James I's obsession, given as gifts of state and trusted more than courtiers in the open safety of the chase, race track and tiltyard. Horses did not conspire. Elizabeth Ryder was employed as Queen Anne of Denmark's lavander at Denmark House, known before and since as Somerset House. A Catholic background, as well as facility in Portugese, Spanish or French, might have helped Elizabeth's appointment to an essentially intimate post which carried qualified status. The queen had two successful pregnancies while in England, several still births or infant deaths, growing children to be laundered for, her own largely female-staffed palace discrete from the king's residences, and an appetite for costumed masques. She and her guests, who included the native American Princess Pocahontas in 1616, generated enough washing to keep Elizabeth Ryder's team of laundresses at the royal laundry in Scotland Yard hard at work. Among the masque costumes and dozens of pairs of sheets in trunks at Denmark House lay Henry VIII's shirts, at least eighty years old! Jeane was brought up with the blending scents of finest Castile and of saddle soap.

The Ryders' Charing house, between Spring Gardens and the medieval Cross, was within easy distance of both parents' workplaces. A survey of 1650 describes Elizabeth de Boussy's home of forty years and two marriages still substantially the four-storey house of Jeane's childhood. With eleven hearths and rated at £50, the largest house on Charing Street after Wallingford House and George Kirke's home, it stood north of widow Rowden's tenement and Lady Naunton's house, west of the Cross.

> Over two large cellars are two halls on [Charing Street] front, behind them two fair kitchens and a pantry … above stairs in the first storey four chambers on the front and two chambers backwards and two closets there. And in the second storey, three chambers and one closet. And in the third storey two garrets. And further backwards adjoining to the Spring Gardens, one small kitchen, a stool house and over the same in the first storey one chamber and a garret over the same. Also four courtyards all paved with [grey] Purbeck [lime]stone, well fitted and jointed.[8]

Immediate neighbours, including the Kingsmills and the Nauntons, were courtiers, some of them Crown tenants. Five doors south of the Ryders, behind the Duke of Buckingham's Wallingford House, lay the passage to Spring Gardens, a semi-public tree and game reserve around a fountain in a corner of the royal St James's Park. In 1635, just after Jeane left home, it was closed on public order grounds, as drinkers, gamblers and duellists were drawn to its bowling matches. It stretched behind the Ryders' back wall;

neighbours cut doors and windows through their walls to access it more conveniently. A stone-throw away, Whitehall Palace was an ongoing construction project, the Banqueting House completed when Jeane was ten. The streets of Whitehall, Charing and The Strand were themselves the Court, and Wallingford House one of its politically powerful palaces.

While the Scots crowded to the Cross when trouble flared, William Ryder had to find lodgings in the area for the visiting retinues of the king of Denmark, the Duke of Holstein (the queen's brother), the Elector Palatine, the Count of Nassau and the marquis of Brandenburg. Royal gifts for visiting servants were Ryder's responsibility to buy and bestow. In 1610, when he was on a mission to Prague, King James sent a supportive message over some incident that he would 'not withdraw any beam of favour from Mr Ryder'. One beam of the king's favour was Ryder's pension of £150 a year awarded in 1608, shortly before his marriage, no doubt prompting the accusation of the Scots cashing in yet again. It may have been connected with an incident in the previous year. Robert Ker (Carr in English), a Scots page, broke his leg during a coronation anniversary jousting in the Tiltyard and was 'instantly carried to Master Ryder's house at Charing Cross [and] the king went initially to visit him'. From that moment Ker became a favourite and joined the inner circle of those attending the bedchamber.[9]

The annual pension – a guarantee that Ryder would be paid, unlike many court officials who depended on venality to supplement or even obtain their income – was also a measure of compensation. Travel abroad was slow, hazardous and uncomfortable, and expenses were equally slowly refunded. One moment Ryder would be heading a delegation leading horses to present to the Duke of Holstein; the next, his facility in speaking German would be employed along the Rhine seeking the best wines for the royal household, with the company and advice of Wolfgang Rummler, the German royal apothecary. Both men were Augsburg-born, Ryder's wife from Brabant and Rummler's wife a Zeelander. To some, Ryder would always be 'a German who lived in England' because of the time he spent abroad.[10]

Meanwhile, a succession of responsibilities landed on William Ryder after Jeane's birth early in 1612. Prince Henry, heir to the throne, died in November, and horses had to be organised for the state funeral. Princess Elizabeth, later known as the Winter Queen because of the sole season she spent in her Bohemian kingdom, was betrothed a month later to the Elector Palatine: servants had to be lodged and Ryder was responsible. The sixteen-year-old royals married in the chapel at Whitehall in February 1613 and stayed for the honey-month, Ryder responsible for lodging the groom's entire entourage. In mid-winter 1613–14, just after seeing his second daughter Anne baptised in Kingston church near Hampton Court, William escorted an English midwife to Heidelberg for the birth of Prince Rupert.

In October 1615 he attended Princess Elizabeth on her visit to London and then escorted her back to Heidelberg.[11] He was no longer young and the travelling took its toll.

In 1616 King James decided to visit Scotland for the first time since leaving it in 1603, although he had pledged to return 'every three years at the least'. The new dynasty, 'rootless in England and uprooted from Scotland' recognised that the two nations were growing apart. The expedition left for six months in March 1617, but only after Ryder had housed and provided for the French ambassador and his retinue at Whitehall, and together with James Maxwell had advised on the reorganisation of the royal households. He then helped uproot and transfer the entire court 700 miles to Edinburgh, another official being responsible for sending furniture by sea to Leith. The overall cost of £100,000 was noticed by the king's enemies. Ryder's superior, George Villiers, Duke of Buckingham and master of the horse, oversaw the moving of the stables; the Duke of Lennox organised the moving of the household. 'A hard journey' of two months to the Scottish border faced the royal retinue of hundreds and their eighty luggage carts; once past the border, expenses were shouldered by the Scottish Treasury. It was Ryder's task as gentleman harbinger to 'stable, service and accommodate the retinue in burghs along the road'; essentially a billeting officer to a small army on the move. While purveyors looked after the food, Ryder provided coach-and-four for formal entry to a city or grand estate; he fixed accommodation, checked on the suitability of road surfaces for horse, coach or litter, provided tents wherever inn rooms were lacking, and arranged veterinary backup. Over thirty staff served 130 horses. Ryder and his colleagues depended on gifts, charges and local payments for their income, although the king did eventually pay their fodder, board and expenses. As Principal Harbinger, Ryder had five aides and five changes of horse with him. From Edinburgh, where the king arrived on 16 May, the visitation ventured as far as Linlithgow, Dunbar, Sterling, Perth, Glasgow and Hamilton.[12]

At Edinburgh, however, William Ryder, 'Gentleman Harbinger, sick in body but haill in spirit', decided to compose his will on 20 May with the help of a local lawyer whose Lowland accent shows distinctly in transcription. He 'beseeched most humbly the King and Queen's gracious majestys to look favourably upon my wife and children and to protect and maintain them'. Harris (Henry) his oldest son was his sole heir; Jacob (James) his second son baptised in 1616 would inherit the properties and rents if Harris died. 'Elizabeth de Bosie, laundris to the Queen's Mejesty, my well belovit spous, [and] James, Jeane and Anna Ryder', were to inherit the house, as long as Elizabeth remained unmarried and the children remained underage. Seiger (de) Huse, Jeane's uncle on her mother's side, was to be 'tutor [guardian] to my bairns' in the event of their mother's death, and to receive Ryder's best velvet suit and hat. Jacob Huse, another uncle, and Elizabeth his sister, also received bequests. Ryder left money to the poor of Kingston upon Thames and of St Martin-in-the-Fields. A gold ring went to each of 'the queen's maidens that wash with my wife'. To a cousin he left 'the best of my five horses presently with me in Scotland', but while his Portugese mother-in-law in Antwerp duly received her guilders, her name escaped him in Edinburgh and 'Maria Paraides' had to be inserted later.[13]

William was seriously ill. Eventually the visitation headed south through the summer. As they neared London in September, the travelling Court stopped at the royal manor of Woodstock for four days. They then bypassed Oxford (to save burdening the town), detouring on 10 September through Bletchingdon, Islip and over Wheatley Bridge on the way to the Norreys' home at Rycote, near Thame, where since Elizabeth I's early years as queen, royal progresses always stopped. It provided spectacle for those living by the route and village churches rang salutes to their passing sovereign. As the procession passed along the wall of Holton Park, just before Wheatley Bridge, a young Thomas and Ursula Whorwood with children, servants and tenants, would have doffed and curtsied at the gate as St Bartholomew's bells pealed gamely but faintly from far behind the park.

William Ryder arrived home to enjoy his new son, Edward, born in mid-September 1617, before his own death in December. He was buried in St Martin's by The Mews. His widow suffered the further loss of their other sons in 1618: Harris at the Kingston lodging and James at Charing. Elizabeth continued as royal laundress until the queen died of dropsy in March 1619. Four cartloads of trunks and cabinets of jewels were retrieved for sale from the queen's palace, and her clothes and accessories were distributed to the ladies who served her. Doubtless the queens' lavander took mementos for herself and her daughters.

The queen's funeral had to be postponed while King James, who did not attend it himself, raised the money to cover it and struggled with his gout at Newmarket. Protocol placed Mrs Ryder [sic] behind the ladies of the queen's bedchamber and the countesses' women, but ahead of the earls' daughters' women, in the state funeral procession which eventually took place in May. It may have been seven-year-old Jeane's first attendance at a state ceremony, but she and Anne had a long wait to see their mother pass. It was the queen's last posthumous masque, and not her best, 'A poor show, a drawling tedious sight, laggingly all along even tired with the length of the way and the weight of clothes', namely yards of broadcloth and plaid, and that in May.[14] By then the royal lavander may not have minded. She had remarried just before the queen's death, with the blessing and the bidding of a king who knew her new husband well, and she was now pregnant. The Ryder 'bairns', acclimatising to a new father figure, watched a new sister being baptised at All Souls, Kingston, in January 1620, 'Elizabeth, daughter of James Maxwell Esq.'. The new husband and father drew the family up from The Mews and laundry into a higher circle of royal favour – Prince Charles's bedchamber.

Notes

1. William Ryder's will called his children, including Jeane, his 'bairns', TNA PROB 11/130, 1 December 1617. 'Scottified' was John Ashburnham's description of Charles I's courtly entourage of 1647; Francis Peck, *Desiderata Curiosa*, 1732, Liber IX, 39, and used of the Scots church in the previous decade, see Michael Braddick, *God's Fury, England's Fire* (2008), 124.

2. George Gater and Walter Godfrey, *Survey of London, XX (St Martin in The Fields, III, Trafalgar Square)* (1940), 7–26; *Survey of London, XVI (St Martin in The Fields, I, Charing Cross)* (1935), 25, 104–10; see also *Survey of London, XVIII (St Martin in The Fields, II, The Strand)* (1937); HMC Report, 6, 323ff, appendix, 'The Accounts of the Gentlemen of Horse to the Duke of Buckingham'; Howard M. Colvin, *Royal Buildings* (1968); Arthur MacGregor, 'The Stuart Courts and the Animal kingdom' in Evelyn Cruickshanks, *The Stuart Courts* (2006), 86–115. The poor rate figures are calculated from the Rate Registers of St Martin's, 1611–31, in Westminster City Archive. They chart the Ryders' neighbours and the widowing and remarriage of Jeane's mother: William Ryder paid his last rate in April 1617, James Maxwell paid his first in April 1621, and widow Ryder paid the intervening years. Jane's first half-sister, Elizabeth Maxwell, was baptised on 2 January 1620, suggesting a remarriage in early spring 1619, or a premature birth: *Register of St Martin in The Fields, 1550–1619*, Harleian Society Register Series XXV (i), 1898; *Register of St Martin in The Fields, 1619–1636*, Harleian Society Register Series XXV (ii), 1936; *Register of All Souls, Kingston upon Thames*, transcript, North Kingston Centre. See also Christopher Durston, *James I* (1993), 14–23.

3. Guy Fawkes's memorial to Philip III of Spain, in Antonia Fraser, *Gunpowder Plot* (1996), 89; Lady Arabella Stewart, 1603, cited in John Nichols, *Progresses of King James I*, I, 1061 (1828); see also John Cramsie, *Kingship Crown and Finance under James VI and I* (2002), 121–4.

4. *Huguenot Society of London Proceedings*, XII (1919–24), 346 (1923); William H. Manchee, *Huguenot London, Charing Cross and St Martin Lane*; James Howell, *A Perfect Description of the People and Country of Scotland* (1649); Christopher Durston, *op.cit.*, 18; Andrew Murphy and Willy Maley, *Shakespeare and Scotland* (2004); Dzelzainis, Martin, Milton, Macbeth and Buchanan, *The Seventeenth Century*, IV, 1 (1989), 55–66.

5. Norman McClure (ed.), *Letters of John Chamberlain*, I (1939), 348–55, 12, 27 May and 11 June 1612, to Dudley Carleton – see title quotation; John Nichols, *op.cit.*, II, 443, 449.

6. *Register of St Martins in the Fields, 1550–1619*, 42 (see note 2 above), 'Janna Rider, filia Mr William'. Jeane's marriage licence from the Bishop of London in 1634 recorded her age as nineteen, a certain falsehood, probably to disguise an age gap. Red hair and its accompanying complexion is nature's way of allowing Vitamin D to be produced in a minimum of light. Some forty per cent of Scots have red hair. See www.scottishdermatologicalsociety, and particular thanks to Anthony Green for an anthropologist's insight.

7. She was variously known as Bonfyn, Bowsie, Bousie, Besyne, Boussie, Bessyne de Podolsko, Besyne, Bosie, Bosy, Bouzey, Boozen, Bouzeen, Bousey, Bussine, Buzein, Buzzine, Bousen, Beusy, Boussine, Boussoyne, Boussoin, Bosy and Deboussy. Her brothers Charles and Frederick lived nearby. The version 'de Bosie' was used in her first husband's will; three decades later her second husband's will spelled it 'de Boussy', which is adopted in this book; her own will written in August 1657 (proved 1659), TNA PROB 11/300, employs 'de Bosy'. *Register of St Martins in The Fields, 1550–1619*, 41, 42, 48, 176; Register transcript, All Souls, Kingston; *Huguenot Society of London Records*, XVIII, 1911; William Shaw, *Denizations and Naturalisations, 1603–1700*, 16, 20, 29, 15 May 1612.

8. Description of the Charing house, visible on the Hollar and Ogilvy maps, 1658 and 1671, *Survey of London*, XVI, 1935 (*St Martin in The Fields, I, Charing Cross*), 105–6 (1935), citing *Parliamentary Survey*, 1650, PRO, E, 217, Middlesex, 6. The poor rate was paid in Jeane's parents' successive names – Ryder, Maxwell, and their title, Dirleton.

9. HMC Salisbury Mss, XXI, 1609–12, 1970, 279; Sir Anthony Weldon, *The Court and Character of King James I*, 29 (1687).

10. CSP 1603–10, XLIV, 499, 501; *Huguenot Society London Records*, XVIII, *op.cit.*, 16, William Ryder born in 'Ausperge, [Augsburg] High Germany'. John Nichols called him 'a German living in England', see *Progresses, Processions and Festivities of King James I* (1828), III, 95.

11. APC 1613–14, XXXIII, 1921, 307; Francis Pell, *Records, Issues of The Exchequer, James I*; Frederick Devon, ed., 1836, 82, 142, 154, 162, 180.

12. John Nichols, *op.cit.*, III, 244–438, also RPCS XI, (First Series), 1894, xviii, 120. Nichols is a hostile source drawing on Anthony Weldon's even more bitter and scatological *Description of Scotland*, which when it was delated to James I in unpublished manuscript form caused Weldon to be expelled from Court. See also William McNeill, *et al.*, 'James I's Tour of Scotland in 1617', *Scottish Historical Record*, LXXV, 1996, 38–51; APC, 1617, XXXV, 125. Privy Council records for 1605–13 perished in a fire at Whitehall. For Ryder's advising on household reorganisation, see *Letters and Papers of King James I*, II, 284, 14 March 1617, Lord Binning to the king. The enormous entourage to Scotland included the Maxwell brothers, Sir Robert, Serjeant-at-Arms, and James, Black Rod, HMC 75, *Downshire Mss IV*, 1995, 307.

13. TNA PROB 11/130, composed May 1617, Edinburgh, probate December 1617, London; *Huguenot Society of London Records*, X, index, (1908); II, 176, 213.

14. Nichols, *op.cit.*, III, 538, 539, 541, 545; for Queen Anne's linen store, see M.W. Payne, 'Inventory of Queen Anne's at Denmark House, 17th April 1619', *Journal of Historical Collections*, 13, No. 1, 23–44 (2001); Nichols, *op.cit.*, III, 545.

3

1619–34: *James Maxwell, Black Rod and Stepfather*

The Union with Scotland made this union [Strand – Charing – Whitehall] between London and Westminster. The Scots, multiplying here mightily, nested themselves about the Court, so The Strand, from mud-walls and thatched houses, came to that perfection of buildings as now we see.
James Howell, Londinopolis, 1657

A gentleman born, but never bred one.
Sir Thomas Roe, on James Maxwell, 1643

James Maxwell, groom of the bedchamber successively to Prince Henry and to Prince Charles, was a good catch and a warm match for Elizabeth Ryder. A Lowland Scot from Kirkhouse, he came to London in King James's entourage. He and Elizabeth baptised a daughter, Elizabeth, at Kingston in January 1620; a son James in 1621, who died in infancy; and another daughter, Diana, in August 1622. Jeane and Anne Ryder became Maxwell's 'step' (*steopbarn*, orphan, Old English) or 'bereavement' daughters, their mother freed by their father's death to remarry; 'daughters-in-law' was also used then to describe Maxwell's legal obligation to them once he married their mother, but such distinctions faded as relationships warmed. To the adult Jeane, Maxwell was 'my father'. He had been the ear stud pincher of 1612 and had served the Crown well for two decades, since being introduced to the Edinburgh court by his uncle, the Earl of Annandale.[1]

He had worked closely with William Ryder on embassies, hospitality and the visit to Scotland. Naturalisation in 1622 allowed him to bequeath his considerable growing wealth made up of land, revenues, rights and titles in both kingdoms, along with money, mercantile monopolies, church advow-sons, and notably a 'great store' of jewels from the Crown, reputedly 'the best in England'.[2] His influence on Prince Charles, the heir apparent, was formative and profitable. Once Charles became king in 1625 more material favour poured in Maxwell's direction. Courtiers were privileged, although their contractual income was arbitrary and irregular: the influence, the com-mand of the king's ear, the promoting (or ignoring) of a letter to him, advice offered casually in the Privy Chamber or, more privily, in the bedchamber, offered an alternative source of income. Privy rewards from the king 'for services' unspecified marked the successful courtier, Maxwell a regular recipi-ent. Diplomats listed his cipher for their correspondence, knowing he had the king's eye, ear and trust. The 'politics of intimacy' earned him and others office and rewards, and thereby a whole circle of friends and relatives became obliged to him. Such income, known as 'supplementation', was customary. Bedchamber servants, particularly the Scots, William Murray, Patrick Maule and James Maxwell among them, and the Englishman Endymion Porter, grew wealthy on royal gifts.

In April 1617 Maxwell earned reversion of the office of 'staffbearer at the Feast of St George at Windsor'; a month later he took presents from the king to the Palatine for the Princess Elizabeth's marriage. By 1621 he was Garter Usher in his own right. He became so rich that he loaned thousands to Charles I to help replace the public revenue lost when King and Parliament dispensed with each other in 1629. On every loan and security to the Crown Maxwell made a profit, amassed lands or came home to Charing with fabu-lous jewels to show for it.[3]

Supplementation was controversial in its day. The Earl of Mar for whom Maxwell had bent the king's ear thought him 'a verrye honest man, nochtwithstanding of that little oversycht committed [on] his brother [Charles, slain by Sir Robert Ker], neere to the king and for one of his quality you cannot find a better'. Sir Thomas Roe, a sophisticated man of the world, thought differently when he reprimanded Maxwell at Oxford in 1643 for selling the post of deputy Garter Usher: 'a gentleman born, but never bred one'. The supplementation culture corrupted even the honest, as greed con-taminated a genuine need to make a living. The cascading of favour did not necessarily flow beyond the favoured courtier. Like the debtor in the parable, Maxwell was servile to those above his rank, and a thug to those in his way below. When King Charles was slow to pay Maxwell and other grooms of the bedchamber in 1627, they jogged his memory, protesting they were never in despair, however late their pay, as they were 'preserved in the circle of his gra-cious care'. Maxwell was well warmed by what the English cynically called 'that sunrise in the North'.[4]

His northern home was a mansion at Innerwick, his lairdship twenty-five miles east of Edinburgh, and his ancestors had been Mary Stuart's wardens of the Western Marches. After her execution in 1586, the Johnstons took the wardenship and blood turned bad. James VI, Mary's son, reinstated the Maxwells to favour a few years before coming south for his English Crown in 1603. Maxwell proved himself even before the coronation that summer when he joined an embassy to Denmark for the christening of a princess. His role was to make formal gifts of money to the successful midwife and wet nurse in an age when ceremonial was core diplomacy. Three years later King James interceded with the Scottish Privy Council on behalf of 'James Maxwell and Sir John Drummond our Ushers', who had spent so long in England they feared they were losing out on fees and rents in Scotland. Complaint was lodged that Maxwell had transferred half of a new usher's fees to his own brother and threatened to charge the usher with 'rebellion' if he did not accept. Twice Maxwell was hauled before the Scottish Privy Council on this issue, twice he walked away unscathed, either on a technicality or after (unrecorded) bribery. He was quick to take others before the Council for debt.

The Crown made up any shortfall in Maxwell's theoretical income of £66 a year. In 1611 he obtained the keepership of Guildford Park and its deer; thirty years later he bought it outright from his cousin the Earl of Nithsdale. Most of his neighbours at Charing already had their country seats. In 1616 he was allowed to farm the anchorage fees of the Port of London. For helping prepare the visit to Scotland in 1617 he received £170 expenses, not to mention gifts from hopefuls on the road and the promise of the office of gentleman usher of the Black Rod to the Lords, when its elderly occupant died. His brother Robert, too, was knighted and confirmed in post as Serjeant-at-Arms to the Commons. Inevitably, resentment rose at the success of this 'ill natured, dogged Scot'. Parliament rejected his naturalisation until 1622, and members muttered darkly before then when he was confirmed as Black Rod, and *ex officio*, Gentleman Usher to the Garter Order. 'The oldest Gentleman Usher is now dead and his places belonging to the Parliament [Black Rod] and the Garter [Usher] are bestowed on Maxwell of the Bedchamber, not without some murmuring, for that their orders do expressly forbid *alienigenam* [foreign born]. It is a windfall.' The wind was compensating Maxwell for the death of his brother Charles in a duel with the king's favourite, Sir Robert Ker, also of the bedchamber, the previous month. Allegedly Charles was defending the honour of the Duke of Buckingham. Caught between favourites, King James found Ker guilty of manslaughter, but forgave him.[5]

Elizabeth and her 'bairns' rose in rank and wealth as the new man in the family grew into his public roles. A groom of the bedchamber had unparalleled confidential access to the king; an usher personified the royal presence, like a living sphinx, in an age when the monarch embodied divine authority. The chief usher of the kingdom represented the king's rule in and over Parliament and his power over the great. A touch of the tipped Black Rod meant instant arrest, a knight's dubbing in reverse; it also brought Maxwell a triple gold chain with pendant, and five shillings per arrest. The highest in the land sampled Black Rod's hospitality at Charing when Parliament remanded them into his custody, before committing them to the Tower to await trial. The prisoner stepped into Maxwell's coach at Westminster Palace and was driven to his house to await Parliament's pleasure – in Laud's case for ten weeks. Backhouse, Rutland, Digby, Strafford, Laud and the two frailest of the Twelve Bishops all paid Maxwell for their house remand. Noblemen on their knees at the Bar of the House had to hand Maxwell their swords, and once under his roof had to pay him exorbitant lodging fees. For fresh air his 'guests' walked out with him from the Charing house, 'anywhere except Spring Gardens or any place belonging to the king's houses, to speak with none, but in the presence of Mr Maxwell'.[6] The king, too, was a visitor at Charing, Kingston, Windsor Little Park Lodge and the Castle apartment which came with the Garter role.

The growing girls were used to seeing the great of the land at close quarters. Prince Charles, twelve years older than Jeane and diminutive even in platform shoes, bowled, jogged and strolled in the noisy Spring Gardens over the Maxwells' back courtyard wall. Beyond lay the prince's home palace of St James's, slowly being eclipsed by the exciting new project of Whitehall. In 1626 a Scot caused a sensation in Spring Gardens by knocking off Buckingham's cap, accusing the royal favourite of disrespect to the king. A child brought up at Charing would have inhaled rather than learned the ethos and protocols of court service, which amounted to a frame of mind and a reflex. At the same time, courtiers were not blind to the humanity which wore the Crown and they trod carefully in the snakepit around the throne in order to survive. With every change of monarch came fresh competition for favour, 'the rise and fall of courtly silkworms', as Gerbier described it.

In March 1625 'all the nobility, privy counsellors and gentry went in hundreds and proclaimed the king at Charing Cross and Denmark House by sound of trumpet', the Cross just yards from the Maxwells' streetside windows. That evening the new King Charles rode down Whitehall from hunting at Theobalds in Cambridgeshire and lodged in St James's Palace, his home until he fled London in 1642; it also sheltered him on the last nights of his life in 1649. Eight thousand filed past Charing Cross in procession from Somerset House to the Abbey for the funeral of King James in 1625. Charing, Kingston and Windsor were exciting front seats for a thirteen-year-old Jeane.[7]

Excitement had its dark side. Five doors from the Maxwells was Wallingford House, between the old and new palaces, purchased by the Duke of Buckingham, the royal favourite, in 1621. King James visited daily when the duchess contracted smallpox. On the birth of a son to Buckingham in 1628, the bells of Westminster pealed a welcome and Bishop Laud of London baptised the child at home. Buckingham, however, was assassinated that year, and his body was brought by torchlight at night to lie in state at the Charing mansion for two weeks. Buckingham was the favourite of two kings; he had been William Ryder's master of horse, and was James Maxwell's close associate behind the scenes. Wallingford House was a personal as well as a physical neighbour to the Maxwell family.

Jeane's half-brother James Maxwell did not survive infancy.[8] There is no record of how he died in 1623, but plague and the 'small pocks' or 'poches' raged intermittently through London. In 1625 Parliament had to adjourn to Oxford, a fall-back capital much further up the Thames than Hampton Court and with cleaner rural air, to avoid the plague in a year when smallpox also struck particularly virulently. In 1628 the most serious smallpox outbreak of all took place, when Jeane was sixteen and particularly vulnerable. At some point in her youth – assuming the 'pocks' noted by Parliamentarian intelligence in 1648 were 'small' – she suffered facial scarring, despite cosmetics such as cream and saffron, or salted beef grease employed to fill the pock holes, an approach which must have overpowered the strongest perfume. Sister Diana's complexion survived unscathed.

Smallpox also killed, and was (to some) 'God's chastisement', although it 'hath taken away many of the good sort as well as meaner people'; 'small pocks' when inflamed or scabbed could even be taken for 'great' (syphilitic) pocks. Between 1618 and 1622 smallpox was a constant theme of John Chamberlain's letters from London to a friend in The Hague. 'The small pocks reign and rage very much both in city and country, for all last year's hard winter and cool summer.' Prince Charles and the Duke of Buckingham sent 'broths and caudles' to Lady Lennox when she contracted smallpox, a kindness she had once shown to her neighbour Lady Buckingham when she had smallpox after childbirth at Wallingford House. Others administered 'beer and saffron', which would rehydrate, and at least taste better than the 'horse dung water' which Lady Fane gave her children – manure liquefied with urine, wine, ale, and masked with herbs. A century passed before the first cowpox vaccination appeared, although it was well known that smallpox did not strike twice. However, even when four out of five survived, the women suffered 'that dreaded scourge of female beauty'. Lady Mordaunt was seized by the small pocks 'with great danger to mar her fair face'. Lady de Vere's five daughters (including Anne, later wife to General Fairfax) were infected within three days, and 'many young ladies and gentlemen are overtaken with them'. The 'pocks seized on Lady Bedford and have seasoned her all over, more full and foul than could be expected in so thin and lean a body, a malady which follows young blood. Lady Suffolk is sick of the small pocks, which would have done her more harm forty years ago.' Even babies contracted it, one child 'pitifully destroyed from top to toe'.[9] During outbreaks people fled London, or went into house quarantine, and the king stayed away from court festivities like Christmas.

The scarring of a young woman's complexion affected her chances of marriage and Jeane's scars would have been of particular concern in a family of four daughters. Her flame-hair and name already marked out her ethnic origin to which popular belief added other negative attributes. Maxwell's colleague William Murray's lively daughters, born in the same parish, also had 'unfashionable red gold hair'. Combined with pock scars this could strengthen character, or burden with self-dislike. The fever accompanying smallpox was bad enough, 'a distemper so violent before the pocks broke out', but the suggestion that it was a judgement and punishment could further damage the soul in a culture where religion – prescribed, exclusive and sometimes retributive – provided the only acceptable interpretation of life's drama.

Maxwell's concern to provide for his siblings who had come south for their fortune was as strong as for his new family. It gave credibility to James Howell's bitter claim of 1650 (when it was safe to speak) that the Scots 'swarms who came after King James sucked him of vast sums of money to serve their rot and luxury', and Anthony Weldon's accusation that 'many Scots did get much, but not more with one hand than they spent with the other'. Maxwell had been unable to protect his brother Charles from the duel with Ker, but he was able to bring in another brother, William, first as joint usher in Scotland to King James, then a week before the king's death to a similar appointment for both of them to attend Prince Charles. William Maxwell received large grants of land at Kirkhouse, as James acquired land by award which was once his father's, and further land confiscated from Lord Maxwell of Herries, a kinsman executed for rebellion in 1609.

Yet another brother, Robert, became serjeant to the Commons, then sitting in choir-formation in the former church of St Stephen's – 'Parliament' is still 'Sant Steffan' in modern Welsh. He brought a Lowlands accent to the role of king's executive officer to the Commons, and he alone carried a sword in the House, in addition to the mace. He had powers of arrest, a duty to confine for execution, was appointed by the Crown and acted under the orders of the speaker of the Commons. His role, however, expired when Parliament rose, which meant a commercial instead of a political life after 1629. When Parliament did sit, his and James Maxwell's Lothian brogue and Scots colouring highlighted, and even exacerbated, tension between the Scots and members of the English Commons and Lords, as increasingly the Stuarts' exercise of authority and patronage was questioned. The most controversial constitutional messages from King Charles to the Commons in the years leading up to the War – to dissolve and to attend the king – came in Black Rod's Lowland accent. It was he who was refused entry to the Commons chamber in 1629 when his brother was forbidden to respond to him. In 1640, when he did not even bother to issue the royal summons to the Short Parliament in person, but through a deputy, the members took it as a 'great neglect and wrong' that it was so improperly relayed, 'dishonouring and undervaluing the House'. In May 1641 he forgot his Black Rod of office, for which the Commons rebuked him.

Sir Robert, a bachelor, exemplified the Maxwell 'courtly silkworms' when, composing his will in 1637 in his white stone house in Savoy parish, he bequeathed his office, along with Mace and court dress, to his sister's son, James Edgar, 'if my said brother James Maxwell can procure the place for him'. Brother James received the white stone house for his role in this naked nepotism.[10] He had already advised on the appointment of his first cousin, John Maxwell, to the Scots bishopric of Ross in 1633, a high church Royalist at the eye of the Presbyterian-Anglican storm, who helped 'blow the bellows' of the religious wars between Scotland and England. Racial and religious antipathy made a volatile mixture and Bishop Maxwell's insensitivity ignited it, one hostile Scots chronicler describing him as 'a pretended bishop, a ranting, lying incendiary'. In contrast, James Maxwell grew so confident of his own authority that he appointed a new deputy to the usherships of Black Rod and Garter, without consulting the Crown, without paying the post-holder, and then demanding a fee from the appointee for the privilege.

Scotland seemed to be a bottomless purse from which to reward Scottish courtiers. Titles brought revenue, privileges and land, which in turn brought more titles. Elizabeth and James Maxwell received some rights and revenues from the barony of Innerwick in 1623, the remainder ('for services to the king from infancy') in 1630, and the barony itself in 1641. Charles I spent his last night in Scotland at Maxwell's Innerwick mansion before returning home by Berwick from his coronation in 1633. Hospitality to the Crown required the sort of money few but Maxwell had, and his six fellow grooms and the pages of the bedchamber present would aspire to the same grandeur as a mark of success. In 1633 James had paved the road to Charles I's coronation in Scotland for 500 servants, Archbishop Laud and other notables; he transported an altar, prepared Holyrood Palace for the crowning in preference to St Giles, and negotiated the episcopalian liturgy against the prickles of Presbyterian Edinburgh; his bishop-cousin, freshly consecrated, interrupted a service in St Giles in the king's presence to remove a minister wearing Geneva gown without surplice. James Maxwell had even travelled to France a year before to buy the wine for the celebrations, but the Sabbath banquet (audible in St Giles) before the Monday coronation outraged Presbtyerians. It was understandably, if unwittingly, Charles Stuart's last visit home. In 1637, almost in revenge, he imposed a new Anglican Scottish *Book of Public Service*, a barely disguised *Book of Common Prayer*, on his Presbyterian people, and banned all unscripted prayer: James Maxwell was his courier. It led directly to the humiliating wars with Scotland of 1639–41.

James Maxwell diversified his income, from land and titles in Scotland and annuities from the Crown, to church, commerce and ultimately to exacting interest from the king himself on loans secured by jewels, properties and trade monopolies. He held the advowson of Wigan and of Innerwick, tenements in Aldgate and shared an estate at Tiptree in Kent with brother Robert. In 1628 he received a twenty-one-year monopoly to export calfskins duty free, from any port save Chester and Liverpool, with an option to renew. In 1631 he took rights to mine lead and iron in Derbyshire. A consortium between him, Patrick Maule – another groom of the bedchamber – and others, won a monopoly just after Jeane Ryder's wedding in 1634, to trade between Scotland and the African Guinea coast for thirty-one years, and to import gold, silver and spice custom free. With William Murray, also of the bedchamber, he obtained in 1630 the commission for the repair and dressing of all firearms. For the sake of his minor trade empire he was allowed to build a coal-fired lighthouse on May in the Forth estuary, for which he exacted a toll from all passing English and Scots vessels. (It now flashes electronic warnings.) He also had a monopoly on all gold, silver and copper mined in the Scottish Okehill hills. Once Sir Robert, the Commons Serjeant, died in 1637, Maxwell took over the right (and fees) of *all* arrests in Parliament. In late September 1642, after the king had declared war and on the eve of Edgehill, Maxwell was still petitioning for a monopoly on importing calfskins.

The tax exemption of so many favoured Scots and others on royal concessions did not go unremarked. When the Ship Money controversy dominated the autumn of 1637, the monopolists' general immunity from tax was used as ammunition against the Crown, but Maxwell was a man to rise, not buckle when attacked. He was particularly ruthless in 1639 over a pipeclay monopoly held jointly with late brother Serjeant Robert and George Kirke, a court colleague and neighbour at Charing. The Pipeclay Company accused the monopolists of not buying their Dorset clay as agreed in the licence, one trader announcing that he 'did not care a [expletive deleted, 1639] for the monopoly or for Kirke and Maxwell'. In revenge – more vindictive than assertive – Maxwell's men broke into a London warehouse, commandeered the owner's pipeclay stock and forced him to repurchase it from them at a 500 per cent mark-up on his original outlay. It amounted to organised crime with the Crown's tacit approval.

Maxwell made many enemies, but the rough-mannered courtier also aspired to a calmer, cultured world as Whitehall became a European centre of the arts in the delayed English Renaissance. The Maxwell brothers, Serjeant-at-Arms and Black Rod, had to be tough. They were the Crown's bouncers in and out of Parliament. Toughness brought them wealth, which in turn purchased culture. They moved among the *culturati* of a Court with the king's expanding art collection at its centre and Inigo Jones overseeing the Whitehall building project to house it. Late in life James Maxwell is thought to have been painted by Lely. The king bought art compulsively through diplomats and agents, and his revival of the Garter 'royal priesthood' of chivalry gave his court a halo. The Scots dynasty had 'made it' and such enrichment stated so, like the Banqueting House ceiling, in a curiously Protestant baroque way.

Robert Maxwell may have inspired the red-bearded North British Serjeant with mace in those ceiling canvases. Rubens, diplomat and artist, spent nine months in London, 1628–9, and Jeane would know of him through her stepfather, who in those same months was channelling royal money to Gerbier, Buckingham's art purchaser, to negotiate pictures from Rubens, van Dyck and Mytens. Jeane's mother's being an Antwerper must have heightened the interest. Rubens returned in 1630 on contract for 'the greatest Baroque ceiling north of the Alps', which trumpeted the Stuart dynasty, the ascent into heaven of James I and the saving of the two kingdoms from the Gowrie and Powder Plots. The Banqueting House was 300 yards from Jeane's home and the completion of the canvases in Antwerp was announced in 1634, just before she married. Rubens attended the first Garter procession organised by Jeane's stepfather as usher. Van Dyck came from Antwerp in 1632 for two years, and later oil-sketched Usher Maxwell in Garter procession for tapestries for the Banqueting House walls. He even married a Scots aristocrat. Maxwell and family were unavoidably caught up in the cultural revolution at Court, and in the summer of 1642, just as War broke out, he made a donation to 'enhance' the faculty of Humanities at St Andrew's which his old friend Sir John Scot of Scotstarvet had instituted and endowed.[11]

Buckingham was murdered in August 1628, and Maxwell part-replaced him as the king's moneyraiser. The pawning of royal jewels made for his most dramatic, colourful and possibly most profitable deal. Significantly, it took place in 1629, three months after the king had ordered Parliament adjourned for eight days in March, at which Parliament defiantly adjourned itself. Black Rod summoned the Commons to attend the king in the Lords, but the House refused his request because it was oral, not written. They were used to his accent, but it probably irked more than usual that day. The speaker reiterated the royal command to close business and attend, but one member defied him, and continued to speak while MPs pinned the Speaker into his chair. Sir Robert Maxwell stood helpless, his Mace still on the table before the overpowered speaker. Black Rod Maxwell came again to the Commons and gave formal warning that the king was waiting for Serjeant Maxwell to lead them to the Lords. Sir Robert was forbidden to leave; the Commons adjourned itself and did not walk to the Lords, nor did it walk back to Westminster for another eleven years.

The king, Black Rod and the serjeant had been humiliated. Without Parliament-approved taxation, royal finances would dry up unless extra-parliamentary revenue replaced it. The king's debt stood at over £1 million, much of it war expense, some from compulsory art purchasing; inflation was also rising. Buckingham was no longer there to help and Charles turned to his canny chief usher, who combined the intimate discretion of the bedchamber with the acumen and wealth of the moneylender. James I had indulged a fortune in jewellery, some of its cutting and setting already out of fashion, and Buckingham had urged him to use the growing surplus as economical diplomatic gifts. In the summer of 1628, when Parliament was still sitting, Charles pawned two giant diamonds (thirty-two and twenty-three carat) through Maxwell for £6,000, which Maxwell then advanced to Buckingham, not back to the king. The money was to be repaid to the Crown by Endymion Porter, art adviser to the Duke, with interest by December 1628. Only a fraction went on art as the Duke was murdered in August; half was handed to his widow, and the balance went unspent. Maxwell kept the diamonds.

Discreetly in June 1629, four months after Parliament dissolved itself, King Charles and Maxwell visited 'the secret jewel house in the Tower' with Lord Cottington, Chancellor of the Exchequer. A major hoard of jewels, easily liquidified, was housed in chests there. Broken, cannibalised, outmoded or worn jewellery weighed as valuable as any bullion once the king judged it 'unfit for use and service in the king's eyes'. Some items were 'defaced by extraction', others, even those of sentimental family interest, received short shrift. The inspection inventories reveal an Aladdin's hoard. Gold collars tangled with sapphire rings, pearl pendants, jewelled cap bands, bodkins and an inlaid Turkish dagger. Prince Henry's damaged pyramid diamond went the way of broken orders, S-collars lacking a jewel or two, ninety-one ropes of pearls and three pearl pendants, a gold looking-glass, girdles and hangers. A girdle of 'red and white roses formed from rubies and diamonds', an M-shaped collett, a Lorraine cross of gold, diamonds and rock rubies, and a 'Jesus jewel', all probably Tudor, lay alongside a gold circlet 'formerly of our late dear mother, Queen Anne', inlaid with eight diamonds, eight rubies, eight emeralds, eight sapphires, thirty-two smaller diamonds and thirty-two smaller rubies. These and many more were sent to four jewellers for valuing, after which Maxwell was authorised to sell them. Four gold collars, two dozen gold bowls, a St Michael pendant and chain and a St Michael gold collar were thrown in. The king already owed Maxwell £225 interest on £5,000 the usher had loaned to the Crown, and owed him other principal amounts, but also paid him £2,100 in November (the balance of the pawn from Maxwell left unspent by Gerbier on the Buckinghams) 'for services performed to the king'. The benefit was mutual. Once the jewel valuation of £12,554 was received in January 1630, Maxwell paid £1,000 balance to the Privy Purse and kept the jewels as security for the outstanding loans. He was now playing his late neighbour's role in a private finance initiative, as lender and pawnbroker to the Crown.[12]

Two months later, an even longer list of jewels was placed at Maxwell's disposal – invoices were coming due for payment to visiting artists at home and disposing collectors abroad. Maxwell became the physical and legal owner of even more royal valuables which included circlets, necklaces, 'billaments and apparels', and he took them home to Charing. Jeane and Anne's young adult awe would counterbalance the noisy excitement of two little sisters begging to hold or try on the fairytale baubles. At the same time, Jeane was learning lessons of double accounting, court finance and commercial intrigue to add to her earlier experience of laundry and stables. In a few years time the four Ryder-Maxwell girls would take some of the pieces in their wedding portions of money, plate and jewels. Now that he was able to afford it, it was time for Maxwell to think about arranging the marriages of his four daughters. Wealth gave him the upper hand in any contract, and his daughters could then wear for real the jewels they now played with. Perhaps they squabbled as they played. Three decades later they were still fighting over them.

Notes

1. Sir Robert Douglas, *Peerage of Scotland*, 1784, 186 [erratic]; Sir James Balfour Paul, *The Scots Peerage*, 1906, III, 126–31 [erratic]; *Register of St Martin in The Fields, 1620–36*, Harleian Society Register Series, XXV (ii), 1936, 11, 20, 178; All Saints, Kingston upon Thames, register transcript, North Kingston Centre: Elizabeth was baptised at Kingston on 2 January 1620.

2. Harry Pitman, *Scottish Historical Review*, XXIII, 92, 1926, 268–74, Delmahoy vs Dirleton, An Old Chancery Suit.

3. HMC, Mar and Keillie Supplement, 1930, 23, July 1622; Bodleian Library, Ashmole Ms 1111, 137–8; CSP 1625–33, March 1627; Scottish Historical Society, Series 2, 17, 1917, 364.

4. For the detailed Court background, see indices to the CSP, 1610–39; *Registers of the Privy Council of Scotland*, 1592–1660, notably 1634–51; *Registrum Magni Sigilli Regum Scotorum*; *James I*, ed. Devon, 1836; Gerald Aylmer, *The King's Servants, The Civil Service of Charles I* (1961), 29–31.

5. *Huguenot Society of London Records*, XVII, 1911, 16, 29; *The Chamberlain Letters, 1597–1626* (ed. McClure), II, 1939, 11 March 1620; John Nichols, *Progresses*, III, 558, February 1620.

6. See, for instance, 'The Hasting Journal of 1621', ed. Villiers, *Camden Miscellany*, XX, Camden, 3rd Series, LXXXIII, 1953, 19, 23, for Lord Backhouse's detention; HMC 9 Salisbury (Cecil) Mss, XXII, 1962, addenda to 1661, 220, for Lord Digby as Maxwell's prisoner.

7. *Autobiography and Correspondence of Sir Simonds d'Ewes*, ed. J. Halliwell-Philips (1845), I, 264. R. Wilson, *Life of King James I* (1653), 264.

8. James was baptised at St Martin-in-the-Fields, 2 April 1621, and Diana on 8 August 1622, *Harleian Society Registers XXV (ii), 1936, St Martins-in-the-Fields: cf,* Note 1 above.

9. Simonds d'Ewes, *Correspondence, op.cit.*, I, 94; John Chamberlain, *Letters, op.cit.*, II, 74–531 *passim*, October 1618 to July 1622; Roger Thompson, *Women in Stuart England and America* (1933), 40.

10. *Register of the Privy Council of Scotland*, 1st Series, XIII, 1898, 65, 9 March 1625; TNA PROB 11/175, Sir Robert Maxwell's will, composed and probate 1637. Jane's step-cousin Edgar, merchant and provost of Edinburgh, corresponded

with Jane and other Royalist supporters, 1646–9, see Chapter 8. Sir Robert left step-niece Anne Ryder £25 for a gown and 'Mrs Cunningham, my brother James's daughter', the same, evidently a mis-remembered married name for Jane Whorwood; David Mullan, ed., *Religious Controversy in Scotland, 1625-9* (1998), 28, 37, 171; James Balfour, *Historical Works* (1824), II, 204, 263–4; Christian Hesketh, *Charles I's Coronation Visit to Scotland* (1998), 1, 6, 7, 9; Dougal Shaw, 'St Giles Church and Charles I's Coronation Visit to Scotland', *Historical Research*, 2004, LXXVII, No. 198, 481–502. James Maxwell also acted in 1629 as courier conveying a proposed early *Book of Common Prayer* to be imposed on the Scots; Charles Carleton, *William Laud* (1987), 24, 155; it was finally imposed in 1637.

11. Indices, CSP volumes 1619–41 and *Registrum Magni Sigilli Regum Scotorum*, IX, 1634–51. Scot of Scotsiret played on his sybillant name with *The Staggering State of the Scots Statesmen* (1654). See also, Roy Strong, *Van Dyck* (1972), 59–63, and *Britannia Triumphans* (1980), 24. The Garter Procession oil-sketch is now in the Ashmolean Museum, Oxford. For the jewel financing episode, including Endymion Porter's account with the king in Maxwell's name for Buckingham's use, see SP Domestic, 1628–9, CVIII, 10, (24 June 1628); ibid., CIII, 46 (Porter's *Accompt*, 7 May 1628, accounted for 27 March 1629). Buckingham was murdered in August 1628.

12. Ibid., CXLIV, 55, (9 June 1629); ibid., CXLV, 10, 15 (20 June 1629); ibid., CLII, 10 (18 November 1629); SP Domestic, 1630, CLIX, 19 (January 26 1630); CLIX, 48, (30, 31 January 1630): CLXIII, 21, (20 March 1630) lists I–IV. In 1649 James Maxwell left to his wife much jewellery, including a portrait of the Duke of Holstein (d.1616) set in diamonds, thirty-four pearl necklaces, and a ruby valued by Maxwell at £1,500 for which he had turned down £1,300 offered by the Duke of Richmond. He also apportioned much jewellery to his daughters on their marriages, see Chapter 4. In 1656 and in 1660 the Hamiltons petitioned Charles II for some of James Maxwell's 'great store' of jewels 'the best in England', mentioning in particular two pearls weighing seventeen and twenty-four carats from 'The Mirror of Britain', and a rose jewel set with diamonds and thirty-five single carat pearls. HMC 9, Salisbury (Cecil) Mss, XXII, 1612–68 (1971), 418; TNA SP 29 1660, 22, 56.

4

1634–42:
Four Weddings: Whorwoods, Hamiltons, Cecils and Bowyers

Lord Cranborne is to be married within the week, but to one who is not worthy to wipe my lady Dorothy [Sydney's] shoes, a younger daughter to James Maxwell, with a great portion …£18,000 and £4000 in jewels. I hate marriages made for money.
George Gerard to Viscount Conway, March 1639

James Maxwell in consideration of an agreement of marriage, freed Sir Thomas Whorwood from a Star Chamber fine and gave £2600 in money, goods, jewels and plate as a marriage portion for his stepdaughter Jane to marry Sir Thomas's son [whose] father's estate would never have come down to him without the help of her friends.
Jane Whorwood in Chancery, 1673

The Ryder and Maxwell girls grew up at ease with the faces and names of Court, and of the smaller 'courts' along The Strand, Charing and King Street. The Cecils ruled at Salisbury House, Anne of Denmark (and later Henrietta Maria) at Denmark House, and nearest the Maxwell home, the Duke of Buckingham steered the king from Wallingford House. In 1632 James, Marquis of Hamilton, husband of Mary Fielding the late Duke's niece, took over the mansion and gave his younger brother William permanent lodging there.

Worldly-wise Maxwell parents would have shared their insider experience and gossip with their daughters, and with no son to distract. Jeane and Anne, the older siblings, had more time to learn than their younger sisters – the Court tales, the fantastical jewels, events in Parliament with father and uncle onstage in costume, not to mention the distinguished, if dejected lodgers who stayed with them on remand. Some of the never-ending royal masque was played out audibly in Spring Gardens, over their courtyard wall.

On Sundays the royal parish church of St Martin's was a crowded meeting point for courtiers whose public worship was *de rigeur*, whether for form or from conviction. In fact, the entire Whitehall experience was an education.

No record describes Jeane Ryder's formal upbringing, but the girls would have had tutors. Anne Murray (later Halkett), another Scots courtier's child, described how her mother 'spared no expense educating. She paid masters to teach my sister and me to write, speak French, play the lute and virginals, dance and a gentlewoman taught us needlework.' Anne's cousins, the red-haired daughters of William Murray, Maxwell's bedchamber colleague, also had the education a wealthy father could afford. Maxwell's daughters were in exactly that position. (Sieger Huse, William Ryder had stipulated, was to be his children's 'tutor', probably guardian, only in the event of their mother's death.) Schools for wealthy girls did exist. The Ladies Hall at Deptford trained 'the children of less exalted courtiers and court officials' in dance, public speaking, acting and evocative embroidery, all (including the embroidery) geared to communicating in public and building confidence, something for which Jeane was remarked on in later life and which her letters exude. She may have spent time in service in another household. Less formal education came from home, religion, the surrounding court and embassies, and of course the king's art world. Inigo Jones lived beyond the Cross, in Scotland Yard; Rubens and van Dyck were guest workers. Buckingham's celebrated collection, some of it at Wallingford House, attracted international interest and was succeeded by the Hamilton collection under the same roof. George Kirke, gentleman of the robes, and his wife Anne, dresser to Henrietta Maria, were among other grandee neighbours. Jeane probably learned to ride, with riding houses on hand at St James' and The Mews. An exotic animal centre was established in St James's Park just before her birth; the novelty, as well as the pranks and cruelties inflicted on its pelicans, crocodiles, camels and elephant, were part of her childhood scene.[1]

She may have had a language from her mother – Flemish, French, or a smatter of Portuguese from distant grandmother Paraides – and perhaps a different imported sense of the role of women. No description of her in adult life calls her Scottish; no brogue peeps through her written words and she was reported by Parliamentarian spies in 1648 as notably 'well-languaged [well spoken]'. She wrote fluently in neat italic script, expressing herself in a complex, almost opaque, courtly style, which suggests formal training. Wartime letters to courtiers and the king, and her appeals to Commons and king later in life, are all couched in the same mannered phraseology. A comparison of her adventures to a 'Romance' in a letter of 1648 is evidence more of defiance than of wide reading, since *novellas* had been banned in 1647. Her one nom de plume, 'Hellen', was inspired either by Troy or, in the 'Scottifyed' circle round the king, the heroine of the ballad of Kirkconnell. Certainly she had the confidence of the trickster, embezzling for the Cause, and in later life neither the Bar of Parliament nor King Charles II's presence chamber at Whitehall daunted her. A stepfather like Maxwell was the best tutor she could have had. He made enemies and the family learned to tread carefully, watching their backs and canny under siege.

Jeane and Anne would have helped bring up Elizabeth and Diana in the two-tier family, but as marriage loomed age differences levelled. Jeane married first. According to Peter Heylyn, Garter prelate when Maxwell was Garter Usher, she was known familiarly as 'Ginne [Jinny] Ryder'.[2] Maxwell arranged for her to marry a country squire's son from Oxfordshire and had the wealth for a generous dowry and portion; Jeane's scarred complexion may explain her marriage at twenty-two to a groom nearly four years her junior, an even greater difference than the 'two or three years' which for Anne Halkett was 'such serious weight with me, as would never let me allow [one suitor] further address'. Jeane's red hair may have deterred others. The father of a suitor for Elizabeth, eldest daughter to William Murray (of the bedchamber), later Lady Dysart, noted 'she is a pretty one, but for her deep coloured hair. Such a pretty witty lass with such a brave house and state as she, might [persuade] a young fellow [to] think her hair very beautiful.'[3]

James Maxwell's wealth helped reconcile the Whorwoods to Jeane, her hair and her pocks. Brome Whorwood was heir to Sandwell Park, West Bromwich, and Holton Park, Oxford. In 1613 Thomas Whorwood of Sandwell had married Ursula Brome, sole heir of George Brome of Holton, recusant and antiquarian. As a customary courtesy, they baptised their first son with his mother's maiden name in Cuddesdon church in 1615. George Brome, who died in 1613, was first cousin to a more celebrated recusant and antiquarian, Henry Ferrers of Baddesley Clinton, from where the Bromes of Holton had originated in the fifteenth century. The family branches remained in constant touch, brought close again in the 1560s when the Windsor sisters, recusant aristocrats from a family favoured by Queen Elizabeth, married a Ferrers and a Brome. Their respective sons, George and Henry, later colluded in recusancy. George spent time in the Gatehouse prison as a child with his recusant mother in the 1570s; he was arrested and interrogated over the Babington Plot of 1586; Jesuits on their way from London to Baddesley Clinton in the early 1590s seem to have used Holton House as a halfway stop; and along with Henry Ferrers, George was on the edge of the Powder Plot of 1605. In his closing years, like Ferrers and other weary recusants, he retreated into books, antiquarianism and refurbishing his decrepit mansion.[4]

Holton House, with its medieval tower, renovated house and modest deer park, was potentially a good home for Jeane, but it was literally in a sleepy hollow. Grandfather George's hundred-tome library did not stock romances, nor did the house inventory of 1684 show musical instruments, embroidery frames or the titles of the few hanging pictures. It was a backwater, with gaming tables in the great parlour and a bowling green in the park.

Lady Ursula brought Holton to the Whorwoods on marrying and retained it for her widowed lifetime, after which it reverted to Brome. Thomas was knighted in 1624, a liability as much as an honour, which increased his sense of superior inferiority. He was considered grasping and disagreeable to his neighbours in two counties and evidently bequeathed his traits.

He was also a familiar figure in Westminster, so frequently was he hauled in from the shires to stand before Chancery and Star Chamber courts. His final indictment was to be accused in Star Chamber of ordering his bailiff to kill a man at Kings Norton in a land dispute. 'James Maxwell, later Earl of Dirleton, in consideration of an agreement of marriage, freed Sir Thomas Whorwood from the fine.' The two understood each other, especially after Whorwood plied the prosecutor with drink to obtain copies of the interrogations. Sentence was reduced to a censure, for which the price was that the Whorwood heir should marry Maxwell's oldest daughter who would bring with her '£2600 in money, goods, jewels and plate as a marriage portion'. In response, the Whorwoods would settle on Jeane '1000 marks [£667] a year as her marriage portion'. Holton and Sandwell estates received a welcome subsidy. Brome, who was later described in Parliament as 'of a savage and penurious disposition, like his father', may also have been attracted to the link with Court.

The contents of the windfall marriage portion are no longer known, but an inventory taken at Holton after Brome's death in 1684 listed a 'Red Trunk' kept for security at Queen's College. It held 'one gilt salt cellar with St George on horseback, six plates gilt and two spoons gilt, 71 ounces'. Small and dated, such a salt had a distinct regal or even Garter theme, and was evidently prized. It would have been too light to be a royal gift, but its gilding suggests luxury, while gilt plates and spoons suggest the dessert course, a woman's area of responsibility. These items were not standard manor house plate and may have been tangible tokens brought by Jeane from the Maxwell hoard.[5]

The marriage was agreed hastily in the summer of 1634, under pressure from Maxwell. Even the marriage licence application was perjured to hide the age discrepancy. Holton was on the 48th milestone from London, in contrast to Charing where the great, the good and the eminently dubious were always passing through. Sandwell Park, the new couple's first home, was twice as far from the capital. Royalty did not stroll through small provincial deer parks, Spring Gardens was a long way away and great parlour talk would have been of tenants, bees, the warren, the sermon, patent medicines, poachers, the mills, the crops and the weather. Holton's last political excitement had been the Jesuits, and Sandwell had not even had that; Frances Curson's elopement from Waterperry House with Oliver Gadbury in 1628 had been a nine-day wonder; the Twelfth Night illegal burial of Aunt Horseman, née Brome, in 1630, a cause célèbre; but compared to Whitehall, Holton was on the dark side of the moon. The Whorwoods had to accommodate a confident, cultured lady from across the 'deep and damaging fault line' which separated the Scots at Court from the English gentry.[6] Jeane from Stuart Whitehall became Jane of the English manor, and she may not have fitted; her mother-in-law, a Windsor granddaughter and kinswoman of Viscount Conway, Secretary of State, may have given her little shrift. Maxwell was notorious as well as Scottish, and in arranging the marriage he commanded the shots.

Jeane had been four when her mother processed Pocahontas's linen during the princess's stay at Denmark House; her mother's family had an 'Ethiopessa' among their servants, baptised in St Martin's when Jeane was five. She had witnessed royal and ducal funerals and her father had organised King Charles's two coronations: 1625 in Westminster and 1633 in Edinburgh. In the year Jeane married, Maxwell bounced from Scots coronation to founding the exotic (and profitable) Scottish African trading company. Holton had a coach, but Emmanuel, Lady Ursula's coachman, would have driven nothing like the heavy emblazoned vehicle with outriders in which Maxwell, sometimes with Jeane and family, rode through London crowds with halberdiers in escort. The few horses stalled at Holton Park could not match the columns of mounts at Charing Mews.

Jeane and Brome married on 22 September 1634, but not in the bride's parish. They obtained the licence exempting them from banns and seem to have exchanged vows in St Faith's, the crypt parish church under the east end of old St Paul's. About 400 weddings were solemnised there each year as it was near the two church licensing offices. St Paul's itself was a building site as the king, Laud and Inigo Jones struggled to make it a basilica fit for London instead of a shopping and strolling arcade. Public subscriptions had been invited which may account for the Whorwood brass erected (for a fee) in the cathedral south aisle just above St Faith's.[7] James Maxwell squeezed the wedding into his busy Court schedule. On return to Hampton Court from attending King Charles hunting at Nonsuch, he went downriver immediately from his second home at Kingston, doubtless stopping off at The Mews to collect his coach to carry bride, sisters and mother to St Paul's. It was small beer to a man who arranged coronations.

St Faith-in-the-Shrouds was also the cathedral burial crypt, but its popular name proved to be an omen. Brome's father died immediately after the ceremony, after completing his will that day, 'sick in body' aged fifty-two. The later brass in St Paul's may have marked the event.[8] His death turned wedding guests into mourners overnight, making an already dubious wedding even more inauspicious. On the following day his widow, Lady Ursula, had to mark the 'year's mind' of the death of Brome's sister, Elizabeth, aged fifteen. Maxwell contributed '£2600 marriage portion besides other great and considerable advantages. [Brome's] father's estate would never have come down to him without the help of the friends of Jane Whorwood.' Jane returned to her new home at Sandwell by way of Holton – customarily a bride spent some initial time with her in-laws – and she would have attended Sir Thomas's funeral there a month later. He was buried in the chancel next to his daughter Elizabeth's fresh grave.

Sir Thomas's death between wedding and consummation also cost the newly-weds a fine. The Court of Wards, under its ailing master, Sir Robert Naunton, Maxwell's next-door neighbour at Charing, fined Brome £500 for defying the Court's wardship by consummating his marriage as a minor after his father's death. It was a legalism, and Brome appealed, but unsuccessfully.[9] He petitioned that

> Sir Thomas Whorwood his late father did enter into treaty of marriage … between the petitioner and Jane Ryder, daughter in law to James Maxwell Esq, one of the Grooms of His Majesty's Bedchamber and the petitioner's father with Mr Maxwell did conclude and under their seal and hand, 10th September last, did agree on the conditions of marriage. In and by the said articles the petitioner's father did propose for a jointure to be made for a second wife. The said marriage, in regard of Mr Maxwell attending on your Majesty [at Nonsuch], did not take effect till September 22nd [1634] on which day the petitioner was married and after the said marriage the petitioner's father the very same day died, the petitioner being not then 21.

While it had the makings of a Shakespeare comedy, it was the Crown using any device to generate revenue in the absence of Parliament. Ironically, Sir Thomas's father had also given a false age for Thomas when he married Ursula Brome, which had allowed him to argue a technically defective contract and so to withhold his portion.

Jane's first child, hardly a product of that breach of law, was born in the autumn of 1635, 'red haired as his mother', remembered Anthony Wood, and was baptised Brome on 29 October at Holton in compliment to Lady Ursula's family. He alone of Jane's four children was baptised there. A second son, James, baptised on 27 December 1636 in Windsor parish church, 'son of Mr Brome and Jane', was buried in St George's chapel barely four months later from Windsor Little Park Lodge on 24 April 1637. The Lodge was an *ex officio* Maxwell residence, along with an apartment in the upper ward of Windsor Castle itself. The funeral coincided with the annual Garter feast for St George's Day, which Maxwell managed as usher. That year, uniquely, the feast for 400 grandees was held twice, for the final time at St George's great hall, Windsor, and for the first time in the impressive new setting of the Banqueting House, Whitehall. Jane probably retreated from Holton to Windsor for her confinements trusting a Court midwife over a rural one. The queen had midwives over from Paris, Elizabeth of Bohemia took English midwives to Heidelberg and Jane's mother's confinements had all been at Whitehall or Hampton Court. Childbirth carried such risk it could not be taken lightly, yet possibly it added to the distancing between her and the Whorwoods. To Jane, however, Windsor town, parks and castle were home from home, ever since Maxwell married her mother and was appointed Black Rod. It was a perfect haven for a mother with a sick baby.[10]

Jane's third child was christened Elizabeth in St Helen's, Bishopsgate, on 10 May 1638, but was buried at Holton less than three years later. The choice of name two weeks before the wedding of Jane's sister Elizabeth was a compliment both to her sister and to her mother. At eighteen Elizabeth Maxwell married William Hamilton, either at St Faith's or St Anne's Blackfriars on 26 May. He was twenty-two, cousin to Charles I and younger brother by ten years to James, Marquess and later first Duke of Hamilton. 'I count writing to you or your brother all one', the king told him in 1646. With his own apartment at his brother's Wallingford House, William almost literally married the girl next door. They celebrated with mixed emotions, since the Marchioness of Hamilton, James's wife, died at Wallingford House the day Jane's daughter was baptised. The widower left Charing for Chelsea almost immediately. William and his father-in-law spent the rest of that year trying fruitlessly to head off war with Scotland, but his marriage at least was a success and one which Hamilton had actively wanted. He and Maxwell were already close as personnel of the bedchamber, the Hamiltons in line of succession to the Scottish throne and the king's lead advisers on, and representatives in, Scotland. English Court life, however, distanced them from the Scottish pulse, rendering them suspect in both countries, even to King Charles. At least the normally hostile Lord Clarendon admitted William was 'more to be relied upon than most Scots'.

'William [Hamilton]'s brother [James] was more careful to think of a future for [William] than he was. He provided a marriage for him that had expectation of a vast fortune. Lady [*sic*] Elizabeth Maxwell, eldest daughter of the Earl of Dirleton [Maxwell's later title] who had no sons and but one [*sic*] other daughter, was reluctant, so he married her in 1638 and stayed at Court.' Elizabeth brought with her £20,000 in cash, jewels and land, but the Hamiltons used much of it to pay off debt and to finance their determined art collecting. The couple were still paying rates on Wallingford House in 1641 when William sat in Parliament for Portsmouth. He hoped to be master of horse to the queen and threatened to move to France when he was not promoted. In 1639 Charles made him Earl of Lanark, and in 1640 secretary for Scotland. On his deathbed as a prisoner after the battle of Worcester in 1651, he ended his last letter to Elizabeth, 'Dear Heart, Your own'.[11]

With repeated good timing Jane Whorwood had another daughter, whom she christened Diana on 22 May 1639 at St Martin's. Her youngest Maxwell sister had married there in April; Diana's marriage raised eyebrows, as she did herself into old age; in another century she would have been a 'dollar duchess'. On 28 March 1639 George Gerrard wrote to Viscount Conway:

> Lord Cranborne is to be married, but not to my Lady Dorothy [Sydney – 'Sacharissa', whose surprise marriage came in July] but to one who is not worthy to wipe her shoes, a younger daughter of James Maxwell with whom he gives £18,000, £4000 in jewels, £800 a year in land in England, half his Scottish land, or the whole if Lord William Hamilton's lady [Elizabeth] die without issue. A great portion! But I hate marriages made for money and they have lost their reputation, both son and father, for this high avariciousness.

In his indignation he forgot to mention the couple's £1,000 annuity.

Charles Cecil, Lord Cranborne, was twenty, Diana Maxwell 'about 16'. The marriage was one of few Anglo-Scottish alliances achieved, although James I had hoped to integrate his kingdoms in this way. Again, as with the encumbered Hamiltons and Whorwoods, Maxwell money resuscitated the family which married it. Cranborne's father, William, Earl of Salisbury – Salisbury House dominated The Strand – was enabled by the Maxwell dowry to afford his daughter Elizabeth's marriage to Charles Cavendish, Lord Devonshire, a month before the Cranborne wedding. Another daughter Anne had married Algernon Percy, Duke of Northumberland, in 1635; another, Frances, had married James Fiennes, later second Lord Saye, in 1631. Becoming a Cecil added status to Diana's looks, both of which preoccupied her for life, although she never became more than Viscountess Cranborne. Within two years of the wedding Cranborne was being sued by Diana's creditors for almost £6,000, incurred despite her generous annual allowance. Her son James inherited the Salisbury title only in 1669, nine years after after Diana's husband died abroad fleeing their creditors.[12]

Diana and Charles, 'both of this parish', married at St Martin's on 2 April 1639, presumably in the Cecil chapel where the Cavendish–Cecil wedding had been solemnised. A Cecil was a good catch, from the family which advised monarchs. James Maxwell was doing right by his daughters and investing for himself in good connections. He regarded the marrying of the four girls with dowries appropriate to their stations – wives to an esquire, a knight and two earls – as more than a duty or achievement, noting when he compiled his will in 1646: 'I have already married my children, they also having had good proofs of the love and affection of my dearest Spouse Elizabeth de Boussy, [now] my sole heir.' Anne Ryder, nearly thirty, was the last to wed in about 1640, as third wife to Sir Thomas Bowyer MP of North Mundham, Sussex. At fifty-four, an East India Company and Levant Company merchant, Bowyer was sheriff of Surrey and Sussex. He had a house near the Maxwells in Charing, and close contact with Usher Maxwell through the early days of the Long Parliament. The two colluded in Wartime, hiding Maxwell's goods from Parliament's bailiffs. Anne had one child with Bowyer, baptised in February 1641, but thirteen stepchildren occupied the rest of her time. Later, she rallied from her own secure financial position to fend for her sisters.[13]

Jane's early married years were formally based on Sandwell Park in West Bromwich, but given the time she spent in London she would have stayed frequently at Holton, halfway along the route. Brome too must have completed the law studies at Trinity College, Oxford, which helped bring him a doctorate after the battle of Edgehill in 1642. For Jane to stay or live at Holton was convenient, politic, even required, and Lady Ursula had a direct claim of interest in her only grandchildren. Holton would one day revert to Jane and Brome when Ursula died; Sandwell could always be tenanted, until Jane's own children inherited. On the young family's horizon, Holton eclipsed Sandwell.

The house stood on slopes, east of Oxford, where the London Way crossed the River Thame on Wheatley Bridge, a medieval span of eight arches. The traveller to Oxford from London by Stokenchurch first saw the turrets and trees of Holton Park from the causeway across the flood meadows of the Thame. This nondescript meander seeped past the Crokes at Waterstock, below the Cursons at Waterperry, across Whorwood country at Holton, by the Gardiners and the bishop's palace at Cuddesdon, and on under Chiselhampton Bridge towards the Thames at Dorchester nine miles away. In Wartime the Thame became Oxford's eastern outer moat. It even had its own poet. John Taylor's *Thame to Thame-isis* (1630) described its fall to the Thames as a journey to the dismantled shrine of St Birinus, 'creeping south under Wheatley Bridge like a pilgrim all alone'.[14] Once over the bridge, past Holton windmill, the traveller to Oxford came to the fork in London Way, west over Shotover Hill to Oxford, and north-west to Worcester, through Forest Hill, Islip and Woodstock.

The moated house was an elongated H, on the front of which grandfather George Brome grafted a matching oriel and porch. It lay in 170 acres of deer park, a tenth the size of the Cecil park at Hatfield and the Maxwell park at Guildford. After Sir Thomas Whorwood died in 1634, his brother Field, a Lombard Street banker, moved to Holton as company and support for Lady Ursula. Brome had younger brothers: William, who became a distinguished Royalist officer; and Thomas, a lawyer, known later for his strident warnings to Charles II. Neither of them married. In 1634 Jane entered a dull, rambling, pretentious house in a backwater, dominated by Lady Ursula and her volatile oldest son.

The omission of Jane Whorwood from all family wills, save those of her blood parents, indicates an early distancing from sisters and in-laws alike. She seems to have crossed those closest to her. As a confident oldest sister she might have been imperious and perhaps impetuous. In later years her declining health and everyone's declining fortunes help explain the isolation, but do not explain why her two sisters, Elizabeth and Diana, with eighteen children between them, failed to name a daughter after her, despite her christening compliment to them both. Of the five Hamilton daughters, three were Diana, Anne and Elizabeth, but no Jane or Jeane; of Diana's five daughters, two were

Diana and Elizabeth, but no Jane or Anne. The split, evidently from before the War, continued until only Jane remained alive. Three of her children were baptised away from Holton, and one was buried at Windsor. Her mother-in-law may have envied her status, disapproved of her strong mind, and later been critical of her leaving her children in Wartime. Lady Ursula not only lost her husband on Jane's wedding day, but the following day had to mark her only daughter's first anniversary, *mater carissima maerens* [fondest grieving mother], as the brass still proclaims in Holton church. Jane was perhaps 'guilty' before she arrived, and Scottish hair in the heart of England did not help. She had 'taken' the son and heir in a sequence of events which to some may have shouted 'judgement'. She may also have given rural life short shrift, although the smell of the sewer-moat cannot have been worse than the leaking sewers she had left behind in overcrowded Charing.

Mutual prejudice between court and country was time-honoured and in 1631, as if to warn against marriages like the Whorwood-Ryder one, *The English Gentlewoman* was published by Richard Braithwaite, a conservative northern squire with Oxford and Grays Inn behind him. He spent time observing the Westminster celebrity world, which provincial folk identified with political, financial and sexual irregularity under its mannered and gilded veneer. Braithwaite's book followed his first guide to conduct, *The English Gentleman*, of 1630. In both he contrasted false court gentility with sincere rural and provincial such. 'Court gloss is like glass, bright but brittle. [They are] more courtesan than courtier, [whereas you must be] courtiers of a higher court.' His lament, 'true mothers be rare', about mothers so busy they delegate even the care of their children, is a timeless complaint, perhaps tinged with envy, but the worthy matron in starch has never been the most appealing model for a lively twenty-year-old bride. Given the book's enormous publicity at the time, gentry friends might have made its frequent reprint a wedding gift – even if a pointed one – to the Whorwoods.[15]

On regular visits to London Jane would have gauged the rising tension between King and Parliament from the table talk at Charing. It was no surprise. Her stepfather and uncle were centre stage in 1629, when King and Commons severed the link. The Court came briefly to Oxford in 1636 when Archbishop Laud's coach-and-six with its fifty outriders passed Holton to inspect the new bishop's palace at Cuddesdon, and returned to open a new quadrangle at St John's. The ending of the Short Parliament in 1640 was followed by the calling of the Long, the king's defeat by the Scots, cousin John Maxwell fleeing his second bishopric, and ominously, the detention of Archbishop Laud in the Maxwell home. Black Rod was central to the stand-off, in his role between King, Lords and Commons. In 1641 he was chief usher at the trial of Strafford in Westminster Hall. Even when bringing 'good news', as in May 1641, that the king had assented to Strafford's execution, he was tactless: 'The gentleman was something transported, as if all the world was out of their wits, for he came without his Black Rod, entered without being called in, and exception was taken, but the news he brought was so agreeable [to a Commons majority] it took off the resentments.'[16]

Other courtiers of the king's personal staff might have felt conflicting loyalties in arresting the king's closest advisers, but Maxwell was tough and made money from his prisoners. Laud praised his consideration over his long stay at Charing in 1640–1, but paid for the courtesy. Jane on a Christmas visit home evidently met Laud: 'Ginne Ryder' described him 'to her Gossips' as 'one of the goodest men, most pious, but silliest fellow to hold talk with a lady'. At Laud's trial in 1644 Maxwell was accused *in absentia* of helping Laud burn incriminating papers at Lambeth the day the archbishop was arrested; but he invoiced him £500 for the two and a half months at Charing, December 1640 to February 1641, before taking him to the Tower in Black Rod's coach, 'followed by a railing mob'. One satirist called it *Laud's Change of Diet*. Maxwell missed no chance of enrichment, demanding from the Commons Serjeant the exclusive right to escort prisoners – and all the fees for doing so. Two frail bishops, Coventry and Durham, were lodged at Charing rather than with their colleagues in the Tower in March 1641; Strafford, the king's closest counsellor, moved into Laud's rooms in the house when they had hardly cooled. Maxwell took Strafford's fees too, as well as his sword, and five years later was still pursuing the right to sell as his own the timber platform on which Strafford was tried in Westminster Hall. Even as late as 1669 a successor Black Rod was still trying to clarify the late James Maxwell's 'customary claim for half fees from the Lieutenant of the Tower' for Black Rod's prisoners.[17] Supplementation knew no bounds.

In summer 1642 the declaration of War divided many married couples, among them two who crossed west of Wheatley Bridge. In May a melancholic lone wolf of thirty-six came to Forest Hill by Holton to collect interest from the Powell family on an old debt owed to his father, a London scrivener. Several generations of Miltons had lived in Holton, Stanton and Forest Hill; John Milton's grandfather had been a ranger in Shotover royal forest and a convicted recusant; another ancestor had been a retainer at Holton Park, with a rent-free home granted in Forest Hill. Milton's father left for London, possibly after disagreement over religion. In June 1642 John Milton and Mary, a Powell daughter, returned to London married, although no wedding record survives. A month later Mary, seventeen, visited her family but did not return, cut off from London by the outbreak of War in August, and apparently unhappy in her marriage. Wheatley Bridge was blocked, guarded and eventually cut, but other interpretations were placed on Mary's remaining: 'two opinions do not well on the same bolster' was the kindest. Milton campaigned heatedly for divorce to be legalised, particularly for those in hasty matches ('prisons') with immature partners. On his lobbying, the Westminster Assembly did advise divorce for desertion and adultery, if not for cruelty. In a patriarchal, increasingly puritan society, women were expected to be subject to men, as childlike emotion had to be to adult reason, and chastised into line when necesssary.[18]

Cary Verney of Claydon House also crossed John Taylor's 'creeping pilgrim Thame' that May. She was fifteen, a distant cousin of the Whorwoods through the Bromes, and had married Thomas Gardiner, son of the Royalist recorder of London. Gardiner's manor house overlooked the Thame from the top of the Cuddesdon spur. Cary arrived just as Parliament expelled her father-in-law to his country seat. He was bitter after months in the Tower and being rejected as Crown nominee for Speaker, although the king did make him attorney general at Oxford. Cary wrote to her Parliamentarian brother and MP, Sir Ralph Verney, 'they bid me very welcome to Cuddesdon. We are abroad every day towards evening in the coach' (when she may have visited the Holton cousins). Ralph was pleased for her and proposed 'if the times are quiet I purpose to visit Cuddesdon this summer'. However, the War showed the Gardiners in a poor light, in contrast to Verney kindnesses across the firing line.[19]

The War certainly helped drive Jane and Brome Whorwood apart. Once War broke out and the royal Court barricaded itself into Oxford after the battle of Edgehill, Jane was back among her own, and her husband exiled himself to Holland. It was all perhaps a welcome liberation from unwelcoming in-laws. Reluctantly, James Maxwell also appeared at Oxford for a royal reprimand. In March 1642 the king at York had summoned him from Westminster to organise the Garter Feast there instead of at Whitehall. It was a test of loyalty. Parliament countermanded that, 'in regard of the urgent affairs of the kingdom, he attend his duty here'. Maxwell was in turmoil. 'I know not what course to take but entreat you to signify this to His Majesty. I cannot be sent to bring up the Speaker and Commons except I go carrying the Black Rod, otherwise they will neither obey me nor come.'[20] Five months later the king appointed Maxwell and Sir James Thynne as co-equal ushers of the Black Rod and of the Garter. Thynne served the Oxford Parliament during the War, while Maxwell withdrew to Scotland exacting a premium of £2,000 from Thynne *and* pocketing his own fees for the post.

Among Maxwell's last, perhaps even for him uncomfortable, pre-War duties was to relieve Sir Richard Gurney, Royalist Lord Mayor and East India merchant, of his regalia: they had been commercial colleagues. On 18 August 1642 Gurney, deposed by Parliament, had refused to hand his insignia and seals of office to any but the king, but he agreed to present them to Maxwell as Black Rod. Maxwell kept them overnight at Charing, and then conveyed them to the newly intruded Lord Mayor, Isaac Pennington, before taking Gurney to the Tower. A week later, when the Earl of Southampton stood up in the Lords to deliver the king's ultimatum of war to both Houses, he was forbidden to speak save through James Maxwell as Black Rod, and when he refused he was silenced and escorted from the Lords by Maxwell.

Back west of Wheatley Bridge, John Gadbury marked his tenth birthday. Dubious rural matches raised eyebrows only briefly, unlike at Court. The Gadburys, prosperous Wheatley yeomen, had sent their son Oliver into service with the Cursons at Waterperry House in 1628. He eloped with Frances Curson and they baptised their firstborn at Cuddesdon in 1632. After the War John rose to rival William Lilly for the role of national astrologer, and Lilly called his parents 'knave' and 'whore'. Although John studied it at Oxford, the value of 'philomathy' as a science was increasingly questioned. In wider society, however, and especially in the insecurity of Wartime, kings, generals, devout puritans, bishops and the more obviously credulous, still looked to astrologers for counsel, healing and forecasts. Even witch-finders used them, careful to distinguish between divination and magic. National politics and military strategy often hinged on the interpretation of astrological charts, and in the next few years, the king, Parliamentarians and Jane Whorwood in particular looked frequently to William Lilly's stars for answers.

Notes

1. Anne Halkett, *Autobiography of Lady Anne Halkett*, Camden Society, NS 13, 1875, ed. Nichols, 2–3; Claire McManus, *Women and Culture at the Courts of the Stuart Queens* (2003), 81–99.

2. Heylyn, from Oxfordshire, left two descriptions of Laud's ten weeks' detention with the Maxwells, December 1640 to March 1641: *Observations on the Reign of King Charles I* (1656), 216–17, and *Cyprianus Anglicus* (1668), 465–6. In both he cites a woman of the house, first calling her 'Maxwell's wife Ginne Ryder' and more vaguely, twelve years later, 'the gentlewoman of the house, and her gossips'. While this may have been a confusion with Jane's mother, Elizabeth Maxwell, he did use a familiar version of Jeane, called her Ryder and, given the amount of time Jane spent in London after her marriage, may really have been referring to her: Christmas was a visiting time. At least he preserved her familiar name.

3. Anne Halkett, *op.cit.*, 5; Thomas Knyvet, *The Knyvet Letters*, ed. Sawfield (1949), 151–2.

4. VCH, *Staffordshire*, XVII, 1976, 60; John Fox, 'The Bromes of Holton Hall, A Forgotten Recusant Family', *Oxoniensia*, LXVIII, 2003, 69–88; Cuddesdon Church Register transcript, Oxfordshire Archives, 13 September 1615.

5. John Nichols, *Progresses of King James* (1828), IV, 982 & note 5; Lambeth Palace Archives, Court of Arches, Case 9938, *Whorwood vs Whorwood*, 1672, E 5/29, 1, 8 (1659 and 1673); *Holton Inventory*, March 1684, TNA PROB 5, 5275(6), 114461. Tim Wilson, Curator of Western Antiquities, Ashmolean Museum, and Philippa

Glanville, former Chief Curator of Metalwork, Silver and Jewellery at the Victoria & Albert Museum, kindly helped me understand the 'Red Trunk' contents and other items listed in the House in 1684.

6. Christopher Durston, *James I*, 1993, 16.

7. *London Marriage Licence Allegations, 1597–1648*, I, Index Library Record Society, LXII, 123 (1937), 22 September 1634; also *Marriage Licences, London, 1611–1828*, Harleian Society, XXVI, 219 (1887). St Faith's registers perished in the Great Fire. The marriage was not solemnised at St Martin's that day, although four others were. See also Jeremy Boulton, 'Itching after Private Marryings', *The London Journal*, 16, 1, 1991, 15–34. Although the licence application stated that Jane and Brome were both nineteen and that 'both fathers consent', Jane's baptism entry at St Martin's on 3 February 1612, and Brome's at Cuddesdon on 13 September 1615, are undisputable. Brome's sister, Elizabeth, was baptised on 8 July 1617 at Cuddesdon, and died on 23 September 1633. Holton church registers survive only from 1633. Brome erected a brass in St Paul's to his parents, which was destroyed in the Great Fire, 1666. (W. Hollar etching 5930, 1656, Guildhall Library Print Room, Cat. 8019631); Sir William Dugdale, *History of St Paul's Cathedral* (1658), 78: Brome and Whorwood quarterings, inscribed: *Ne cippi sepulchrales et sacra majorum monumenta etiam perirent*, BROME WHOREWOOD *arm: filius et haeres* THOS WHOREWOOD *eq: aur.* Et URSULAE *filiae unicae et haeredis* GEORGII BROME *de* HOLTON *in agro Oxon Arm: Monumenta haec (alias ruitura) secondo condidit.* Ironically the east end of St Paul's collapsed into St Faith's in the Fire, destroying everything. The Brome motto was *Domine dirige nos*; the Whorwood motto, *Nunc et Semper.*

8. Will composed 22 September, Jane's wedding day; probate 27 September 1634, TNA PROB 11/166; Lambeth Palace Archives, *Whorwood vs Whorwood, op.cit.*, E/529, 1 (1673).

9. CSP 1638–9, CCCCVIII, mistakenly dated 1638, but the words '10th September last' place it in 1634–5.

10. Holton church register, 29 October 1635; Windsor, St John's parish church, Register, baptism recorded 27 December 1636 (transcript in Windsor Public Library); Edmund Fellowes, ed. (1957) *Registers of St George's Chapel, Windsor*, p. 194, burial entry, James Whorwood, 'died 24th April, 1637, at Little Park Lodge'; Ashmole Ms 1132, 135, granting the Lodge, 29 November 1629, to Maxwell as Garter Usher, *ex officio.*

11. *Marriage Licences Allegations, London Diocese 1597–1648*, Index Library, LXII, 17, 26 May 1638; *Marriage Licences*, Harleian Society, Register Volume XXVI (1887), 235; St Helen's Bishopsgate Register, Harleian Society, Register Series XXXI, 25 (1904); Holton church register, burial 23 February 1641; Gilbert Burnet, *Memoirs of the Dukes of Hamilton* (1677); *St Martin's Poor Rate Registers*, 1641, Westminster City Archives; SP Interregnum 1656, CXXX, 104–7. An undocumented portrait 'probably' of Elizabeth Hamilton in widow's weeds, *c.*1652, Picture 714, school of George Jameson, at Lennoxlove House, is of a woman older than thirty-two,

possibly even Countess Dirleton, Elizabeth Hamilton's and Jane Whorwood's mother. Thanks are due to Rosalind Marshall for pointing out this picture.

12. *St Martin's in The Fields Register*, marriage 2 April 1639; ibid., baptism, 22 May 1639; Mary Keeler, *The Long Parliament, 1640–41: A Biographical Study*, entry 'Charles Cecil' (1954), 130; Garrard to Conway, CSP 1638–9, CCCCXV, 65, 622; David Cecil, *The Cecils of Hatfield House* (1973), 168. *Marriage Licence Allegations, London, 1597–1648*, Index Library Vol LXII, p. 184, 1 April 1639; *Marriage Licences*, Harleian Society, Register Volume 26, p. 241, for marriage at St Martin's or St Mary Savoy, Diana 'about 16', Cranborne 'about 20', and registered 2 April at St Martin's. Their portraits from after 1645 still hang at Hatfield.

13. David Cecil, *op.cit.*, 165; James Maxwell's will, Edinburgh Consistory Court, probate 28 July 1652, CC8/8/66, was composed 26 March 1646, expanded (codicils) April 1650 before his death at Holyrood, 26 April 1650; Mary Keeler, *op.cit.*, entries 'Christopher Lewknor' 251, 'Thomas Bowyer' 112; CCAM, II, 421; Holton church register, baptism of Brome Whorwood junior, October 1635; Lady Anne Bowyer died May 1683. Sir William Bowyer, of Denham Court, her stepson, married Frances Cecil, a daughter of Diana Cranborne and thereby Jane Whorwood's niece. The Bowyers of Denham featured in their cousin, Jane's daughter, Diana Master's will, 1701, TNA PROB 11/460, and characteristically in dispute.

14. cf. Bernard Capp, *The World of John Taylor, The Water Poet* (1994); *The Works of John Taylor*, Spencer Society, Manchester (UK), 1869, vols 2–4, 1870–8, vols 7, 14, 19, 21, 25.

15. Richard Braithwaite, *The English Gentlewoman* (1631), 70, 72, 109.

16. John Nalson, *An Impartial Collection of the Great Affairs of State*, II (1682), 195.

17. William Laud, *History of the Trouble and Times of William Laud* (1695), 60; Peter Heylyn, *On the History and Reign of King Charles I* (1656), 145, 216–17; Peter Heylyn, *Cyprianus Anglicanus* (1668), 485. HMC 8, Appendix 137a, Claydon House Mss; HMC 4, 52; HMC 7, Appendix 103; HMC 7, App. ff. 123.

18. John Aubrey, *Lives*, of Milton; Sir John Brome's will, TNA PROB 11/42A (1558); Anna Beer, *John Milton* (2007); Robert Graves, *Wife to Mr Milton* (1943), employed literary licence to interpret the Milton marriage, and in the heat of a World War dismissed the English republic as 'undisguised fascism'.

19. Lady Frances Verney, *Memoirs of the Verney Family*, II (1892–9), 58–79.

20. Ashmole Ms 1132, 35.

5

1642–46:
'Madam Jean Whorewood',
Gold-Smuggler Royal

One Mistress Whorwood in Oxfordshire, was wont to bring in intelligence to the late king, as well as to Oxford as to the Isle of Wight. She was sent several times of messages.
Thomas Coke, interrogated in the Tower, May 1651

Sir Paul Pindar sent several sums of money in gold to Oxford (by the hand of Madam Jean Whorewood, yet living) in 1644, for the transporting of [the then] Prince of Wales and the late Queen, his mother, to France.
Pindar Family Petition to Charles II, 1680

As lord of Sandwell Park, Brome Whorwood owed the provision of two cavalrymen for the king's use. The armour, weapons and buff coats were still hanging there in 1684. In Wartime the link between the landed gentry and their horses gave the Royalists an initial advantage – and the ambivalent nickname 'cavalier'. In 1639, however, Brome Whorwood, and many like him, failed to answer the muster for the Scots or Bishops' Wars, the king's rash attempt to wage war without Parliament.[1] When England's own war broke out in 1642, Brome evacuated his family away from hostile neighbours, taking Jane, now thirty, Brome junior, seven, and Diana, three, into refuge with Lady Ursula at Holton. In 1646, when Brome attempted to redeem Sandwell Park from sequestration (confiscation), the Staffordshire committeemen took so long to detail their objections that Parliament accused them of contempt.[2] When they did file, they overreached themselves with malice, accusing Brome of

having many arms in [Sandwell] in 1642. He did accordingly send them to Warwick when the [Royalist] Earl of Northampton besieged the Castle there.

His neighbours told him they would stop him and he said 'Let them do so if they durst [as] he and other gentlemen have £500 each and would spend it all in the king's service'. The king was in the right and Parliament's courses were destructive. He and [they] would spend and lose their blood before the king should be beaten down. He then cursed the adherents of Parliament and swore he would *lose his whole estate* rather than they should prevail.

Brome, a trained lawyer, rode to Sandwell in 1646 to expose the lie in person: sequestration was not introduced by Parliament until spring 1643![3]

He insisted in 1646 that he had been 'no way conscious of any wilful delinquency' in 1642, although he did send arms and money to the Earl of Northampton, then besieging Warwick to secure its magazine and provisions for the king. However, a relief force defeated Northampton on 22 August; the day the king declared War at Nottingham and marched south. Brome and family reached Holton before the end of the month. Oxford had declared for the king and blocked its bridges on 13 August. With Uncle Field Whorwood, the city banker then living at Holton Park, and their Curson neighbour at Waterperry, Brome welcomed Sir John Byron's Royalist force into Oxford overnight on 28 August; the mayor and vice-chancellor billeted the arrivals. In the presence of these same gentry, the mayor paraded the town militia exhorting them to join the university for the king, but the town bailiff called the Crown a 'tyranny', and Oxford remained more or less divided, town against gown, for the duration, due as much to local resentment of Chancellor Laud's grip on Oxford town as to any national issue. On 10 September Lord Saye's column took Oxford back for Parliament, and ten days later abruptly left.[4]

Cary Gardiner in her exposed new home at Cuddesdon was scared: '1200 soldiers came here [Oxford] this day and I am afraid they will make a great massacre of all the books. What cannot be billeted in the Town is sent to all the towns about. I am in a mighty fright.' (In May 1643 the Gardiner manor house was looted by Parliamentarians.) Her cavalryman husband, Thomas Gardiner junior, had joined the king at Nottingham, leaving Cary with a bitter father-in-law who hated her 'neutrality' and her continued correspondence with brother Ralph. Sir Thomas even forged a letter from her, to turn her family, but they were not fooled: 'If I were you,' wrote Sir Ralph's wife Mary, 'I would not purchase my welcome to any place at so dear a rate.' Cary's husband remained above the quarrel, writing to Lady Mary, 'were not your Parliamentary officers so busy in stopping and opening letters, I would write oftener to you. I hate to have my secrets laid open, read openly in Westminster Hall, and proclaimed at the Cross. Neither king nor Parliament has any quarrel against women who never did hurt, save with their tongues.'[5]

Sir Thomas soon swallowed his pride to ask Sir Ralph to safeguard a trunk of valuables. 'You have been pleased to do me a favour and you may well expect thanks. We could trust the trunk here no longer. One extravagant word spoken by one man is enough to confiscate the goods of a whole family to the Parliament soldiers. Conscience enters not into vulgar hearts.' Brome, meanwhile, returned to the Midlands, to a commission of array before the king at Perry Common on 19 October. He may have fought at Edgehill, thirty miles away, on 23 October when Ralph and Cary's father died holding the king's standard; Anthony Wood of Oxford certainly believed Brome had 'stuck close to the king in his necessities', despite his unacceptable (to Wood) Whig stance after 1660. From Edgehill field the king's columns rode to Oxford where Brome, 'sometime gentleman commoner of Trinity', was created doctor of laws with thirty-two others on the first day of Convocation at St Mary's, on 1 November, donning scarlet robe and black cap with Prince Rupert, the Duke of York, and his own cousin Sir Christopher Lewknor, MP for Chichester, whose mother was a Holton Brome.[6] The king used the occasion to appeal to the wider nation beyond Oxford, 'give me, as God's second, your hearts', and to warn it that 'to fight against God's Vice-Gerent is to fight against Heaven'. At root, the war was about authority, civic and religious, but it found varied expression in terms of race, class and ritual.

The king marched on London, failed to enter it and fell back on the college 'palaces' of Oxford, fifty miles away, which offered attractive winter quarters. Oxford was the first Stuart exile from a capital since Queen Mary Stuart fled Edinburgh seventy years before, and it presaged refuges to come. Wintering at Oxford would be little different from the plague summer Parliament of 1625, or the royal visit of 1636 when Whitehall requisitioned the town. The town walls could be strengthened with bastions and the Thames and Cherwell rivers could be engineered into a moat for a long defence. Oxford folk were used to an itinerant court, although not to an occupying army with it. Charles garrisoned 4,000 troops on 8,000 citizens and a distracted university whose shrinking numbers were balanced by incoming refugees from Parliamentarian territory.

Soldiers filled the villages and took winter fodder, grain and animals. Farms nearest the city, including Whorwood fields in Marston, lost trees and topsoil for improvised earth bastions forward of the medieval walls. Receipts ('billets') promised payment, but on victory. Hooves, boots and wheel rims scoured crops and grazing; local men hid from conscription; horses and wagons were requisitioned; gentry surrendered plate and money on Charles's crude appeals. 'Whatever you lend, I shall see, in the word of a king, justly repaid. I shall take especial notice of such who shall be backward.' He threatened 'speedy course with refusers, as persons disaffected', and wrote to the 'well-affected' in person to make private agreements. With other gentry, Brome was ordered to impress men and to raise quartering money.[7] Months later he opted for neutrality. 'Not minding to have to do in the unhappy difference between the king and the Parliament, [Brome] did in the beginning thereof, travel into Holland and other foreign countries in the Continent until the month of December 1645.'[8]

He left Jane, the children and his mother at Holton. An extramarital relationship with Katherine Mary Allen, a Holton servant, which was to last until
his death in 1684, may have already begun in 1642, increasing pressure on
him to leave to cool his ardour, but however strained the marriage, Jane disapproved of his leaving. She testified in Chancery in 1659 that 'in or about
1643 Brome absented himself from [her] wilfully and without cause and went
beyond the seas'.[9] It may have added to a growing resentment between her
and Lady Ursula.

Holton Park was literally on the front line, half a mile west of Wheatley
Bridge. Early in 1643 a Parliamentarian deputation to Oxford agreed that 'His
Majesty's forces should advance no nearer Windsor than Wheatley [Bridge]
and shall take no new quarters above 12 miles from Oxford'. The talks collapsed, leaving Wheatley Bridge with one arch already cut, drawbridged,
and guarded as a *de facto* demarcation point, to be proposed again in talks at
Uxbridge in 1645. The respective sides fell back on defending Oxford and
London as capital bases from which to sally across England. Oxford became
a fortress. John Taylor poeticised its inner moat as 'flowing putrefaction', in
contrast to the Thame in its clean flood meadows. London also threw up
earthworks, 'the Lines of Communication', but unlike Wheatley Bridge and
Oxford's works they were never tested in anger.

The warring sides fought with words as they formed their armies. Puritans
called Oxford a 'papist garrison'. The taunt 'roundhead' or 'rattlehead' (crop-
headed apprentice, skinhead) was met with 'cavalier' (*caballero, cavalière,*
horseman, foreign and Catholic-inclined). 'Godly puritans' were dubbed
'fanatical rebels', and they dubbed their enemies 'malignants' and 'delinquents'.
Cavaliers pleaded that their vices (women and wine) were human, but puritan vices (hypocrisy and pride) were devilish. Later, two Parliaments clashed,
Westminster calling Oxford 'anti-Parliament', Oxford decrying Westminster
as 'traitors'. Initially, Charles called them *both* 'the Lords and Commons assembled at Oxford and Westminster', but after Westminster snubbed 'those at
Oxford who have deserted your Parliament', he retaliated against 'those at
Westminster who call themselves a Parliament'. (Privately, to his wife, he called
his Oxford Parliament a 'mongrel' with its majority of Lords and minority of
MPs.) As the taunting escalated, Sir Paul Pindar, the Royalist City merchant
patriarch, summed up the War: 'our age is as children falling out and fighting
about the candle until the parents come in and take it away leaving them to
decide their differences in the dark.'[10]

In January 1643 James Maxwell appeared at Oxford, to explain his not
attending the Garter Feast at York, and his selling of the office of deputy Black
Rod with the help of his son-in-law, Lord Lanark. Questioned by the king,
Maxwell shrugged: 'everyone would do the best for himself'; Sir Thomas
Roe, Garter Chancellor, cut him to size: 'a gentleman born, but never bred
one.' As Black Rod, Maxwell was in an impossible position between King and

Parliament at war. In May he left with Lanark for Scotland with the agreement of 'both' Parliaments.

Lanark, secretary of state for Scotland, had a rougher reception at Oxford than his father-in-law, and just as the king ordered him out in May, the Estates summoned him back to Edinburgh, saving his face. He and Maxwell – Lanark spent that summer at Maxwell's Innerwick home – carried north the king's condemnation of any Scots alliance with Parliament. They lobbied hard, but unsuccessfully, and remained in constant touch with the king. Both eventually allied themselves with the Covenanters against the king and Jane did not see her father again until 1647. Lanark reappeared briefly at Oxford in December 1643, and understandably was arrested. In 1645 Maxwell loaned the Scottish Army of the Covenant in England about £8,000 (sterling equivalent) for food. In London his locked home at Charing was forced by English bailiffs to raise a war levy, but Parliament ordered it repaired and protected. Westminster appointed its own Black Rod in Maxwell's place, while Maxwell's deputy, Sir James Thynne, served the king and his shadow Parliament at Oxford.[11]

London's trade and supply lines were severed by Royalist garrisons stretching from the Midlands to the south-west, although eastern England remained closer-linked to the capital. Westminster and St Martin's were 'distinctly underpopulated'; London and Oxford were vulnerable to spies and smugglers. On market days intelligence flowed in and out of Oxford over Wheatley Bridge. (Cromwell halted dragoons there in 1645 to question folk returning from the market before riding to an attack at Islip.) Sentries gossiped and men removed or turned the sashes and ribbons which passed for uniforms on the outbreak of the War. Inns at Tetsworth, the last stage before and the first stage from Oxford on the London Way, were notorious for loose talk. Pedlars and chapmen carried intelligence round the countryside. Men urinated below an open window in one Oxford street, passing notes over the sill as they did so; the notes were taken out into the Parliamentarian countryside by 'city gardeners' and left in ditches. A jingle described such messages from Oxford to London, 'written by owl light, intercepted [collected] by moonlight, posted by twilight, dispersed by daylight, and read by candlelight'. Couriers were rewarded, or hanged if caught, in a war as brutal as any tribal feud. In April 1643 Parliament ordered that anyone nearing London from Oxford be punished 'as spies or intelligencers'.[12]

Besides her father and brother-in-law, other faces from court familiar to Jane crossed Wheatley Bridge, past Holton Park and over Shotover to Oxford. With Christ Church 'palace' only four miles away, and with a grandmother and servants to look after Brome junior and Diana, she had time to visit old friends. Old Johann Wolfgang Rummler lodged in St Aldate's, the royal apothecary who had travelled Europe with her father buying *restoratifs* for King James. The widowed duchess of Buckingham, an old neighbour at Wallingford House, was at Brasenose College with Lady Mary whom Jane had known as a child. Within weeks of Edgehill, Sir Peter Wyche, Sir Nicholas Crispe and Sir George Benyon, East India men and commercial colleagues of her father, took refuge. Her brother-in-law, Anne's husband Sir Thomas Bowyer, and Sir Christopher Lewknor of Chichester, a Brome cousin, also came fleeing Parliament. Possibly Mark and George Ryder billeted in St Aldate's parish were her blood cousins.[13] Inevitably, Jane was drawn into the War. While 'royal service' or 'the cause' was an impeccable alibi, it may not have found approval at Holton, yet she had noble precedents. Prominent Royalists left their children in care for a higher cause. Sir Edward Walker's wife left theirs with relatives so she could join him in Oxford; the Verneys left theirs when they went into exile, and the queen herself left her children for so many years she never saw some of them again. The king's acid test of loyal friends was ruthless: that they 'forsake themselves'.

'One Mistress Whorwood,' confessed Thomas Coke in 1651, 'wife of Mr Brome Whorwood in Oxfordshire, was wont to bring intelligence to the late King [Charles I] as well to Oxford as to the Isle of Wight. She was sent several times with messages privately to the late king.' Coke, an MP in the Long and Oxford Parliaments, 'held the secrets of all His Majesty's designs and friends in England'. His father, Sir John, was a friend of the Nauntons, neighbours to the Maxwells at Charing. What messages Jane carried to Oxford or from whom went unspecified, but Coke knew her from there. Secretary Edward Nicholas called Coke's confession 'a disaster' for the Royalist cause, as Coke knew so much.[14]

Jane's red hair, even with a linen undercap, marked her out in Oxford, as Anthony Wood recalled years later. The Scots were slow to enter the War, but the threat was as real as the feeling against them. John Cleveland composed *The Rebel Scot* at Oxford, likening the word 'Scot' to 'poison with no antidote, unless my head were red'. He called Scots 'lice', 'Jews', 'witches', 'wolves', 'infections', 'leeches', 'zoo animals', ending his litany of hate with 'haemorrhoids'. John Taylor was gentler: 'must Oxford and sister Cambridge both learn of St Andrew's and Aberdeen?' The Hamilton brothers returned to Oxford in December 1643, ahead of the invasion they had failed to prevent, and were immediately imprisoned; William escaped to London with the help of his Scots page, and into the protection of Parliament now that Scotland was its formal ally. He reconciled with the Covenanters, as his father-in-law evidently had also done; his regiments of foot and horse were in the Covenanting Scots Army and he, an army commissioner. Lanark's loyalty was seriously torn between his countries: the one personified by his fiercely Covenanting mother who actually bore arms in the 1639 war; the other in the person of his cousin the embattled king. John Maxwell, now an archbishop, also took refuge at Oxford from his Irish diocese of Tuam where he had been appointed after being chased out of Scotland. In the garrison he was honorary preacher to the king, but of little other use. Despite the dangers, Jane presumably kept links with her own, but only from 1648 does evidence show how close she was to her Lanark sister and brother-in-law (see Chapter 8).

Traffic in intelligence and unlicensed publications flourished. Messages in books were smuggled to and fro by 'certain adventurous women. It was easy to sew letters privately in the covers of a new book and give the book a secret mark.'[15] Books were stored wholesale in London river barges on a river commercially navigable above Oxford. Jane would have been wasted (and conspicuous) on such service, but in 1648 she did use an advance, marked copy of a book to smuggle intelligence from London to the king on Wight. Another garrison Scot, Kate, Lady d'Aubigny (*olim* Stuart, later Newburgh), the king's cousin, obtained a pass from Oxford to London to settle her late husband's affairs early in 1643. She smuggled the king's commission for an uprising in the capital in the spring of 1643, intended to prevent the blood-shed of the first campaign season, but she was discovered and spent a year in the Tower before returning to Oxford until the surrender in 1646. Later, she and Jane conspired together in the king's escape attempts, and Jane's mother included Lord Newburgh, Kate's third husband, in her will.

The evidence for Jane Whorwood as royal intelligencer is credible coming from Coke, who knew firsthand her activities in Oxford, and in the light of her known work after 1646. However, it lacks any detail. In contrast, her gold-running into Oxford is documented. It centred on the Royalist merchants of the East India and Levant companies who had traditionally supported the king in peacetime, particularly when he ruled without Parliament, 1629–40, and when the City was synonymous with wealth, 'the liver of the Italian goose, drawing all the nutrient and riches to itself'. The merchants were James Maxwell's commercial colleagues, several of whom fled to Oxford. When Maxwell became a money-lender to the king in peacetime, his capital came from trade and commerce, monopolies, exemptions, and notably his Scottish African company's exclusive importing of gold and silver. In peacetime, the raising of money for the Crown without Parliament's authority was illegal and in contempt, but astonishingly, even after War broke out, City gold still flowed into the king's coffers and credit was given. This was despite the defeatists, Parliament's control of London, the collapse of trade and customs, and the roadblocks on the way to Oxford. East India and Levant company merchants provided much, if not most of that cash flow from their personal wealth.

Sir Paul Pindar and Sir John Jacob, leading East India men, were admitted to Grays Inn in 1631 on the same day as James Maxwell and other prominent Scots courtiers, a mark of how closely entwined commerce and the Court became in the absence of Parliament. Sir William Courteen, grandee of the East India Company and close partner of Pindar and Jacob, called Maxwell 'my respectful friend' in his will of 1636. Jane's daughter Elizabeth was baptised in Pindar's home parish in 1638. In 1640 Maxwell's younger stepdaughter, Anne Ryder, married Sir Thomas Bowyer, one of a family of East India merchants, and Bowyer made Maxwell his executor in 1648. Pindar himself, a veteran maritime explorer from Queen Elizabeth's reign, was the king's most generous financier. In his eyes, loyalty to the Crown was both honourable *and* profitable, the Crown as eternally safe a bet as the divinity behind it. The king saw Pindar's City colleagues as a 'silent volcano' of loyalty, *his* merchants sworn to allegiance on their aldermanic oaths. Levant and East India merchants needed safe seas, particularly the Mediterranean, so they supported the king's peace with Catholic Spain and the hated Ship Money, which built ships to fight North African pirates. Leading merchants Job Harby and John Nulls helped Henrietta Maria pawn Crown jewellery in Holland in 1642, to purchase and deliver supplies to Oxford in 1643. In effect, pre-War royal finance had been largely privatised, and only private capital could meet the even greater expenses of Wartime. Maxwell, like the merchants, had invested and profited, to the point where supplementation, loyalty to the Crown, self-enrichment and family considerations became inseparable.[16]

One significant commercial gamble, however, returned to haunt Maxwell. In 1640 the king purchased compulsorily all the pepper in the East India warehouses for £63,000 on credit, to be repaid through future concessions; he sold the pepper at a loss for £50,000 ready cash for his Scots war. The merchants, locked into their cycle of assumptions – royal promise, low risk and solid long-term expectation – acceded pliantly, if uneasily: 'this will give good satisfaction to the king and cause him to give our Company favours in matters formally requested.'[17] At least the deal was better than his seizing of the bullion in the Tower to force a loan in June 1640, or his threat to issue brass coin; but Parliament returned to Westminster that year, indignant after a long enforced absence. It confiscated the pepper to punish the City's long-term contempt, and fined the merchant culprits £168,000.

Paul Pindar, Peter Wyche, John Nulls, John Jacob and Nicholas Crispe, all knights, aldermen and merchants, had allowed Maxwell to help underwrite the king's pepper credit up to £4,000. On his depositing of that sum he would be insured 'harmless' from liability for the royal debt up to £100,000. The king, however, lost his Scottish wars and could not pay creditors, despite selling off land and timber; in defeat, his bond, privy seal and word were worthless. The English War soon followed, and with it Parliament's revenge.

Royalist merchants had gambled with peacetime cards. The last civil war had been between the Roses 160 years before, and they only knew the slow but sure profits of peacetime: the outbreak of War made their commercial experience irrelevant. After 1642 trade and customs slumped, the king could not enforce monopolies or repay loans, the merchants lost civic and commercial power and finally control of their companies as Parliamentarian merchants took over. The Royalist merchants suddenly found themselves in a minority and their diminishing wealth trapped in London where Parliament could levy heavily, force loans and confiscate any money discovered loaned or given to the king.

Abroad, the Royalist ambassador in Turkey, Sir Sackvile Crowe, was even more alienated from the companies, then Royalist, now Parliamentarian, which had nominated him in 1633, and the final straw came when his property at home was sequestrated. Crowe compensated with his version of supplementation by collecting Levant Company dues and his own imaginative levies on English ships in Turkish ports. The pepper came back to haunt Maxwell when he was arrested in 1649 and held liable for the *whole* of the king's pepper debt. In 1664 Lady Anne Bowyer, Jane's sister, produced the £4,000 bond in a bold attempt to claim £100,000 maximum liability from the merchants, and in 1675 Parliament did at least award her back the £4,000 deposit with thirty-three years' interest! Maxwell trained all his daughters well.

Despite increasing war losses, the merchants stood remarkably firm by the king. Nicholas Crispe claimed to have lost £300,000. Sir Paul Pindar, perhaps the major donor, died bankrupt in 1650. His pre-War syndicate – Crispe, Nulls, Jacob, Harby, Wyche and Eliab Harvey (a close friend of the Maxwells) – rented from the Crown the collecting or farming of customs. They paid lump sums (six paid £200,000 for the 1640 contract, approximately £35,000 each), waited for their profit and received honours for their patience, but the returns evaporated. Abraham Dawes acknowledged that loyalty to the Crown had a double price and he was willing to 'pay it and pay *for* it'. John Jacob spoke from the heart: 'Though I give all I have, I can be no loser; if not, though I keep all, I can be no saver.'

Pindar exhausted his fortune on the king, then borrowed widely to continue lending, thereby bankrupting others whom he could not repay. By 1645 Parliament was finding his creditors everywhere, each owed between £500 and £5,000 by Pindar, and all of it instantly forfeit on discovery. Dorothy Seymour, for example, spinster maid-of-honour to Henrietta Maria and known for her greed, began to feel the pinch at Oxford and wrote to Pindar in 1644 asking for the interest on £5,000 she had lent him. Parliament intercepted her letter, took the £5,000 from Pindar, on top of a £20,000 loan and a £3,500 war levy which they had already imposed on him. At the Restoration in 1660 the Crown owed the grandee families of Pindar and Courteen approximately £250,000 on debts incurred before and during the War, but Charles II could not cope with the wider multitude of creditors demanding repayment for his father's frantic borrowing. Pindar's heirs were still pursuing their dues forty years later; Dorothy Seymour received two-thirds of the £5,000 she had lent Pindar, but without a penny of eighteen years' interest.

In 1680 Pindar's executor claimed that

out of great zeal and loyalty towards the preservation of the Royal family, [Pindar] sent several sums of money in gold to Oxford (by the hand of Madam Jean Whorewood, yet living) in the year 1644, for transporting of His Majesty

[Charles II] when he was Prince of Wales, and the late Queen his mother, with their servants and goods to Brest in France.[18]

It was summarised in 1679 as 'money in gold to a considerable value for the protection of the Royal family'. Jane was key surviving witness, and prime actor. Before the War, insisted the executor, Pindar and Courteen had also paid for the funeral of James I, the relief of La Rochelle, the upkeep of the exiled Winter Queen, the Irish expedition 'and made several disbursements for diamonds and other jewels of the Crown', amounting to £85,000 in 1638–9 alone. Charles II felt a debt of honour to Pindar for the queen's escape abroad in 1644 (he left England only later, in 1646), and promised the Pindar heirs a part-payment in 1667. It would not be a direct payment by the Crown, nor would it carry interest on the twenty-seven-year delay, but it would be a refund of Pindar's £35,000 share of the 1640 Customs rent of £200,000 (see above), to be taken from the 1667 Customs Farm revenue earned by Crispe and other syndicate survivors of 1640. Oxford 1644 was ancient history; the Customs Farm 1667 was a going concern, as indispensable to Charles II as it had been to his father. The confidence of the participating merchants had to be maintained, but predictably, Nicholas Crispe took care that no money was ever handed over.

Even had the gesture payment of £35,000 actually been made to Pindar's estate, his executor protested in 1680, 'it doth *not extend to half the value of the gold* sent to Oxford *as aforesaid* [author's italics]'. Pindar, therefore, on the estimate of his executor with well-rehearsed figures before him, sent *more* than £70,000 to Oxford in 1644 alone. If a conservatively assumed 10 per cent (£3,500) shortfall is added to the £35,000 (which 'doth not extend to half'), and then doubled, the guesstimated total principal of gold sent into Oxford by Pindar, 'by the hand of Madam Jean Whorewood' in early 1644 alone, amounted to £77,000. However, Pindar had also sent gold to the king in 1642–3, again through 'Mistress Horwood'.

The sole account ledger to survive from royal Oxford was signed off in October 1643. Any formal record of gold delivered in 1644 or later (the queen left Oxford in April), or in the last quarter of 1643, was burned with four years of records in June 1646, just days before Oxford surrendered. The surviving *Accompt* was the responsibility of John Ashburnham, treasurer at war and paymaster for eighteen months from April 1642, and after the battle of Edgehill, based at Corpus Christi College, Oxford. Ashburnham had been a groom of the bedchamber with James Maxwell since 1628, and was father-in-law to John Jacob, an East India Company Royalist donor. His mother was a Villiers and he a protégé of the late Duke of Buckingham. Once established in the Oxford garrison, he delegated the account-keeping to his gentleman retainer, John Browne, evidently a lawyer, in November 1642. Browne recorded and back-recorded Royalist cash contributions from April 1642 until he relinquished the accounts in October 1643 – a total of £162,117, of which he handed £82,903 to the army quartermaster. Outgoings were meticulously reconciled. Other donations to the king were presumably either recorded elsewhere, by others, or not at all. The importance of ready cash to the royal war effort cannot be overstated, just as when Charles sold the pepper at a loss to procure cash for the Scots wars. Years later, when Commonwealth officials tried to make Ashburnham reveal who had advanced the king money during the War, so they could fine the lenders and confiscate the equivalent sums loaned and any bonds or securities held for them, he concealed his accounts, and in the panic 'scarce had time to eat'. The *Accompt* survived the search parties to be published only in 1830.[19]

'Moneys are the nerves of war,' the king reminded his Oxford Parliament in April 1644, 'expedite supplies of it by subscription or excise.' Manor house plate and 'contributions' were not enough. The *Accompt* recorded Lady Ursula Whorwood's widow's mite of £158 and her '36 plate trenchers [valued at] £89' from Holton House.[20] They would be minted into coin and never repaid, but if the St George salt and gilt dessert settings recorded in 1684 were at Holton as early as 1643, Lady Ursula concealed them. Ashburnham's gentleman also recorded rich men's donations, some of them East India and Levant company loyalists with whom Ashburnham, James Maxwell and Lord Cottington, Chancellor of the Exchequer, had worked closely for years. Cottington was already in Oxford; merchant financiers there, Nicholas Crispe and George Benyon, even acted as treasurers to the parishes where they were billeted, St Peter's and St Ebbe's.

Browne showed a lawyer's caution with many donors, masking them behind initials or anonymity. No entry is dated. 'A woman employed in secret service' received £20; 'Sir W.G.' had £50. The majority, however, were named, and had the *Accompt* been found by Parliament's Committee for the Advance of Money, it would not have cost an astrologer's fee to identify the initials. Merchants' contributions were not widow's mites; only City men could afford to gamble four-figure donations on the royal cause. Five donors known only by initials gave a total of £11,040: IH (? Job Harby) £2,500; IN (? John Nulls) £3,000; II (? John Jacob) £1,040. AP, who gave £2,000, and LH, who gave £2,500, remain obscure, but the first three, if correctly identified, were Pindar's syndicate colleagues and leading East India men.

The largest individual contributions came from 'PP' (Paul Pindar) himself, who first gave the king £2,995 'through a Mr Markham'. PP next gave £2,000, perhaps once the king had settled into Oxford and first appealed for money. Finally, 'Mistress Horwood for PP and others at times [paid in] £6,041', the largest single donation recorded by Browne over eighteen months.[21] Pindar, therefore, paid around £8–10,000 in 1642–3, allowing for the 'others at times' who contributed to the £6,041. In addition, he later gave the estimated sum of £77,000 in gold smuggled to Oxford early in 1644.

No clue survives of any donation he may have made later in 1644 or in 1645–6, but then funds were running out. Had Ashburnham/Browne's ledger evidence of Jane Whorwood's money-smuggling been discovered, Parliament could have used it against her and those for whom she acted. They did punish her in 1651, on an unrelated exemplary charge of corrupting the chairman of the parliamentary Committee for the Advance of Money. Browne and others were successful in concealing her and others' names.

Other East India and Levant men gave to breaking point: Sir Peter Wyche loaned £30,000 and fled to Oxford; Sir George Benyon sent £5,000 to the king at York which was intercepted and confiscated before he fled to Oxford; MarmaDuke Roydon came to Oxford in 1643, spent his fortune on the king and died as governor of Faringdon. At the other end of the scale, smaller amounts were recorded in Browne's columns. Mr Adams (£50) was possibly Alderman Thomas Adams, the ex-Lord Mayor who sent funds to the king through Jane Whorwood in 1647–8. Sir Edward Bowyer (£50), was brother-in-law to Jane's sister Anne, and others lurk behind initials in the *Accompt* still to be identified.

The known sum of £85–87,000 from Pindar alone (£8–10,000 in 1642–3, and £77,000 in 1644), is a minimum; a conservative estimate based on fragmentary records, and those only for the first two years of the king's four years at Oxford. The approximate £83,041 which Jane is known to have smuggled for Pindar 'and others' in the same period, is also a minimum, the two sums approximately the same money. Pindar was used to working in syndicates, and the 'others' may have been part of his and Jane's smuggling operation. His calculated minimum contribution amounts to almost the output of the Wartime mint in Oxford, and to more than the army quartermaster's entire revenue over eighteen months, April 1642–October 1643. It was also cash, not credit, essential for paying (and retaining) soldiers, as well as financing royal escapes; in neither circumstance would credit have been acceptable. Pindar's contribution through Jane Whorwood was significant, and while we do not know its full extent, even at its minimum it was a great weight of metal.

The contract for minting gold at the Tower Mint, 1642–5, stipulated that forty-one *laurel* or *unite* coins be struck from one *troy* pound of twenty-two carat gold. If the respective Pindar or Whorwood figures are rounded to £85,000, it means that Jane organised the smuggling of a known 2,073 lbs *troy* of gold, 1,705 lbs *avoirdupois* (775kg) for Pindar alone, and evidently more than that 'for others at times'.[22] The conveying of gold in such bulk would test anyone's ingenuity. Uncle Field Whorwood at Holton, a Lombard Street goldsmith and financier, might have advised. Holton Park, so close to the main road, offered a natural dropping point and many hiding places. East India Company merchants were expert bullion traders and knew about transporting it. Frequently in peacetime they had outbid the Mint and caused shortage of coin. Even small gold weighs heavily in bouffant hair, a body belt, the hem of a dress or a book binding, and in bulk it has been known to defeat bullion thieves. A contemporary believed Sir Nicholas Crispe's agents smuggled 'thousands in gold', one 'riding on his way to Oxford in [between] a pair of panniers like a butterman going to market … [another] a porter … [another] a fisherman … [another] a merchant'.[23] Crispe may have been one of the 'others' working with Pindar and Whorwood. Most likely, Jane learned her smuggling and intelligencing skills from other women, not from merchant bankers, and her confidence allowed her to be an obvious organiser. In the trafficking of gold she was unlikely to have been a mule, although she may have travelled to London in the organising of it.

In 1642–3 an air of unreality still hung over the roads (and waterways) between the warring capitals which invited smuggling. Passes were relatively easily obtained. 'Sentries at town gates,' wrote the French ambassador to Scotland after visiting Oxford, 'are little exact in remarking dates [on passports] and for the most part are unable to read.' Respect for the Crown, traditional protocols and courtesies were observed, albeit against a backdrop of increasing hostility. Well-bred women with a pass and confident manner were less likely than men to be searched. Lady Mary Stafford – her husband was of the queen's household – entertained the Dutch ambassador in 1652 with her account of having smuggled 'the king's crown and a great quantity of other jewels to Oxford at his request when he was there with his army, and the ruses she had to employ to hide them, without ever being caught'. The Journal of the House of Commons confirms she was not exaggerating. Four times in 1643 she obtained passes to visit London, twice by coach, with Lady May and Lady Grey. They lodged in St James's Palace, the king's pre-War home, and literally helped themselves for his cause. Parliament finally barred their visiting London and banished them permanently back to Oxford.[24] If the crown of England could be smuggled to Oxford, anything could.

At one point Parliament voted to allow the king to retrieve spare stockings from Whitehall. In June 1643 alone he paid £190 for clean ruffs and cuffs. Laundresses were allowed passes, along with soap consignments, for the cleaning of linen and clothes; like Jane's rural midwives, Oxford washerwomen were not good enough for the royal body and its apparel. Soap also served as an enema in a city under siege where the diet and water were deficient and exercise limited: constipation from ration packs still haunts soldiers. John Ashburnham paid 'Mistress Burgenny, laundress, £20', and 'Mistress Freeman, the Prince's Laundress, £5'. In July 1643 Parliament allowed Mistress Elizabeth Wheeler, 'laundress for His Majesty's body', to go from London to Oxford with her servants, but without soap her journey was pointless. Peacetime London produced some 700 barrels of soap a week and the barrel was the ubiquitous weather-proof and damage-proof container of the day. Barrels went from Oxford University to London carrying books for safe keeping; John Dale, bursar of Magdalen, hid college plate among the tomes in barrels;

publishers transported new imprints wholesale and dry in barrels. Thomas Coke, prior to the battle of Worcester in 1651, confessed to his interrogators that pistols and powder were being smuggled, as he spoke, by Royalist rebels into London 'in barrels under the name of soap'.

Jane grew up in a world of Castile soap, manufactured in Antwerp with fine thistle ash; Huguenots brought soap production to London, and her Antwerper mother was the queen's laundress. Merchants competed for the soap monopoly through a 'whiter and sweeter' soap-and-linen competition judged by the Lord Mayor. Monopolists (Patrick Maule, Maxwell's colleague of the bedchamber, was one) had the right to test soap and assay-mark the barrels, the largest of which weighed 26 lbs empty and held 254 lbs of guaranteed Castile. Barrelsful transported by wagon, too greasy, deep and cumbersome for a roadblock picquet to even want to examine, offered ideal cover for gold. Laundress Elizabeth Wheeler worked so closely with Jane Whorwood after the War, carrying messages between London and the king in his various prisons, that the alliance may be assumed to have begun earlier in peacetime Westminster. They were about the same age, one from Charing, the other from Kensington, and Jane knew the laundry routines and royal laundresses from her cradle. She would have been quite at home *incognita* as a member of the travelling team. In January 1649 Wheeler and Whorwood were even confused with each other as they waited in the wings (See Chapter 10) before the king's execution. Thomas Coke, too, named them to his interrogators in the same breath in 1651: 'Mrs Wheeler, laundress to the late king, *likewise* brought letters to him on the Isle of Wight.'[25]

William Lilly, the astrologer, was privy to the secrets of both sides in the War. Safe under the Commonwealth, he wrote a cynical account of Charles I:

> Citizens of London assisted the king with their flatterings *and large gifts* [and] in his latest extremity *relieved him with considerable sums of money, even at Oxford, in soap barrels*, yet he slighted them, thought them too rich, and intended for them a secret revenge [author's italics].

Angrily, Sir Edward Walker, Royal Secretary at Oxford who took over the War accounts from Ashburnham in October 1643, denied that the king was vindictive or that the 'sums' donated were all that 'considerable'. He admitted that citizens (*prominenti* of the City of London) did send contributions and in soap barrels, but his priority in 1653, like Ashburnham's in 1651, was to conceal their names. Ashburnham, Browne and Whorwood were already heavily implicated, and Walker's reticence reflected the very real risk of severe financial retribution against anyone discovered to have been a Wartime donor to the king. Many faced financial ruin already because of the king's defeat.

It would have been, Walker continued, 'justice [for the king] to punish those of the City that had rebelliously opposed him, [but] *if any of them supplied him in his extremity it was done as good subjects [ought]'*. He certainly had in mind the Royalist merchants and went as close as he dared to acknowledging them when he praised *'City aldermen of the better and discreeter sort. I am sure His Majesty had many most loyal and affectionate to him as their actions and sufferings have sufficiently demonstrated* [author's italics].*'* The king's restraint towards the newly Parliamentarian merchant companies who had been less loyal, Walker insisted, had actually saved London from destruction.[26] 'By the hand of Madam Jean Whorewood' Paul Pindar, alderman, knight and London citizen, a survivor of Drake's era, sent the king at least three-quarters of a ton of gold, in weight the equivalent of more than six gross barrelsful of soap (127kg, 280 lbs each), spread across many barrels and many months: and probably much more.

Lady Ursula or Uncle Field may have funded Brome's neutrality through Robert Abbott, the family's banker. One trace from his exile in France remains. In August 1645 he wrote from Paris to his cousin Ralph Verney in Rouen about the impending marriage of Margaret Lucas, the queen's maid-of-honour, to William Cavendish, Duke of Newcastle. Brome was Verney's distant cousin, not even on the Verney cipher list. Lord Lucas had asked Cavendish to care for his sister who, along with Mary Gardiner of Cuddesdon, attended the pregnant queen from Oxford, via Exeter, to Brest in 1644, the escape for which Jane Whorwood conveyed Pindar's gold. The queen knew nothing of the marriage plan. Margaret, nicknamed 'Mad Meg' for her imaginative intelligence – she once quizzed an amused Bishop Wilkins, a serious astronomer, about moon travel – hated the exile court in Paris, 'a place of much censure', profligate and gossipy, 'court devils in their dissenting hell'.[27]

Rouen was cheaper than Paris, and Verney was a Parliamentarian, avoiding all contact with the Royalist exiles at the Louvre whenever he visited the capital. Brome informed his 'Honest Cousin' he had just been at St Germain, the exile queen's summer palace, and that he had a letter for him from Sir Ralph Sydenham, former courtier and MP; he had also seen Mary and Margaret at Verney's request. 'I did obey your command to them [and] Mistress Gardiner presents her service to you and my Lady cousin.' Verney may have been wary of Mary Gardiner because of the way her family treated his sister Cary at Cuddesdon, and for her intrigues among the émigrés. Brome promised, but failed to come to Rouen.

A month later he asked that his courier may 'kiss your hands and present my love and service to yourself and my dear cousin Mary [Lady Verney]. I have obeyed your command to get two virgins of honour [bridesmaids] who I have not seen this day for I came late [to St Germain] last night from Paris and this morning write before I visit them.' He promised to come to Rouen soon, 'but will not prefix any certain time. If you see my lord of Devonshire [Charles Cavendish] and his lady [Elizabeth Cecil, sister-in-law to Jane's sister, Diana Cranborne] pray present my service, Thy affectionate kinsman and servant.'[28] Like Verney, Cavendish had absented himself from Parliament, and the colonies of exiles from both sides and from none often did not mix. He and Brome returned after the battle of Naseby to submit to a Parliamentary ultimatum in December 1645 and were fined and pardoned. Naseby spelled the end of the king's cause and many came home from abroad, tails between their legs, as bankruptcy for a war already lost seemed pointless. 'Men do well to compound in time and be wise, for the king is in a most low and despicable condition.' Brome left behind him arrangements which ended in a secret marriage in the English ambassador's chapel and Henrietta Maria's passing displeasure.

Cary Verney left Cuddesdon for Bedfordshire early in the War. When her husband was taken prisoner by Parliament, Ralph Verney had him released. Her fears for Cuddesdon had been well-grounded. The Gardiner house on the spur was looted in 1643 and Governor Legge of Oxford ordered the house and the bishop's new palace torched in 1644 to prevent their becoming enemy vantage points west of the Thame. Cary's husband, Captain Thomas, returned to fight and was killed in action in 1645; three months later his younger brother fell. Their father attended both funerals in Christ Church as mourner-in-chief and his bitterness still showed in his will ten years later. Cary lived off the charity of relatives. A consultation with William Lilly in 1645 about her disabled daughter cost fees and was a measure of her desperation. By then, the eighteen-year-old widow was a lifetime older than the fifteen-year-old bride of 1642, excited by summer evening coach jaunts.[29]

Jane Whorwood certainly emerged from the shadows after Oxford fell. In 1647 the records, despite their fragmentary nature, begin to reveal a seasoned agent who had for some time already proved her ingenuity and trustworthiness. She had access to court, the king's ear and had earned expressions of his personal confidence (see Chapter 7). She had helped create and maintain networks and channels in Oxford, the obscurity of which was their Wartime strength, but which sadly remains their chief characteristic.

There is reason to believe she was still at Oxford when it surrendered in 1646. Certainly Elias Ashmole, who served in Oxford from late 1644 to December 1645, the only period when their time at Oxford ever coincided, 'knew her well'. His commission there was to oversee the eastern defences at the Eastgate, the approach from Wheatley Bridge and Holton. By 1646 Jane had nowhere else to go. Just before the king fled from Oxford to the Scots outside Newark late in April 1646, the king entrusted John Ashburnham with a jewel cache. They may have been the broken Garter Stars, Georges and other jewels which Charles obtained from a lady in Westminster after his trial in 1649. Perhaps they were among 'the great quantity of other jewels' retrieved by Lady Stafford from St James's Palace in 1643. Jewels were often

Charles I's comfort cushion when isolated and bankrupt. Then, as now, the richly ornate Garter insignia had to be returned to the monarch on the death of the holder; Garter membership was freely conferred in Oxford garrison years and the necessary jewels were available. Ashburnham must have passed on his cache – Garter jewels or other – for safekeeping, as neither he nor the king could escape with them across guarded countryside. John Browne left Oxford ahead of the king's escape, when the roads were still open, and may have carried away his master's old *Accompt*, but royal jewels were still too much to risk on the highway. The tradition persisted that Jane Whorwood looked after them, and that they were the Garter pieces in the unnamed Westminster lady's possession in 1649. Jane would have been an appropriate guardian, as the king's gold-smuggler and daughter of the Garter Usher. In a letter to Sir Edward Nicholas from Newcastle on 24 June 1646, the day the Oxford garrison marched out, Charles asked, 'send me word where my jewels are which 449 had and if my cabinet or p[?ortmanteau] which I left with you be at ad.[?] or not'. These may have been two distinct items: jewels in a box or cabinet, *and* a case or cloak bag (portmanteau) of papers; they may have been three items: jewels, a cabinet of private correspondence, and a bag of papers.[30]

The king may have worried more about losing the correspondence, after the Naseby experience when his and the queen's letters were captured, published and mocked. Nicholas interpreted '449' as Ashburnham ('IA'), and in Jane's lifetime Dugdale the historian from the Oxford garrison claimed that a jewel 'cabinet' was retrieved by Sir Thomas Herbert from Jane, two nights before the king's execution, she 'then living' in Westminster. His authority was Herbert himself. Anthony Wood, the Oxford diarist, document collector from Dugdale, Ashmole, Lilly and Herbert, and confidant of them all, remained convinced that 'Jane Whorwood is the same lady mentioned [by Herbert] in *Athenae et Fasti Oxonienses* II, 523, where King Charles I had put into her hands a cabinet of precious jewels to be by her kept until such time that he should send for them, which he did a little before he died' (see Chapter 10). This was despite a last-minute change of mind by Herbert before he died.

In 1646, encircled, walled Oxford, on the verge of surrender, was no place to hide valuables. The roads were blocked, the king in Scots hands and London was out of bounds; 20,000 Parliamentarian soldiers were about to occupy the small dilapidated city. Kate d'Aubigny was refused an exit pass in May, as were Prince Rupert and the Duke of York, despite their private pleading. Jane's Holton home, however, out on the edge of garrison territory, under New Army guard as General Fairfax's personal quarter from 1 May, was about the safest place to hide anything. Six weeks later the Naseby generals celebrated a Cromwell family wedding at Holton House and lodged there, possibly yards from the king's jewels.

Notes

1. TNA PROB 28/387, 114461; CSP 1638–9, CCCCXII, 9, 2 February 1639.

2. CCAM, I, 84, 106, 162, 166; II, 648; CCC, II, 966; III, 1813.

3. TNA SP, 1642, XIX, 63.162.167.

4. HMC Report, XI, House of Lords, Misc. Mss, Addenda 1514–1714 (1962), 322–33, 352, 17 September 1642, 'Grievances at Oxford' concerning events on 1 September.

5. Lady Frances Verney, *Memoirs of the Verney Family*, II (1892–9), 58–79.

6. John Ashton, *The Story of West Bromwich* (1964), 27; Frederick Hackwood, *A History of West Bromwich* (1895), 56; Anthony Wood, *Fasti*, II, 43, 1 November 1642.

7. See also CCAM, II, 996–1005, Oxford Engagement; William Black, *Docquets of Letters Patent under the Great Seal at Oxford, 1642–46*, I (1837), 97, where even *in absentia* Brome Whorwood – or his Holton estate – was liable to provide soldiers in November 1643, along with his cousin Christopher Lewknor, Nicholas Crispe, Thomas Gardiner and many other gentry sheltering at Oxford.

8. Basil Henning, ed., *History of Parliament: The Commons, 1660–90*, III (1983), 714–16.

9. Lambeth Palace Archives, Court of Arches records inherited from Commonwealth Court of Chancery, *Whorwood vs Whorwood*, Case 9938, 1672, E 5/29/10.

10. David Lloyd, *Memoirs* (1668), 633 citing Pindar.

11. HLJ, V, 498; VI 576, 621; VI, 54; Ashmole Ms 1111, 137–8, Bodleian Library; Mary Keeler, *The Long Parliament 1640–41: A Biographical Study* (1954), 360–1.

12. Seventeenth-century news sheets, accessible as 'Periodicals' in Early English Books Online; Anthony Wood, *Pamphlets*, 632, Bodleian Library; Margaret Toynbee and Peter Young, *Strangers in Oxford* (1972); Frederick Varley, *The Siege of Oxford* (1932); Frederick Varley, *Supplement to the Siege of Oxford* (1935); Rosemary Kelly, *A City at War; Oxford 1642–46* (1987); Stephen Porter, ed., *London and the Civil War* (1996), notably Chapter 6, 149–74; Ian Roy, *A Cavalier View of London*, and Chapter 7, 175–204; Stephen Porter, *Impact upon London of The Civil War*.

13. Margaret Toynbee and Peter Young, *op.cit.*, 252–3.

14. Camden Society, NS 50, 1880, Nicholas Papers I, 237, Edward Nicholas to Edward Hyde, 3 May 1651; HMC XIII, Portland I, 1891, Appendix I, 603, 28 May 1651: Thomas Coke (or Cooke)'s confession, made between March and May 1651, was reported in full to the Commons (ibid., 576–609). Coke was Sir John Coke's younger son, an MP in the 'mongrel' Oxford Parliament of 1644, who collaborated in Royalist espionage with his brother John. Austin Woolrych, *Soldiers, Writers and Statesmen of the English Civil War* (1988), 86.

15. Peter Barwick, *Life of Dr John Barwick* (1724), 58–64, on intelligencing and smuggling to Oxford; Ashmole Ms 1112, 61–4, Bodleian Library; 'Richard Royston', *ODNB*, 2004. John Barwick acted as a smuggler and courier but did not know

'what other private agents the king had in London'. The Earl of Pembroke, he claimed, provided passes for smugglers between London and Oxford, by whom intelligence and 'sometimes money and ammunition furnished by certain citizens was conveyed to Oxford'.

16. *Grays Inn Admissions Register*, 191–2, 1 March 1631; Richard Ashton, *Court and Money Market* (1960), 78, 175; Robert Brenner, *Merchants and Revolution* (1993), for the London merchant companies' role in the War, notably 53–107; Robert Brenner, *Past and Present*, 58 (1973), 53–107, 'Civil War Position of London's Merchant Community'; Robert Ashton, *The Crown and The Money Market* (1960), and *The City and The Court, 1603–1643* (1979); A.C. Wood, *The Levant Company* (1935); Alfred Wood, *The Levant Company*, Oxford thesis, 1934, Bodleian Library. For Crispe and Benyon's humble responsibilities in St Peter's and St Ebbe's parishes, Bodleian Library, Additional Ms, D114–15.

17. *Calendar of Court Minutes of the East India Company, 1640–43*, ed., Sainsbury (1912), 82.

18. 'Madam Whorewood' in George Carew, *Several Advertisements concerning the Services and Sufferings of Sir William Courteen and Sir Paul Pindar for The Crown of England* (1680), 1, copy in Huntington Library, California, Wing/S2748. Carew was second successive administrator of Pindar's will, thirty years after Sir Paul died. Also, *The Humble Address of the heirs …of Paul Pindar*, 1679, Wing/H3380AC, and Edward Graves, *Brief Narrative of the case …of Paul Pindar to Both Houses of Parliament*, 1679, Wing/G1605. The Commonwealth Parliament agreed in 1653 that the Customs farmers were owed £276,000, but the merchants failed to agree and the offer was reduced, each farmer being assessed at the bare £4,000 agreed in 1649 with James Maxwell. William Foster, 'Charles I and the East India Company', *EHR*, XIX, 1904, 456–63. See Chapter 10.

19. 'John Ashburnham', *ODNB*, 2004; Henry Cary, *Memorials of the Civil War in England* (1842), I, 109; John Ashburnham, *Narrative and Vindication* (1830), to which the *Accompt* was first published as an appendix. Browne was apparently Jane Whorwood's companion on the Medway in 1648 and attended the Newport talks. See Chapters 8 and 9.

20. Lady Whorwood's 'widow's mites' were recorded on sheets vii and xi of twenty-four pages of undated revenue entries. Assuming some chronological order, she gave early in the War, perhaps winter 1642/3, when the king first requested money. She was lodging in Oxford in spring 1644 but was certainly back in Holton by December 1645 (and probably much earlier), when her son wrote to ask her for details of his property to help him compound with Parliament. See CCAM, II, 648.

21. PP's three donations were recorded on pages vi, viii and xiv of the *Accompt*, the last just over halfway through the revenue entries, therefore possibly early in 1643. 'PP' has been interpreted in the past as 'Privy Purse' and 'Peter Perceval', but the evidence for 'Paul Pindar' is compelling.

22. Christopher Challis, *A New History of the Royal Mint* (1992), 282–3, 305–20, 689, 740.

23. David Lloyd, *Memoirs* (1668), 628–9; CSP 1641–3, 498, 11 September, 11 October; *Camden Miscellany* 8, Camden New Series, 1883, 'A Secret Negotiation with Charles I', 1643, 1–2. The weight of £85,000 in gold is calculated based on the 1588 standardising of *troy* and *avoirdupois* pound weights. Gold bullion prices rose beyond $900 per *troy* ounce in May 2009, at which rate Jane's gold was worth $22,388,400 (£14,925,600 at exchange rate $1.50) in modern times.

24. Lodewijck Huygens, *The English Journal, 1651–2*, tr. Bachrach and Leiden Collmer, 1982, 81; HLJ, V, 559, 641; VI, 235; HCJ, III, 1662. The Crown was, in the second draft of the Oxford Surrender Articles, 1646, to be handed over with 'seals and all other insignia of office and honour'; it was omitted from the first draft. Bodleian Library, Additional Ms, D114–15.

25. Clarendon Papers, 16109, 1694, Bodleian Library, 66, 3 June 1643; CCC, I, 196, 511; PRO E 134, East 14, 19 Charles II; 'Paul Pindar', 'Peter Wyche', 'John Shaw', 'George Benyon', 'Nicholas Crispe' and 'MarmaDuke Royden', *ODNB*, 2004 articles; Mary Keeler, *The Long Parliament, 1640–41: A Biographical Study of its Members* (1954) for articles on Nicholas Crispe, John Jacob, William Masham and John Nulls; for further merchant and courtier donations to the king at Oxford, CCAM, II, 996–1005, Parliament's enquiry into 'The Oxford Engagement' of 4 July 1643, in which many had pledged donations, including the Benyon brothers, Thomas Lawrence, silkman, Henry Pratt, Matthew Bradley, George Strode, all of them merchants, and Judge Thomas Hyde who assisted Jane during and after the Commonwealth. This investigation into twenty-two of the king's key donors at Oxford continued until December 1653. Before that, all bonds, securities and cash loaned to Charles were forfeit to Parliament, which now needed the money as desperately as the king had a decade before. Field Whorwood, Lombard Street goldsmith, lived at Holton House with his widowed sister-in-law, Lady Ursula, from 1634. He issued England's first known banknote. For Eliab Harvey's financial involvement with Jane's mother and stepfather, see Chapter 10. 'Paul Pindar', *ODNB*, 2004, notes that Parliament was pursuing Ashburnham in May 1651 for evidence against Pindar for shipping gold to Oxford. At the same time Thomas Coke was informing on Jane Whorwood's work for the king. A month later she was fined and imprisoned for bribery and on the same day, 25 June, the investigation into the Oxford Engagement donors intensified.

26. HMC, XIII, *op. cit.*, 582; Sir Edward Walker, 'Letter to William Lilly', 1652, 5, in *Historical Discourses*, ed. 1707, 238–9, responding to Lilly's *Monarchy or No Monarchy in England: Observations on the Life and Actions of the Late King Charles I* (1651); HCJ, III, 157, 3 June 1643, permit for Mrs Wheeler to go to Oxford.

27. Letter in Claydon House Papers, Bodleian Ms 1249, 1644–5, 15/25 August 1645, Paris. Margaret asked Bishop Wilkins of Chester where she might stop off for the night if moon travel were feasible. He replied that she had so many 'castles in

the air, you may live every night at one of your own', Arthur Stanley, *Westminster Abbey* (1886), 217.

28. Paris, 16/28 September 1645. Brome was a distant cousin to the Verneys through the Dentons of Ambrosden, near Bicester, into whose family his great-great-aunt Magdalen Brome had married.

29. HMC Report 7, Verney Letters, 1 September 1645, Henry Verney to Sir Ralph Verney; Sir Thomas Gardiner's will, 1656, TNA PROB 11/259; Lady Gardiner's will, written in February 1647, TNA PROB 11/301, 1660, made no mention of her widowed daughter-in-law: she had borne them no grandson and by then had remarried.

30. British Library, Additional Ms 78264, f. 98; also printed in John Evelyn, *Diary and Correspondence*, ed. W. Bray, 814; Cordell W. Firebrace, *Honest Harry*, 51 (1932). Sarah Poynting of Keele University kindly pointed out that the letter is to 'IA' (John Ashburnham) and not, as Firebrace wishfully misread, 'IH' (Janna Horwood), see British Library, Egerton Ms 2550, 52, for cipher '449'. Anthony Wood, *Secretum Antonii*, Tanner Ms 102, cited in *Life and Times of Anthony Wood* (ed. Clark, 1891–1900), I, 1632–63, xxix–xxx. For the jewels and the lady who held them in 1649, see Chapter 10.

6

1646: *The Cromwell Naseby Wedding at Holton House*

My daughter had a husband worthy of the title of my son-in-law, Ireton my best of sons ... It was thy [Bridget's] fate to love him ...what will become of that fine monument thy careful father did erect for thee, next to thy husband?
Lady Cromwell's ghost, the Roundheads, Aphra Behn, 1682

God our refuge and our strength ...maketh Wars to cease ... He breaketh the bow and cutteth the spear in sunder, He burneth the chariot in the Fire.
Psalm 46, sung at the City Thanksgiving for Naseby, 1645

Oxford, 'the source of all our evils', surrendered a year and a week after Naseby. Its final six-week siege was a ritual anti-climax. With as many as 7,000 defenders, reputedly sufficient provisions and unbroken fortifications, the 'royal head garrison' could have held out longer, even if pointlessly. Morale, however, was not good, and the king fled to the Scots outside Newark in April; from Scottish custody at Newcastle he ordered an end to all resistance. According to Bulstrode Whitelocke, political adviser to the siege commanders, 19,300 New-Modelled Army men dug in around Oxford.[1]

Normality had been well acted out in Oxford for three summers. While Lord Essex skirmished and raided west of Wheatley Bridge in 1643, and smallpox scarred the town, the bishop's son studied for his degree, John Taylor wrote awful poetry, Jane Whorwood took a lover and King Charles sat for yet more portraits. Bodley's librarian famously refused to allow Charles to take away a book; even-handedly he later refused Cromwell the same. A minor victory at Chalgrove was good for morale and allowed Henrietta Maria to parade a relief column of supplies, troops and horses into town via a stormy landing from France at Bridlington. She preened herself in her mother's language, *La Generalissima*; Taylor deified her as 'Venus returned to Mars' (after pawning Mars's rubies to pay for the convoy); aptly her last role in a court masque in 1641 had been as Queen of the Amazons. By 1644 Oxford was overcrowded and dirty; typhus followed smallpox and plague, and fire followed them both. Crime was rife, the air fetid and the news of defeat at Marston Moor in April 1644 depressed morale. The king adjourned his Oxford Parliament.

That gloomy Easter Lady Ursula Whorwood paid the highest rate in the parish on Oxford High Street, where she lodged in a packed city, perhaps in a Whorwood townhouse. She heard the mandatory prayer in All Hallows for the safety of king and city, Jane perhaps, and certainly the grandchildren with her. Evacuees packed colleges and houses, swelling rate revenue but straining resources. Beyond the earthworks, Richard Symmonds, Life Guard captain, rode over to Holton from visiting Wheatley chapel, noting 'Lady Whorwood or Horwood lives in a fair house near this town, but is in the [?Leaguer].'[2] That same April the pregnant queen fled from Oxford to Exeter, attended by Mary Gardiner of Cuddesdon, on a road which led to France. Essex's army failed to consolidate an attack on Oxford, prompting Taylor to rank 'Mount Headington, vulgarly called Headington Hill' with Olympus and Parnassus. Vulnerable though Holton was, and despite Wheatley death rates rising by 200 per cent in 1644, the park air was healthier than that of the packed, marsh-bound city, where burials increased by 600 per cent and pigsties and cattle pens took up every space.[3] Lady Ursula did not stay in town.

A year later, Fairfax and Cromwell encircled Oxford with the remodelled army, intent on trapping the king; Taylor alerted citizens to 'Agamemnon and his Blazing Comet' outside. They built a bridge across the Cherwell, but had no artillery; the king escaped and the siege ended prematurely. Instead, they pursued the king's force, catching up at Naseby village as the Royalists wheeled south, ironically to relieve Oxford. A crushing royal defeat on 14 June was compounded when they published Charles's captured correspondence with the queen: 'the letters showed him governed by a woman', sniped Milton, who later taunted his own General Fairfax in similar vein.

The king's garrisons fell back like dominoes towards Oxford: Bristol and Hereford in 1645, Chester and Exeter in 1646. 'I am closed in on all sides', Charles wrote to his wife in April 1646, after she failed to land a French force at Hastings. Commissario [quartermaster] General Ireton brought up advance regiments mid-month to the eastern bank of the Thame by Wheatley Bridge 'for the closer blocking of Oxford'. On 24 April at night, the Duke of York's French tutor came to Ireton's quarter at Waterstock House begging terms for the king. Ireton rebuffed him and informed Parliament. To the north,

Woodstock House fell on 26 April, the day Ireton contacted Parliament: 'The king is still in Oxford, but now (it is thought) does again intend to get away if he can. We shall be as vigilant as we can to prevent it and do our utmost duty if he attempt it.' That the king did escape on the 27th increased Ireton's animosity.[4] Charles fled to the Scots outside Newark, not leading 500 horse as planned, but at night, crop-headed and disguised as a servant, demeaned enough for one poet to compare him to a despoiled monastery. Parliament heard he was making for London and at dawn they searched the home of the Lord Mayor, East India merchant Sir Thomas Adams. The Duke of York remained in Oxford with Princes Rupert and Maurice, all *incommunicado* as Parliament banned contact.

Fairfax force-marched from the south-west to join Ireton. Waterstock House was home to Mary Croke, widow of a respected Parliamentarian judge; the Whorwoods lived two miles away. On 1 May Fairfax's horse 'appeared in the fields east of Oxford and began to keep guards. Himself had his headquarters at Holton'. Parliament was duly informed that the army was now 'on both sides of the river [Thame] intending closely to begirt the city'.[5] Wheatley Bridge was secured, no enemy relief force loomed nearer than Ireland, and time was on Fairfax's side. A siege leaguer was built on Headington Hill to hold the London Way from Shotover to East Bridge, and sappers rebuilt the bridge of 1645 across the Cherwell at Marston. Under orders to pay for everything, the blockaders lived off the land. A free market was announced from local pulpits on 4 May, which won local approval and tantalised the garrison. Late in the afternoon of 18 May, Ireton, a lawyer who had negotiated at Exeter, began surrender talks in a Marston house belonging to a Croke nephew.

Holton Park afforded Fairfax a haven. He was sick, racked with gout, stone and 'riddled with wounds' from professional soldiering abroad and at home.[6] Lady Anne, a soldier's child and, like General Waller's wife, 'a pretty portable army' in her own right, had caught 'Ottery fever' while sharing her husband's hardships in Devon; Lucy Hutchinson recorded that Anne 'followed Fairfax's camp to the siege of Oxford and lay at his quarters there all the while he abode there', some days into July. The sick couple then took the waters at Bath. Affectionately, Cromwell assured them 'you and yours are in my daily prayers' and teased Anne as 'the Generaless', playing on Henrietta Maria's '*Generalissima*'. (Detractors called Anne '*Queen* Fairfax', claiming she ruled her husband.) As second-in-command Cromwell may even have shared the Fairfaxes' quarter at Holton, along with their personal army chaplain, William Dell. Lady Ursula's mansion boasted eighteen fireplaces, large enough for any general staff – and a wedding party.

Love was better timed in 1646 than in 1642, when the Miltons and Gardiners married, but Bridget 'Biddy' Cromwell's intensity worried her father. She was twenty-two and his first daughter. Henry Ireton, ten years older, had been deputy governor to her father at Ely, the Cromwell home town, where the couple met. 'Little Geneva' was good soil for youthful Calvinist piety. Cromwell's own 'breathing after God' had mellowed with age, and life – as a farmer, Cambridge student, MP, family man, notable equestrian, and formidable civilian soldier (Fairfax was the professional). For all Cromwell's blindspots, his mature Calvinism was more inclusive.[7] His daughter's ghosts may have been raised by Calvin's pessimism about original sin; the devil, the world and particularly the flesh sometimes sat uneasily with the Incarnation; Plato and Augustine shaped the puritan, ranking the spiritual above the corporeal; Calvin's God saved the predestined, which left the confident to assume and the rest to fret. Human love, where Cupid disturbed even Calvinist psyches, could be a nettle bed of scruples, although puritan theologians, like others, did debate the shifting marital priorities and demands of procreation, passion and prayer. Another Cromwell daughter, Elizabeth, who married at sixteen in January 1646, also had 'perplexed thoughts. She seeks her own carnal mind [wishful thinking], but bewailing it.' Anxiously, Cromwell advised Bridget, 'that which is best worthy of love in a husband is the image of Christ he bears. Look on that, love it best and all the rest for that.'

He had a soldier-farmer's earthiness, which allowed him to enjoy an evening campfire and command the Commons to remove 'this bauble', the revered mace. Henry Ireton's intensity concerned him as much as Bridget's. Five months into Bridget's marriage, when she was at Cornbury under tuition from Lady Fairfax in front-line partnering and pregnancy, Cromwell wrote to her knowing she was racked with scruples. Married love, he reminded, complemented the divine,

> but [I am not writing] to your husband, because one line of mine begets many of his, which makes him sit up too late. Dear heart, press on. Let not husband, let not anything cool thy affections after Christ. I hope [Henry] will be an occasion to inflame them. I pray for thee and for him; do so for me. My service and dear affections to the General [Fairfax] and the Generaless. I hear she is very kind to thee. It adds to all other obligations.

In raw reality, Bridget may have found Ireton harsh, awkward and intense, and she may have been homesick. Her corresponding letters are lost.

Cromwell heard years later that the couple were still haunted, 'tempted, and breathing after Christ, [Ireton particularly] much crying to God in secret'. Mary Cary, a puritan visionary, who 'breathed after Christ' while abhorring cleavages and facial beauty spots, dedicated a tract to Lady Cromwell and Bridget Ireton, 'virtuous, heroic and humble' puritan models, defending them against Royalist satire. After Ireton's premature death at Limerick in 1651, Bridget married Charles Fleetwood, army commander. She was an old-young, twice-married veteran mother before her younger two sisters had even married, yet the scruples persisted. With classic déjà vu, Cromwell advised Fleetwood: 'Bid her beware of a Bondage spirit – Fear – if I had done this, if I had done that. The antidote is love. Poor Biddy.'[8] Today he might have begged her to 'lighten up' or 'let God be God'. Ireton was a hard man, Lady Fairfax an exhausting model (although Cromwell welcomed her kindness to Bridget), and being the oldest Cromwell daughter did not help. Two years later, 'Queen' Fairfax publicly denounced Cromwell during the king's trial, as guards aimed muskets at her and called her a whore. The *esprit* of Holton was short-lived.

In 1646 a lieutenant-general's pay and booty helped Cromwell provide dowries for four daughters. Ireton impressed him, although he was more hostile to king and monarchy than Cromwell could yet be. Henry was an oligarch, an elitist conveniently predestined by God, property and rank. He would have England run by ardent young men like himself, but the older Cromwell had a vaguer, more hesitant idea; the younger advised by the older, the older refreshed by the younger, in a pooling of strengths to inspire a godly Parliament and constrain a king. As a civilian, Cromwell knew a settlement had to be a civilian one, and ten years later tried to effect it. The consuls of republican Rome were part of every gentleman's classical education. Cromwell and Ireton had proved themselves in battle, returning to the Commons (as consuls to the Senate) with the confidence of veterans. Fairfax, who had appointed them both, was sick, just when Army and Parliament needed strong reins, and the two virtually took over. By 1651, when Ireton was Lord Deputy in Ireland and Cromwell Lord General, the 'consulate' was evolving. Cromwell's and Ireton's names had long been mouthed in the same breath, Ireton said by Royalists to be 'hovering about Cromwell as an evil genius'; Whitelock observed them both before Oxford and at Holton, 'no man could prevail so much, nor order Cromwell as far as Ireton could'; Bishop Burnet called Ireton 'a Cassius', while Levellers called him 'Prince Ireton'. Lilburne went the furthest, seeing him by 1649 as 'an absolute king'.[9]

Henry's more modest role before Oxford was to negotiate the surrender; the symbolic end of the fighting War although isolated garrisons held out until months later. Force was a serious option, but the Council of War decided to 'approach' Oxford with terms rather than storm or starve it. It would be a coup for Ireton to achieve the surrender *and* his marriage by the first anniversary of Naseby. Exactly when (or if) Mrs Elizabeth Cromwell and family came to Holton is unrecorded, but Bridget hardly travelled alone from Ely. Oliver had missed Elizabeth's wedding there in January and the family had not yet moved to Westminster. Roads were muddy from the wet summer and vagrants abounded, but a military escort would have been provided. Wheatley Bridge now marked a dwindling patch of royal territory, although the technicality still mattered. Uncle Field Whorwood at Holton, Milton's father-in-law Richard Powell at Forest Hill and Edward Stampe, the Holton estate steward living in Headington, were all accused by the sequestration committee of having 'joined the king's garrison' at Oxford simply by living at home west of that boundary.

Arranging a wedding in this no–man's–land was problematic. The Anglican church framework had vanished, its primate executed after four years in prison in 1645, the year Bishop Skinner of Oxford was deposed with all other bishops, and his palace at Cuddesdon destroyed by his own side. The Scottish episcopal church had gone the same way in 1638. From a rectory in Bicester, Skinner ran a recusant-style underground church, while his few besieged clergy west of Wheatley Bridge remained openly Anglican under the king. When Parliament abolished the *Book of Common Prayer* in 1645 and replaced it with the *Directory of Public Worship*, Charles had demanded that bishops be reinstated, and that only *Common Prayer* be used. 'We shall require a strict account and prosecute' he warned, as Parliament ordered fines and imprisonment for refusing the *Directory*. Like enemy weapons, *Common Prayer* books were to be surrendered by September 1645. It was Scotland repeated. Archbishop John Maxwell, late of Tuam, as of Ross, hounded out of both dioceses in three years, took up his pen at Oxford to defend kings and bishops, but Charles's Oxford edict was increasingly unenforceable as the royal writ shrank.[10] However, if a wedding were to be held at Holton House, within the garrison perimeter, before Oxford surrendered, by whose writ and rite was it to be formalised, when the two rituals were reciprocally banned by the rival authorities?

Alban Eales, rector of Holton, was only months in his isolated post. Days before the wedding the vicar of Forest Hill was expelled and ex-bishop Skinner was deprived of Cuddesdon rectory; Thomas Thackwell at Waterperry might have sympathised after decades coping with Jesuits in hiding there, but essentially Eales was alone. He and William Dell, Fairfax's chaplain at Holton, came to an agreement, perhaps over a shared pipe of Virginia, a glass of sack and with the encouragement of the devout Lady Fairfax – she turned against Dell and his fellow-Independents only later when they put the king on trial. Dell was to solemnise with the *Directory* rite, and Eales was to register. Already across England rectors and vicars were 'ministers', and their churches 'meeting houses'; by 1653 churches would only register marriages (and births instead of baptisms) after the civil magistrate solemnised them away from church with a toast not a blessing.[11] By then, the (revised) *Directory* rite was the only recognised wedding format. Eales conducted and registered just three marriages at Holton, 1645–60; none of them after 1653.

The *Directory* required that marriage be celebrated 'in the place appointed by authority for public worship', and Fairfax was the authority in the field for a drumhead service. Holton parish church was visible from the house, but they settled for a semi-public wedding in front of household, guests and formal witnesses. Lady Fairfax dared not risk a drenching in the record summer rain which was even threatening the harvest. The Laudian trappings of Holton church made it an impossible venue for puritans: the communion table placed against the eastern wall like a pre-Reformation stone altar (instead of in the chancel, Geneva style) by decree in 1634, had triggered desecration in other places, as had stained glass. Rain on a wedding day was also a bad omen, and to impose an enemy service on a church within the unsurrendered garrison perimeter would have contravened the civilities of war. The choice was really Holton House or a wet field.

William Lilly called the *Directory* 'the threepenny *Directory*', but waited until 1668 to say it. John Taylor mocked it at the time as 'the *Alcoran*', outraged that 'the merry lords of misrule at Christmas had been suppressed by the mad lords of bad rule at Westminster'. On the other side, Milton called *Common Prayer* 'an English mass book from King Edward's time', guarded by royal chaplains, 'yeomen ushers of devotion'. At his billet in Magdalen College, Henry Hammond, the king's favourite chaplain, was more thoughtful, commending *Directory* ideas on prayer and preaching, but warning that 'spontaneous prayers' easily degenerated into sermonising. Informality, he complained, reduced services to 'parlour and closet prayers', and he asked whether kneeling at home was now forbidden. Ceremony and ritual (including wedding rings), to some the 'beauty of holiness', to others 'papistical superstition', had been Laud's preoccupation. The *Directory* replaced theatre with reflection, scripture and silence, a stress on the Word rather than the flesh, perhaps more consonant with Bridget's and Henry's scruples.[12]

The *Directory* could have been the *Common Prayer* of a second Reformation, but many refused it and more drifted from it, especially as Parliament failed to establish in law an English Presbyterian church, or revert to compulsory attendance. It sank without trace after 1662. Its composers had argued that *Common Prayer* was 'lip labour', its language a century old, its worship 'burdensome and disquieting'. They acknowledged openly the boredom of 'longsome services'. Their remedy was that 'nothing is to be rendered tedious', nor were preachers to 'burden the memory, trouble the mind with obscure terms, or detain the heavens with endless propounding, or raising old heresies from the grave'. Parliament also demanded reciprocal reform from the pews: 'no gazing, sleeping, private whisperings, conferences or salutations or reverences to any persons present or coming in.' However, Parliamentarian and Royalist alike still 'enlisted' a partisan God. One side asked delivery from 'the tyranny of the anti-Christian [puritan] faction and the cruel oppressions and blasphemies of the Turks'; the other prayed equally tendentiously for the king to 'save him from evil counsel', and 'for the conversion of the [Catholic] Queen, and the religious education of the Prince [of Wales]'.

Oxford's impending surrender, the wedding and the first anniversary of Naseby were synchronised excuses to remove sword-belts and 'to leap and smile'. It would be an ideal occasion for Fairfax to wear the Naseby jewel on its blue collar riband presented to him in Devon by Parliament the previous winter. On 10 June Boarstall, an outpost in the defensive ring around Oxford, surrendered and, as local schoolboys were allowed time off to watch the ceremonial march out with honours, Fairfax marked it by sending a gift of venison, veal, mutton, lamb, capons and butter across the lines into Oxford to the thirteen-year-old Duke of York as a token of goodwill and a gentle reminder not to delay the talks. As his own standing orders required, he would have paid Lady Ursula for any venison from Holton Park. Coincidentally that day, King Charles ordered Oxford to surrender. Four days later the Naseby anniversary fell on a Sabbath ('Sun-day' was unbiblical) when weddings were discouraged, but the feast was moveable and the wedding was held on Monday 15 June.[13]

All the general officers present, Fairfax, Cromwell and Ireton, had fought at Naseby, the New Army's first victory. Ireton's pike wound to the thigh and halbert scar on his face matched his seniors' injuries. Before the battle, Fairfax overrode Parliament to demand Cromwell be his lieutenant-general of horse and second-in-command; Cromwell in turn requested Ireton, one of Fairfax's first New Model colonels, as his sergeant major general of horse, and promoted him in the field to commissary general. The other Naseby general officer at Oxford, Philip Skippon, sergeant major general of infantry, may also have attended the wedding. He was supervising the entrenchments around Oxford, but sick, elderly and still recovering from serious wounds, he may have been invited to share the Holton sanctuary. Dell, too, had served as a regimental chaplain in the battle.

Cromwell, Fairfax, Lady Anne, Henry and Bridget were there, with the two clergy and Lady Whorwood, the presiding matriarch, all gentry, and Fairfax a baronet. If Mrs Cromwell attended, Bridget's three sisters and two surviving brothers probably came too. The Cromwell parents' relationship was close: they wrote frequent notes during Oliver's War, '[he to her] dearer than any creature, I could not omit this post though I had not much to write'; '[she to him] my life, I have only half a life in your absence'. They fretted at the silences when notes went astray. Ireton's relatives may also have attended, together with messmates, including Charles Fleetwood commanding the outpost at Brill on the Oxford to Aylesbury road.

Jane Whorwood had no other bolthole. Oxford was too 'close girt' for her to travel, passes were consistently refused to everyone regardless of rank, and at the other end of the road suspect Royalists were banned from London. The king was in Newcastle, Sandwell had been closed off since 1642, her father was in Scotland, her mother presumably with him. Sister Diana was in the enemy camp, Elizabeth with husband Lanark in Scotland, and Anne Bowyer in Sussex on the far side of enemy London. For better or worse, Jane and the children had been with Lady Ursula at Holton or in Oxford for the entire War. The fragmented records of her smuggling, 1642–4, Elias

Ashmole's remembering of her there in 1645, and the Ashburnham jewel tradition, are the sole evidences for her Wartime years in Oxford. Uncle Field Whorwood and Thomas, Brome's younger brother, also seem to have been at Holton. Brome, back in London from France, was still a delinquent, and crossing Wheatley Bridge to Holton would repeat his delinquency. Captain William, his youngest brother at twenty-two, chafed at the bit in the Oxford garrison, defiant but trapped. Bulstrode Whitelock, MP and adviser to Fairfax and Cromwell, was in the Commons on the wedding day, despite promising on 9 June 'to wait upon the General next week', but he did appear at Holton two weeks later.[14] He was also a friend and counsellor to Jane's mother. There were worse places for Jane to be.

According to the inventory of 1684, Holton had truckle beds and bolsters in every upper chamber and eighteen fireplaces to heat the house. It could lodge several families, though with much creaking of floorboards, panelling and bedframes. No oratory was recorded and the 'small remnant of the chapel', seen in the half-demolished medieval tower on the north-eastern side of the house in 1803, was probably fanciful. Manor house oratories were modest cubicles, not wedding venues, and sometimes improvised out of an available space. The Brome family's recusant record would have caused an oratory licence to be withdrawn years before. In 1684 a Bible of 1638 was noted in a Bible chest, possibly bound with a *Book of Common Prayer* for household use. Domestic prayers on Sundays and special occasions, daily under Lady Ursula, perhaps only in bad weather under Brome, would have been held in the great hall, where even a wedding might be accommodated. Only modestly 'great', at twenty by fifteen metres, it was still the main communal room.[15]

Rector Eales had no *Directory*, but Parliament had decreed that chaplains and senior officers be presented with copies. It also ordered 'A register is to be carefully kept [with] the names and times of the marriage [and] fairly recorded in a book provided for that purpose.' Eales' predecessor, John Normansell, had begun a parchment volume for Holton in 1633, after failing to find the register from the previous incumbent's fifty-year tenure. Eales brought the leather-bound document up to the house, probably accompanied by John Ives his elderly churchwarden. Both later signed it off as a true record.

As the guests assembled, staff would have craned to see from the screen passage between the hall and kitchen. The three refectory tables, trestles, chairs and benches in the hall in 1684 would have been supplemented, the fire irons polished and the chimney-breast picture (subject unknown) dusted. Perhaps the sedan noted in 1684 was not yet parked there. Midsummer flowers from the estate might have been strewn and garlanded. At a signal for silence, Dell reminded that marriage was 'no sacrament, but common to mankind and of public interest'. He then invited 'a competent number of credible witnesses to solemnise' it. No ring featured in the new rubric (it was only *explicitly* banned in 1653) as Henry and Bridget 'hand fastened' to exchange promises.

Ireton was deaf and might have stalled or cupped an ear at Dell's prompt, but Dell had a field preacher's voice. 'I do take thee to be my lawful married wife [husband] and do in the presence of God and before this congregation, promise and consent to be a loving and faithful husband ['loving faithful *and obedient* wife'] unto thee until God shall separate us by death.' Death did end it five years later, but effigies of Henry and Bridget lay side by side throughout the 1650s on their joint tomb in the Henry VII Chapel at Westminster Abbey.

'Prayer to this effect' followed, and a puritan couple would not kneel. Dell then preached, taking his cues from the *Directory*: 'a new frame of heart, fit for their new estate … to perform the duties, enjoy the comforts, undergo the cares and resist the temptations which accompany that [married] condition.' He pronounced them man and wife 'without further ceremony', save a warm dismissal to 'watch over each other with love and good works'. Fifty miles away, 'citizens of London city' were delating his Oxford sermon of 7 June to Parliament, and accusing him of more 'sesquipedalian verbosity … old Malignancy in new forms', in his preaching at Marston the day before the wedding. Influential citizens, Presbyterian in politics and religion, had visited Oxford as siege tourists ('having never seen a Leaguer before') and stayed in an inn in occupied Wheatley, expecting to hear Dell preach. They considered him too radical, independent, over-tolerant, a congregationalist hostile to the idea of establishment, Anglican or Presbyterian. 'If I saw anything of God in anyone, I reckoned him as a brother to us', was Dell's religious democracy, born of shared army hardship and experience; 'honest men' fighting for 'liberty of conscience', as Cromwell described Naseby to Parliament.[16]

A scratching quill, scraping penknife and blotting sand on vellum might be faintly audible as eyes turned to Rector Eales. He made one mistake (which he knifed), one omission (which he inserted) and dried the entry. Perhaps he was nervous.

Henry Ireton, Commissary Generall to Sir Thomas Fairfax and [erased, illegible] *Bridget Cromwell, daughter to Oliver Cromwell, Leftenaunt generall of the horse, to the said Sir Thomas Fairfax, were married* [inserted] *by Mr Dell in the Lady Whorwood her house in Holton, June 15th 1646.*

'Parchment [certificate] and witnesses [signatures]' may be assumed, as can maids of honour, perhaps Bridget's sisters, and purses offered to the clergy. Flagons would do the rounds for a toast in sack or canary; gifts, probably including traditional white gloves, appeared, the volume of chatter rose and perhaps an honour party fired a *feu de joie* over the moat. Wedding portraits came months later, Bridget and Henry inclining towards each other in 'my father and mother's pictures which are half lengths', still treasured by their son in 1710, along with 'my father's picture set in gold, crystal and a case, also my Grandfather Cromwell's picture in oil colour, and his picture enamelled'. A gilt cage cup with cover and a Cromwell portrait by Walker are traditionally linked to the Holton wedding; a flagon said to have been used at the celebration was last seen in 1860.[17]

Cromwell would have paid for his daughter's day, all would have paid for their billets, and gifts to Lady Ursula for her hospitality would have been appropriate. Cromwell, like other Parliamentarian commanders, despite the atrocities at Basing House, showed chivalry (and some confusion) towards women left defending homes alone. Lady Ursula was never punished for her financial and moral support of the king, or her offence of going to live in Oxford, and Cromwell may have intervened. Eight months later she wrote her will, refusing a *Directory* funeral; a decade later, Cromwell allowed a *Common Prayer* funeral to Archbishop Ussher, and *Common Prayer* weddings to his remaining two 'little wenches'. In the end, Parliament had to cut through a tangle in 1660 with blanket validation of all weddings since 1645. To be sure of being wed, some had married three times: an early *Directory* service in church, a later revised *Directory* rite before the JP, and an illegal *Common Prayer* service in secret before an obliging ex-clergyman. 'Married without a ring' was an uneasy status.

Despite Wartime conditions, the wedding would have had a feast with the commissariat's help, venison from the park, and perhaps soldier pipers and fiddlers in the gallery over the screen passage. Puritans could 'leap and smile' as well as any. The Fairfaxes hoping for a quiet wedding in 1637 had a great crowded feast sprung on them by family and friends. Bridget and Henry would have presided facing down the hall towards the screen from a dais, the St George salt perhaps before them. Midsummer light would allow dancing outside, rain and smells from the moat permitting. (Today, immediately south-west of the moat, a black mulberry, horizontal with age but still fruiting, may mark an important Holton marriage.) The participants were not yet the grave elders of portraits: Ireton and Bridget at thirty-two and twenty-two, Fairfax and Lady Fairfax at thirty-five and twenty-nine, Eales at thirty-seven, Cromwell and Elizabeth at forty-five and forty-six, Jane at thirty-four, and Dell about thirty-five. Brome junior, nine, might have played about the men, while Cromwell's daughters, Elizabeth, sixteen, Mary, nine, and Frances, eight, would have had time for Jane's seven-year-old Diana. Cromwell, 'naturally taciturn', enjoyed a drink and a party, 'among his friends diverting and familiar, in public grave and reserved'. In expansive mood, according to the Commonwealth Vice-Chancellor of Oxford, John Owen, he would place a hand on the shoulder of friends with whom he talked. At Frances's wedding in Whitehall, 1657, the wine flowed, food (and wigs) flew, and the orchestra played until dawn. By then Cromwell's 'wenches' were virtual princesses and he all but regal. As Protector he relaxed playing the organ at Whitehall and Hampton Court, although the sensuous instrument had no place in his worship. To begin the Holton supper he may have read aloud from his field Bible which dated from Naseby.[18]

Cromwell doted on his children and was at ease with others. When lost at Allerton in 1651 he called on Lady Stewart and her sickly son of ten. His gentle approach to the frail child, 'my little captain', and his present of wine to the lady, 'a staunch royalist', made her 'abate much of her zeal'. He attended councils of state with granddaughter Bridget Ireton on his knee. He and Fairfax had lost family in the War and the Holton wedding was a healthy change of mood on the eve of peace. Fairfax might have stammered, talking army 'shop' or theology. An introvert off the field, he wrote copious reflections on sermons, scripture, female beauty and even pock-marked bridesmaids. The two Naseby enamels, in their diamond-studded locket, were an eye-catcher – and a topical icebreaker; he may have indulged guests and servants to see them at close quarters.[19]

Jane and Lady Ursula had common ground with Ireton, four years older than Brome, but a fellow lawyer and graduate of Trinity, Oxford; brother Matthew Ireton had matriculated at Magdalen Hall with Thomas, Brome's younger brother, in 1635. Dell and Eales might have explored past experience and current issues over canary and pipes: the rector of Yelden, a temporary army chaplain baited by Presbyterians; the rector of Holton soon to pit himself against a violent lord of the manor. Twelve years previously, in Northamptonshire, Eales had been publicly insulted by another squire as 'no better than a ploughman'. Both men were accomplished preachers, Dell able to rally the respect of seasoned soldiers, Eales later appointed to Canterbury in 1665 as canon preacher. Dell became master of Gonville and Gaius, Cambridge, and an educational reformer, but with the humility of his mentor, John Calvin, he ordered his burial to be unmarked in a wood.

If Ireton drifted men-wards, Bridget had her mother, Ladies Anne and Ursula, and Jane Whorwood. On a quieter day after the wedding, they might have brought down the genealogy charts from grandfather George's study and spread them out in the window bay of the hall, or on the 'great table' in the great parlour next door with its rugs, bay window, playing tables and cheerful red curtains. Henry Ferrers of Baddesley Clinton, a noted genealogist, and Lady Ursula's cousin, who died only months before Jane married, had complained that Sir Thomas Whorwood forever pestered him for these charts.[20] They showed Lady Ursula's great-great-aunt and great-great-grandmother as Hampdens, and Henry Ferrers' grandmother as a Hampden, making Lady Ursula's grandmother first cousin to John Hampden's grandparents. Ursula's second cousin, Henry Ferrers, was third cousin to Oliver Cromwell, whose aunt was John Hampden's mother. Cromwell and Hampden were first cousins. Lady Fairfax and Lady Ursula were both great-nieces to the Earl of

Oxford, one by blood, the other by marriage. Unravelling such complexities could easily occupy a wet afternoon. Genealogy was a serious business, and that generation was fine-tuned to it, but laughter always helped those lost in its maze.

The couple would have had the 'best chamber'. In 1684 it was carpeted, had velvet elbow chairs, damask curtains, down bed, blanket and quilt, en suite facilities (two closed stool pans in cedarwood), an olivewood-framed full-length mirror, walnut and cedarwood tables, couches and a velvet window seat strewn with satin and velvet cushions in red, green, gold and white. Red and gold curtains matched a red couch. A landscape-decorated screen shielded the stool pans, and a fire warmed the newly washed. The walls were hung with canvas *faux* 'tapestries'. Bridget and Henry may have been seen to bed with some laughter and, if not a bell tied under the bed, at least a cup of sack posset shared in it to encouragement from outside. It was an age still close to the earth, whatever the religious overlay.

The following morning Fairfax rode to Water Eaton House, stopping by Headington Leaguer where he wrote to the Commons for a pass for the Earl of Bristol, and read the king's order forwarded by Parliament on 15 June for the ten remaining royal garrisons to surrender.[21] Cromwell returned to his desk and national despatches, Ireton to chairing the parley at Marston, possibly returning each evening for a rationed honeymoon. That day the Powell home in Forest Hill was judicially looted for their 'adhering to' the garrison. They spent winter 1646 in London with son-in-law Milton, who found them noisy and distasteful, but sheltered them for reconciliation's sake. Cary Gardiner, now widowed, never returned to Cuddesdon, where her first married home and the palace above it were burned-out shells. She remarried, more happily, and stayed away from the Gardiners. The broken silhouettes of the War – bishop's palaces, royal hunting lodges, gutted manor houses – joined the abbey ruins which marked an earlier dissolution of tradition.

A ceasefire was ordered on 17 June, just as Eales conducted his last funeral by *Common Prayer*. The restraint shown by both sides had preserved the dignity of the defeated. At the outset, Fairfax had stated, 'I desire very much the preservation of that place from ruin, so famous for its learning, which inevitably is likely to fall on it, except you concur', to which Governor Glemham insisted it was the king's decision; he would 'submit to the fate of the whole kingdom [but not] distrusting his own strength'. The king in Newcastle was realistic. 'You are not to expect relief so I give you leave to treat for good conditions. Let those of Exeter be your example. The addition must be the taking care of the University.' Prince Rupert and Cromwell had ridden out of Bristol together after its surrender in 1645. Cromwell had confided, 'If ever it would be in my power, I will recompense this [humiliation]', but at Oxford such compensation was not in his gift.

Oxford was not cowed, but it was strangled in its flood plain with full moats. Twenty-five Royalist officers rejected the surrender, among them Captain William 'Harwood', Jane's brother-in-law.[22] After the king's second order to 'quit and disband', the young bloods fell into line, but mutiny still threatened. A routine of truces developed; rain dampened military ardour, and no one wanted to die for a lost cause, especially in wet weather. Those outside the walls spoke of those inside 'drooping in posture', and mocked a garrison of 'Lords debating, Council of War consulting, Clergy prating, Townsmen meeting, and Soldiers asking what to do'. Rumour had the garrison already packing on 13 June for its exit, and shortly afterwards they burned their records. In 'a cessation of arms between besiegers and besieged, divers of the [Parliament] soldiers came to the Ports and drank with ours'. As in 1642, honorary degrees were hurriedly conferred in convocation at St Mary's, last-minute awards for service and suffering.

Negotiations concluded, terms were ratified at Water Eaton House and at Christ Church, the king's recent palace, where the surrender was formally signed. Royal commissioners included the Marquess of Hertford, Royalist chancellor of Oxford. On the Sabbath, 21 June, Fairfax reflected at Holton on the 'great mercy of God that this place was so regained, considering what blood might have been spilt around it, and more treasure it would have lost than the [confiscation of] the estates of those within it could have satisfied'. The following day the princes James, Rupert and Maurice rode out across Eastbridge for the Wycombe road past Holton. Next day a column of gentry followed. On 24 June, old Midsummer's Day and St John's Day, now Parliament's Day of Public Humiliation and Fasting, the city was handed over to Fairfax at 10 a.m., a guard posted on the Bodleian Library and after noonday two columns totalling some 3,000 armed soldiers, one led by Governor Glemham, left the city by the north and east gates in driving rain. A Parliamentarian guard of honour a mile long saluted the thousand or more who crossed Eastbridge for Shotover Hill.

They passed Holton Park, crossed Wheatley Bridge and marched to Thame where arms were stacked, ammunition handed in, and safe-conducts distributed. Anthony Wood and schoolmates at Thame enjoyed their second surrender spectacle in two weeks, pestering the tired rankers. More than half the garrison chose 'to go on foreign service' to the end-battles of the Thirty Years' War. Others, like Captain William Whorwood, were allowed home unmolested, on condition that they did not fight Parliament another day – which Whorwood soon did. When he reached Holton Park the distinguished guests were still there: the Fairfaxes, the Iretons and Cromwell. Dell had been detained in London after taking to Parliament the formal news of the surrender; he forfeited his £50 herald's reward and was being investigated by the mainly Presbyterian Parliament for preaching Independency and tolerance.[23] London was now the stage and neither Captain William nor Mistress Jane stayed long at the park. Oxford was no longer where events unfolded.

Notes

1. On 12 May Fairfax asked the Commons to release Bulstrode Whitelock as his political adviser before Oxford; both the *Diary of Bulstrode Whitelock* ed. R. Spalding (1990), 185–7, and Ruth Spalding, *The Improbable Puritan* (1975), 109–10, give an impression he was with Fairfax from then until late June. The Speaker advised discretion lest Presbyterian jealousies be aroused, and Whitelock tactfully took home leave to Henley instead, 'but a little way' from Oxford. Commons records, however, show he was active at Westminster in mid-June, notably on the day of the wedding, Monday 15 June, HCJ, IV, 576–8.

2. Margaret Toynbee and Peter Young, *Strangers in Oxford* (1973), 249, 250. British Library, Harley Ms 965, f. 64, 14 April 1644. 'Leaguer', a military, frequently a siege camp (hence be-leaguered), from Dutch 'leger'.

3. Wheatley chapel entries in Cuddesdon Register transcript, Oxfordshire Archives. Some deaths were from disease, some from war: 1642 saw twenty-two burials from Wheatley, 1643, fifty-three and 1644, sixty-nine.

4. British Library, Sloane Ms 1519, 133, 25 April 1646, and two other letters, same to same, 23 and 27 April; John Ashburnham, *Narrative* (1830), 71–2; Nicholas Papers, I, 1646–52, Camden Society, NS 40, 1880, 66. Sir William Fleetwood approached his brother, Colonel Charles, at Brill for a safe conduct for the king and was rebuffed, as was Prince Rupert on 9 May when he asked Fairfax for a 'place of safety and liberty for me', Sloane Ms 1519, 143. The surrender of Oxford was to be honourable, but without favour.

5. Sir William Dugdale, *Life, Diary and Correspondence* (1827), 86, diary entry 1 May 1646; Bulstrode Whitelock, *Memorials of English Affairs*, ed. Hamper (1828), 14.

6. On 'ecumenical Calvinism', see Conrad Russell, lecture at Sydney Sussex College, 1999, quarcentenary of Cromwell's birth; Theo Hobson preferred '*liberal* Calvinist', *Sunday Times* review, 9 November 2008.

7. Andrew Hopper, *Black Tom* (2007), 179.

8. Thomas Carlyle, *Oliver Cromwell's Letters and Speeches* (1849), ed: XLI, 25 October 1646; CLXXIII, 3 May 1651; CLXXXVII, 1652; Mary Cary, *The Little Horn's Dream* (1651); Henry Nevile, *News from the Commonwealth of Ladies* (1651). ('Hugh Peters keeps mighty intelligence with Mistress Ireton, as Cromwell with Mrs Lambert.')

9. David Farr, *Henry Ireton and the English Revolution* (1969), 202, 128; Henry Perrinchief, *Life of Charles I* (1693), 182. The wedding was too early to be a ruling dynasty marriage, but it cemented an alliance in which power soon concentrated, 1646–51.

10. John Rushworth, *Historical Collections: 1659–1701* (1722), I, pt IV, 208, at Oxford, November 1645. John Maxwell, *The Burden of Issachar*, May 1646, Thomason Tracts 55 E. 336(3).

11. Lady Anne Halkett, née Murray, described her *Directory* wedding: 'Holding the *Directory* in his hand, [the JP] asked if we wished to marry, then says he,

"I pronounce you man and wife". So, calling for a glass of sack, he drank and wished us much happiness and we left him, having given his clerk money who gave us parchment on the day and witnesses, but if it had not been done more solemnly by a minister afterwards, I should not have believed it was lawfully done', *Autobiography of Anne, Lady Halkett*, Camden Society, NS 13, 1875, 102–3; J.T. Johnson, *A Society Ordained by God: Puritan Marriage* (1970); Geoffrey Smith, *In Well Beware* (1978).

12. William Lilly, *History of His Life and Times* (1774), 86; John Milton, *Eikonoklastes* (1649), 63, 77. Some Quakers were made to read the Qu'ran in prison, see G. Ricksdell Smith, *Without Truth or Dishonour* (1968), 170; Henry Hammond, *A View of the New Directory and a Vindication of the Ancient Liturgy*, Oxford, 1646.

13. Frederick J. Varley, *The Siege of Oxford* (1932), 145; Sir William Dugdale, *op. cit.*, 89.

14. British Library, Sloane Ms, 1519, 143. Bulstrode Whitelock's mother was a Croke of Waterstock and presumably he knew Waterstock, Waterperry and Holton. It has been argued that the destruction of his house at Fawley Court inspired the painting *When Did You Last See Your Father?* by William Yeames, 1877.

15. Inventory of Holton House, 1684, TNA PROB 5/5275, 114461, although forty years later, it gives an idea of the house and its customary furnishing; Oxfordshire Archives, PAR 135/17/J1/2, 'Diary and Notebook of Frances Biscoe', who saw the deserted house before its demolition in 1804. The remains of the south-western foundations of the house still allow calculation of room dimensions.

16. *Reliquiae Liturgicae*, III, 1847, 60–3. *Directory* services were banned in 1663, but the rite was 'revived' west of Wheatley Bridge in 2004 in one of Mick Jones's many community and radio plays, *Swallows on the Moon*, inspired by local history and community enthusiasm; Anon, *Complaint of Christian Readers*, London, 1646. Wood Pamphlets, 514 (17), Bodleian Library.

17. Holton Register entry, 15 June 1646. Nerves dog marriage registers – in 1945 Registrar Wagner mis-spelt his own name certifying the wedding of Hitler and Braun. Holton churchwardens 'viewed' the Ireton-Cromwell entry in 1675 as evidence for Henry Ireton junior in a law suit. The 'Holton Cromwell Cup' is an Augsburg-made gilt cup and cover, reputedly given by Cromwell to Ireton, and by Ireton to Lady Ursula. However, its maker, Adolf Gaap, worked a decade later; its base was inscribed in Oxford about 1850 and neither it nor its story are recorded before then. It was left to Lord Sherbourne, a distant relative, by the last, landless Whorwood of Headington Manor: Gloucester Record Office, D2026/E; *Notes and Queries*, 9th Series, IV, 9 December 1899, article by Lord Sherbourne; Christie's *Catalogue*, 9 May 1889, Lot 91, withdrawn after servants tried to sell it; *Notes and Queries*, 7th Series, VII, 29 January 1889; *Notes and Queries*, 9th Series, VI, 9 December 1899; John Henry Parker (annotated copy) *Architectural Antiquities in the Neighbourhood of Oxford* (1844), Bodleian Library. 'Escutcheon polishing' may lie behind such traditions, as when William Earle-Biscoe of Holton claimed

that the wedding was in Holton's *private chapel*, in the time of Rector Alban Earle, see *Notes and Queries*, 6th Series, VII, 30 June 1883, 514. 'A flagon said to be from the Ireton wedding' was last seen in Hungerford in 1860, *Journal of the Archaeological Association*, XVI; Bulstrode Whitelocke died at Chilton Lodge in 1676, a family home near Hungerford, and did stay with Fairfax at Holton during the surrender talks. 'The Holton Cromwell Portrait' is now Oxford University's formal portrait of its former Chancellor, and a copy is at Cornell University. Tradition had it presented to Holton House after the wedding. However, the Biscoe family, who bought Holton in 1801, were collateral descendants of Colonel John Biscoe, a regicide living in exile after 1660, and may have brought the portrait to Holton, although this was denied: Bodleian Library, Picture 417, and Bodleian Library Records, *c.*1328. The wedding portraits feature in the will of Henry Ireton junior, 1710, proved in 1712, TNA PROB 11/525.

18.　James Weland, *Memoirs of The Most Material Transactions for the Last Hundred Years* (1699), 94; *Correspondence of John Owen*, ed. Peter Toon (1970), 32; for the later Cromwell daughters' weddings, see Edward Holberton, *The 17th Century*, XX, 1 (2005), 'So Honey from the Lion Came, the 1657 Wedding Masques for the Protector's Daughters', 97–112. For Cromwell's four-part field Bible, inscribed on the flyleaf, *Who ceases to improve ceases to be good*, see *Sussex Archeological Collection*, III, October 1848, 18.

19.　Fairfax's reflections, British Library, Additional Ms, 4929, and poetry, British Library, Ms 11744. By 1646 he had been married eight years. Faded beauty was 'a starless night', 'a saintless shrine', 'an unlit torch', 'a godly ship without her sail'. On a bridesmaid's pock-marked face (like Jane Whorwood's and Anne Fairfax's), 'they have foolish sotts, that beauty ought to have no spots; why should not a maid of honour have them, if even Venus had one'; Horace Walpole had the Naseby jewel from John Thoreseby who had it from the Fairfax family.

20.　John Fox, 'The Bromes of Holton Hall, a Forgotten Recusant Family', *Oxoniensia*, LXVIII (2003), 88, for Henry Ferrers' complaint about Whorwood and the genealogy charts. For the later furnishings of the 'best chamber' and other rooms at Holton, see *Inventory* (1684), *op.cit.*

21.　Henry Cary, *Memorials of the Civil War in England*, I (1842), 106–7, Letter to Lenthall for safe pass for Lord Bristol, from Water Eaton.

22.　Margaret Toynbee and Peter Young, *Strangers in Oxford* (1972), 28–9.

23.　The Dell-Ireton link continued. Dell married in 1647 and returned to minister at Yelden. King Charles declined his (and others') offer to pray with him before execution in 1649. Ireton's nephew and niece witnessed the will of Dell's wife, Martha, in 1684. Dell and John Bunyan were close; Bunyan was arrested and jailed by Sir Francis Wingate of Harlington, and William Dell junior married Elizabeth Wingate; as a minor he had been Sir Francis's ward. (Information from Alan Dell, descendant of William Dell, August

2005.) Alban Eales was recommended for a Canterbury preaching canonry by All Souls College in May 1665, was collated Rector of Aldington, Kent, for his living and died there in 1670. *Archbishop's Act Book*, 1, 140, Canterbury Cathedral Archives, DCc/Carta Antiqua, Z 15; DCb/BT1/3. Afterwards, his daughter became gentlewoman to Jane Whorwood's daughter Diana at Holton House.

7

1647: 'Mistress Whorwood, Committee Chairwoman?'

[In 1647] Sir Robert Banastre asked the Messenger from the Committee for the Advance of Money, whether Mistress Whorwood were Chairwoman of the Committee?
Evidence given before Parliamentary Enquiry, 1651

The lady is of my ancient acquaintance. I believe well of her affection to your service, but truly sir, my own dear bought experience of that sex, by my own folly, makes me generally to judge them to be vessels too weak for the retention of strong liqueur.
Sir Lewis Dyve to the king, apparently about Jane Whorwood, 1647

In February 1647, eight months after the Naseby wedding, Lady Ursula spent a week composing her will, 'revoking all other[s]'.[1] She was to be buried in Holton chancel, 'privately according to the Ancient [*Common Prayer*] of burials'. Brome was to have the cattle and swine, with Holton Park. She had withheld enough plate from the king for her other sons, two silver cups to Thomas and two silver bowls to Captain William. Her only two grandchildren had her silver warming pan and basin, while brother-in-law Field Whorwood had her silver-lidded tankard. She also left to the younger sons bonds, cash and linen, with any remaining cattle and horses. Park keeper, butler and personal maid received legacies, as did the local poor; everyone, in fact, 'my sons, grandchildren and my brother [Field] Whorwood shall have mourning, and my servants likewise, and my sons' servants, and my brother Whorwood's man, cloth for a cloak'. She could not have excluded her daughter-in-law more pointedly – as if dead.

By then Brome had returned home and Jane had gone to track the king, the two children left with their father and grandmother. Brome later deposited an affidavit with Robert Abbott, banker to leading Royalists including the Maxwells and the Whorwoods. Abbott looked after their papers, laundered Royalist funds, and helped those facing fines and debt.

> [*Undated*] In the late time of Rebellion, [Jane Whorwood] without any just cause departed from the defendant's house unknown to him, came to London and other places as she pleased, and put him more in debt which he paid and used all other means possible to have by all fair means her company at home again where she was plentifully provided for [and he] paid vast sums of money for her.[2]

Brome could have been describing 1647.

Among 'other places she pleased' to visit seems to have been Newcastle, where her father, now Earl of Dirleton, once more attended at the captive court, and her brother-in-law, Lanark, negotiated as a Scots commissioner, both reconciling themselves uneasily with the king. Charles remained in Scots custody until early February 1647, while Parliament and the Estates negotiated the compensation due to the Scots for their Wartime alliance. £200,000, half the agreed debt, was paid with the balance to follow. It was uncannily like a ransom, and the king was handed over to the English, despite his request for a Scots escort. James Maxwell, who had loaned £8,000 sterling to the Covenanter Army in 1645, recouped half of it in the agreement, even as he waited on the king.

Jane conducted parallel negotiations with the king at Newcastle, lobbying while visiting her father, as well as by courier, for Sir Thomas Bendish, her reputed lover, to be appointed ambassador to Constantinople. The posting, once the Levant Company's own appointment, had become a Crown gift for 'court cormorants', (a reference to the royal sport of fishing with obedient trained birds). As with bishops, the king's candidate was compulsorily 'elected' by the company, although they could nominate others. Sir Sackvile Crowe, Royalist incumbent in Turkey since 1633, but dismissed in 1646, now refused to resign and made up his losses at home by poaching company revenues. The company, now with a Parliamentarian majority, wanted him out, nominating in his place its long-serving consul in Aleppo, Edward Bernard. The king would not confirm, at which Royalist minority members of the company 'rejoice greatly'. William Murray, gentleman of the bedchamber and now Earl of Dysart, 'puddled the clearness of that business much' by demanding of the company 'near £3000, as if without that the king would not consent', in return for his promise to influence the choice. It was a loyal scam played on all candidates to secure 'cash for honours' for the king's funds. Even Bendish was not exempt and likewise paid £3,000.[3]

Other hopefuls tendered bids. Sir Lewis Dyve, ex-governor of Abingdon imprisoned in the Tower, supported City and Parliamentarian moderates for compromise with the Crown. He corresponded frequently with the king throughout 1647 when the Tower gave him a listening post and a friend in 'free-born John' Lilburne, the Leveller leader who warned against the Cromwell–Ireton 'consulate'. In January 1647 the Levant Company approached Dyve for support for Bernard; he informed the king that this would be 'direct opposite to my own interests', reminding him of a 'most sacred and inviolable' promise of the post to himself. He was confident that Charles 'would not dispose of it in the meantime to any other, although I am told that some now about Your Majesty give great assurance of effecting it on the performance of those offers [of money] that were made by merchants to approve it'. This he had been told by 'a man of much credit in the City'. He felt the company should not be rewarded in view of its Parliamentarian majority's Wartime support for Parliament; neither, he felt, should Sackvile Crowe be 'called off in disgrace on the complaint of those who deserved so little favour'. Jane Whorwood was Dyve's named courier by early summer, 1647, and had been for some time. They kept each other informed.[4]

Queen Henrietta Maria weighed into this strong field, reminding Charles that Sir William Killigrew was her nominee, a hero of Edgehill whose daughter attended her in Paris. 'Next to him,' she added, 'you are engaged for Sir Robert Browne', ambassador in Paris, also close to the exile court. Endymion Porter of her entourage was convinced Browne 'will carry it. The Turkey Company has presented him to His Majesty to be their ambassador.' Browne had appeared in Oxford in January 1646, to press his case after applying for the post in mid-1645; his daughter's attending on the Princess Royal strengthened his petition with Henrietta Maria who had a virtual Regent's role in the matter, corresponding with Crowe in Charles's name. The king had actually delegated her: 'I give thee power and desire thee to fill up the blanks for the Turkey business as [you] the Queen shall find fit.' However, she had been away too long to know the king's mind or the pressures upon him. 'I am daily importuned with letters from the Turkey Company', he told her in November.[5]

The king retained the appearance of deciding, but Sir Paul Pindar, helpless, sidelined and bankrupt, 'squeaked like a goose divided into semi-quavers' in protest at the lobbying. Charles finally approved Bendish on 8 January 1647; Parliament assented three weeks later, and agreed that the king might commission him. Assistant Royal Secretary Nicholas Oudart wrote from Holland on 18 February (in lemon juice on the back of a fictitious wool merchant's letter) to Secretary of State Sir Edward Nicholas that 'the [Levant] Company are now discontent and begin to think Mistress Harwood [*sic*] did avail more for Sir Thomas, her paramour, than the friends [and payment] they employed for Bernard'.[6] James Maxwell may have helped his daughter bend the king's ear, in a bitter contest. Parliamentarian commissioners in the king's entourage even tried to prevent Bendish's obtaining the king's signature and seal.

Oudart shrugged, 'perhaps the project may come to naught and Sir Sackvile Crowe continue'. Far away, Crowe hoped in vain for his own lobby.

If Oudart's barb was accurate, Jane's affair with Bendish had begun in Wartime Oxford. The reputation of the fortified city had been 'London with all its vices on the banks of the Isis, where Minerva, not to say Diana, gave place too much to Venus'. Intimations of mortality made for impromptu bedfellows and gossip thrived on garrison dalliances. Bendish was Jane's age with a wife and children in Essex; both were on royal service separated from partners and both featured for special service in John Ashburnham's garrison *Accompt*. If they were 'paramours', it must have been in the early years, 1642–3, as Bendish spent twenty-two months in the Tower, 1643–4, and on release was confined to London until 1646.

Early in 1647, Jane's husband agreed a loan of £300, 'between me and Sir Thomas Bendish, baronet, on behalf of [my wife] for the performance thereof, she and Sir Thomas Bendish did about the same time enter into a special obligation of the sum of £300 [to me] conditional on [a bond]'. The purpose of the loan was not stated, nor the month, but Bendish left for Turkey that spring. It may have gone towards the £3,000 Bendish gave to the king 'out of his own purse', and it proves that Brome knew of Bendish and Jane's working relationship. Jane may have flattered Brome that he was being drawn into the loyalist circle around the king; in 1648 she wrote a fiction to 'my bedfellow' from the Medway to decoy a spy. Later, she seems to have relieved Brome of his copy of the bond, to protect her case for separation and alimony.[7]

Although the king's request to negotiate in London was rejected, he rode south on a virtual progress towards the capital. Taylor saw 'a passenger in a Hackney chariot', and Fairfax warned of 'a golden ball cast before Parliament and the Army'. On 14 February Charles halted in Northamptonshire, at Holdenby, a refurbished royal lodge. Jane shadowed him but could not enter Holdenby, despite her father's role there. However, her sister, Countess Lanark, evidently did visit the king on her way from Edinburgh to France, offering to 'do anything in [the king's] service and promising to find a way to send the letters of the king and queen, which she will communicate to [the French ambassador] in passing through London'. She had even invited the French ambassador in Edinburgh to accompany her to meet Charles. She began a parallel courier network to the one Jane was constructing in southern England, but most of the evidence for it has vanished.

For four months Charles led a decorous, convalescent schedule of bowls, golf, rides to Althorp, chess and prayer. Maxwell and other veteran courtiers around the king were 'narrowly watched' by Parliamentarian commissioners and servants. In March, Charles articled Bendish to Turkey, but without the divan traditionally given to the ambassador. By September 1647 the baronet was in Constantinople with his wife and six children, bribing his way through the last barriers to the Ottoman presence and despatching Crowe back to the

Tower. He held the post until the Restoration. In 1661 Jane received £139 expenses agreed by Parliament in 1648, which may have been for her work for Sir Thomas.[8]

On Wight, in January 1648, the king asked Abraham Dowcett 'who was she that brought me the first letter at Holdenby?'[9] Nicholas Oudart in Holland noted on 4 March 1647 that while Jane's father attended the king, 'Mistress Harwood herself, with [despite] all her father boldness and art [daring and cunning], dares adventure no farther than Northampton. The king is so narrowly watched that nobody can privately speak with him nor present to, nor receive from him anything but what his overseers admit.'[10] Holdenby is seven miles north-west of Northampton where, in February, Nicholas Oudart believed Jane was loitering. In April, Major William Bosvile came from Holland and, disguised as an angler, passed a packet of letters from the queen to the king as he dismounted at a narrow bridge near Althorp. The handover was spotted, the letters confiscated and Bosvile arrested. Later that month John Browne, Ashburnham's right-hand man, brought a letter to the king from his master in The Hague. Browne and Mary Cave, daughter of a deputy lieutenant of Northamptonshire, who delivered it, were also arrested and interrogated. The king had stayed overnight with the Caves on his flight from Oxford to Newark. Mary admitted trying to deliver the letter, but she knew nothing of its content and Browne admitted to involving her.

Evidently, Mary had approached a lady friend near Holdenby to arrange for her a routine audience to kiss the king's hands. The audience was effected through the landlady of a Parliamentarian officer, but the landlady's husband informed the officer of the plot. Accordingly, when Mistress Cave and her unidentified friend came to Holdenby on 11 May she was searched, but the letter, hidden in a petition and probably written in lemon juice, was found only afterwards behind wall hangings by which she had been close-searched. She and Browne were held by the mayor of Northampton until Parliament agents arrived to question them. Ashburnham's letter promised 'a good war for your recovery', a Dutch army and an Irish force, but warned Charles not to give away too much. '389 (? the queen; Jane at one time was '390', and the king '391') hopes you have burned all your letters and ciphers. If you have not, for God's sake do it. You will still remember the alphabet.'[11]

Jane Whorwood was not implicated and already in London from the beginning of May, but she had certainly been near Northampton in April, and continued to shadow the royal road show to Hampton Court in August. Other business had occupied her at Passenham, twenty miles south of Holdenby. Sir Robert Banastre, master of the household to James I, and colleague of Jane's father and stepfather, bought Passenham manor in 1625. His son Lawrence married Mary Dynham from Boarstall near Holton, second cousin to Lady Ursula. Charles I stayed at Passenham in 1633 as he returned from his coronation in Scotland with James Maxwell in attendance.

Sir Robert's estate was sequestrated in 1645, subject to a redemption fine of nearly £3,000. As sheriff, Banastre had collected Ship Money as ruthlessly as if it were supplementation. Despite hostility to Parliament, he claimed that he had paid over £2,000 on 'public faith' during the War, to be offset against his fine, leaving about £600 balance owing. At the end of April 1647, Jane returned to London from Northampton with a letter from Lady Banastre to Alderman Thomas Adams, an old friend of Sir Robert and a fellow native of Wem:

> it will be very fit that you engage yourself upon good reasoning to Mistress Whorwood for the payment of the £600 upon the Committee's discharge of Sir Robert's assessment of £3000, upon a promise from her that she provide in public faith [evidence of allowances] for the money which Sir Robert paid to the late Earl of Essex [and] the Committee for Northamptonshire.[12]

Three days after Adams had Lady Banastre's letter, an officer of the Committee for the Advance of Money at Haberdashers Hall reviewed the case. A day later, Jane secured a discharge for Sir Robert from four committee members chaired by Lord Howard of Escrick and signed for the committee clerk in his absence. Women were acceptable pleaders on behalf of 'masculine malignants', but 'it was perceived by the officers of this Committee that Mistress Whorwood had applied herself to the Lord Howard who was instrumental in that business'. She had some hold over Howard which Lady Banastre, the more obvious 'solicitor' for her husband, did not have. Jane may have known him from his visits to her neighbours at Wallingford House after his marriage to Buckingham's niece. When a Parliamentary courier requested £14 outstanding expenses from Banastre, the old man dismissed him, saying 'he had paid Mistress Whorwood these charges and it had cost him dear. He was sure it was £640 [£40 plus his fine] and if anyone ought to pay his charges, Mistress Whorwood ought to do it and willed him to repair unto her. He was cholerick with the messenger and asked him, "Who is Chairman of your Committee?"' The courier later testified to the actual words, 'Is Mistress Whorwood *Chairwoman* of your Committee?'

The shortchanged courier asked the clerk to issue a summons to Jane 'to satisfy him with his charges, which was granted, and delivered to Mistress Whorwood'. She refused to accept the summons and threatened to confront the committee. The next morning, Lord Howard, chastened by the blackmail threat, brought back her summons paper, demanding of the clerk why he had issued it without committee approval. The clerk protested his right to do so, to which Howard replied, 'call the messenger to me and I will see he shall have satisfaction. Lord Howard was not well pleased, although the summons was regular.' Despite Jane's £40 surcharge, the final payment of an apparent £600 was a bargain for Banastre, but it was not paid to the committee and Howard paid off the courier to silence him. Jane was then paid £600 by Alderman Adams to make up for the £600 she had supposedly paid the committee. The total embezzled, possibly £1,200 less any bribe to Lord Howard, went to the king's account. It may have formed part or all of the 'thousand pounds in gold' which Adams was later alleged by William Lilly to have 'collected' and transferred to the king, 'five hundred pounds of which was put into Jane Whorwood's hands'.[13] Ex-Lord Mayor Adams, sixty-one, and Banastre, seventy-eight, were fellow Shropshire men, contemporaries of a Dick Whittington generation made good; Adams became Banastre's executor in 1649.

In June 1647, shortly after the Banastre discharge, the king was taken from Holdenby by force, by a cornet with several hundred troopers from Oxford, acting apparently on nods from Fairfax, Cromwell and Ireton to keep the king and Parliament apart. James Maxwell helped hold the king's apartment door against the officer, 'keeping firm to their resolution that he should not enter, [but] the noise was so loud it awakened his Majesty'. Charles was escorted to army HQ at Newmarket, then to Childersley (where he met with the Naseby generals and Dell, having 'most conference with Cromwell and Ireton') on the summer road to Hampton Court. Ahead of him the army moved on London to take it in a bloodless pre-emptive strike, a response to a purge of Independents by the City and Parliament. Once Fairfax had control of the capital, Thomas Adams, the senior alderman, was remanded with others to the Tower in September. Back in April 1646 he had been suspected of harbouring Charles in flight from Oxford, and he 'hath made a party in the City for the king'. He and Sir Lewis Dyve in the Tower kept in touch with Royalists through Jane Whorwood and raised money.[14]

Dyve's surviving letterbook from the Tower contains thirty-six letters to Charles in 1647, and another seven to John Ashburnham. He 'intelligenced' the king between Newcastle and Hampton Court, reminding him that while City merchants had supported Parliament under duress in the War, they now feared instability as the Army challenged the rule of Parliament. On 24 May he advised of '200 citizens who, if they get only moderate fines [from you for Wartime disloyalty] will yield a million to your Majesty'. These included many former Royalists of the East India and Levant companies, although others in the Royalist minority like Adams, Pindar and the customs farmers had proved unswerving. In March Oudart had advised Nicholas, probably after listening to Edward Andrews, the Surrey Royalist, 'the City is subject still to be ridden by any party rather than endanger trade'. Dyve even spoke of Cromwell's latent loyalty to the Crown, warning the king that Cromwell thought him 'bloody and inconstant in word' and feared his vengeful streak.[15]

Jane acted as courier between Dyve and the king, and probably for Adams too after his arrest in September 1647, and between the three of them and the City, just as she had done at Oxford and when lobbying for Bendish. On 18 June

'Mistress Whorwood undertook the care to convey [my second letter that day] to Your Majesty. A seasonable opportunity.' Dyve was already used to trusting her. He had sent a very different first letter unsealed through official Army channels as a lure, before giving her the second. By then Charles was at Newmarket. Once the Army marched on London, Charles having brushed aside their relatively moderate proposals, Dyve became so guarded he omitted all names from his letters. On 6 August he told Ashburnham:

> I received a ticket [note] of yours this morning from a lady who sent a young gentleman to me [for] the cipher you wrote of to decipher a letter she sent me from the king, but I knew the character to be none of his … I offered to have it deciphered for her, which the gentleman that brought it declined, whereby the letter remains useless to her until I receive further order from the king … make my excuse to His Majesty as his service may suffer.

Dyve's 'ever great care' was understandable. The king wrote post-haste and Dyve

> immediately repaired [my error] on sight of yours of August 7th. The character in the letter [from Ashburnham] being different from that with which I was acquainted, and the messenger that came from the lady for the cipher being a young man and a stranger to me, made me unwilling to part with it without your express command. *The lady is of my ancient acquaintance and I believe well of her affection to your service* [author's italics], but truly sir, my dear-bought experience purchased by my own folly which I have had of that sex makes me generally to judge them to be vessels too weak for the retention of strong liquour, though I intend not the application to her particular, having a warrant sufficient for me to rely upon from your judgement. Yet, the cipher [now] having been out of my hand and it not being impossible that some copy may be taken thereof, I send Your Majesty another cipher here enclosed.

Despite muddling his biblical 'vessels', it is likely he was describing Jane Whorwood in correspondence with Ashburnham and the king, using her cousin, Captain John Maxwell, Lady Dirleton's twenty-year-old nephew and retainer, as her courier (see Chapter 11). Another unnamed 'noble lady' who carried Dyve's letter to the king at Hampton Court in September, and spoke of her husband's 'singular zeal and loyalty', may also have been Jane, never loath to 'use' her husband when it helped.

Dyve's 'ancient acquaintance' with Jane went back to St Martin-in-the-Fields where he once had a townhouse, and where as a courtier and MP he knew James Maxwell. Later, as governor of Abingdon, he was in and out of Oxford where Ashburnham's *Accompt* recorded payment to him for special service. Dyve boasted of his ability to judge character, 'an observer of those who upon all changes of fortune and times of greatest extremity have always continued firm and consistent in their loyalty and duty'.[16] His sweeping judgement about 'the folly of that sex' was mistaken in Jane's case, yet she, the king and others did commit one major continuing folly which helped undo them: they confided continuously in William Lilly.

Lilly had spent the War in London and was no Royalist. He and George Wharton, the Oxford soldier-astrologer, had fought star wars like lethal divas. Lilly made money from fear, loss and uncertainty. His surviving case notes reveal separated lovers, the loser of a cloak in Covent Garden, Royalists seeking the fate of the king, the losers of loved ones in battle, prison, at sea, in exile, and those with pocks and other health problems. He erected his charts, counted pock scars and inspected urine in a mélange of mathematics and astrology. Increasingly, the claim that 'philomathy' was a science was being contested by those who thought it a charlatan's stall. In wartime, claims to read the future and find the lost are always taken more seriously, but by 1654 Dorothy Osborne dismissed Lilly as 'worse than an old woman that passes for a witch, a simple impostor'.

The king consulted Lilly, if reluctantly. Just before his trial he declared: 'I do not care for him. He hath always been against me [yet] he understands astrology as well as any man in Europe.'[17] In 1648 Parliament took Lilly to Colchester siege to bolster army morale. London clients asked him who would win the War and would the king be safe. Fairfax interviewed him ('he understood it not'), and Hugh Peter, the radical chaplain, checked that his almanacks were 'lawful and agreeable to God's word'. Puritan divines did distinguish between necromancy, magic and what Lilly was doing, no 'charms, sorceries or enchantments'. Ironically, he replaced Saints Roch, Jude and Anthony, and the crucifix which in pre-Reformation piety comforted the contagious, the hopeless, those who had lost property, and those haunted by demons. The solace of praying for the dead had long been illegal, but Lilly offered reassurance about them too. Like a good medieval shrine he also took offerings: Jane Whorwood paid £20 in gold from the king's fund for a series of consultations and Cromwell gave him £250 for his services. He took his income from, and was *confidant*, to both sides, yet his loyalty and his tongue was with Parliament.

Lilly's clinical notes survive incomplete, but show Jane consulted him on 2 May 1647, after she left Passenham; two days later Bendish's sister came to ask whether her brother had arrived safely in Turkey. Jane's appointment at Lilly's house where Strand Lane met The Strand was less than a week before she appeared at Haberdashers Hall on Banastre's behalf. The reason for her visit was not recorded, but Lilly reversed her name, *Doowrohw Lady*, to hide from prying eyes, just as he wrote other entries in Latin. On 3 June '*domina ex Oxford de amico* [lady from Oxford about her friend]' consulted him, and he noted, 'soldiers came to Holdenby *hac die* [today] and they removed the king'. Three days later, '*De exercito. Quod addendum* [about the Army. What more]?' Two weeks later someone asked 'if Parliament and the Army should agree?', and in July, while the king talked in earnest with the Naseby generals at Childersley, three clients consulted Lilly '*de Rege* [about the king]'. By August, London was under army command, the City leaders purged, and the king installed at Hampton Court Palace up river, healthier in every way and, as England's Escorial, more fitting.

For three months Charles held 'his last running Court' there. Courtiers later harked back to 'halcyon days, a court it now appeared to be, an amnesty by consent'.[18] The Holton wedding party, wives and all, had audience and dinner there with Charles in September, though Ireton refused to kiss hands. 'I am free-er than I was at London and at Holdenby', the king remarked. James Maxwell continued in attendance, and Peter Lely painted, his sitters including the king and apparently Maxwell. Scots commissioners Lauderdale, Loudon and the blunt and open Lanark, Jane's brother-in-law, in the lead, talked with the king from the end of September. 'Things seemed as if they were drawing to a conclusion and great hopes appeared of the accommodation of peace.' The king kept to his parole not to escape, even when the Scots brought a fifty-strong escort of horse to free him while he was hunting at Nonsuch Park. The one 'cloud on the fairest day' was the army, six miles away from Hampton at Putney, where in October and November rank and file debated frankly and heatedly with general and field officers about the future of English government. 'Free-born John' Lilburne was even released from the Tower on bail. Fairfax stood aloof; Cromwell tried to moderate; Ireton fired it up, demanding that an oligarchy replace the monarchy. Ominously, a trial of the king was also mooted. Lanark believed the king was about to be removed from Hampton Court, but when a letter signed 'E.R.' warned Charles that his murder was being planned, he withdrew his parole arguing that the army had broken its word. Honourably, he informed Colonel Whalley, his guard commander. Lanark begged him to escape and head for Berwick, near enough to Scotland but still in England. Charles did escape on 11 November, but not northwards.

John Ashburnham was expelled on 1 November, after the general public was first barred from the palace. The king's freedom to ride out was curtailed shortly after that and the 'halcyon' mood evaporated. Lewis Dyve heard about it immediately, presumably from Jane, his courier, and wrote to Charles two days later, 'the way is not so blocked up as to hinder free passage'. On the evening of 11 November the guard was light. Whalley reminded Parliament afterwards that the king was 'never in custody as a prisoner, any more than a bird in a pound'. Despite advice to flee to Berwick or France, the king landed on the Isle of Wight. That Colonel Robert Hammond, his chaplain's nephew, had been appointed governor of the island in September 1647 was coincidence, although Hammond had been introduced to the king at Hampton

Court by his clerical uncle. Cromwell may have been trying to give Charles
an opening to go abroad, or to isolate him from supporters in London and on
the mainland, but Ashburnham, who had returned secretly to the palace from
his house at Ditton to lead the escape, was suspected ever after of colluding
with Cromwell.[19]

Jane Whorwood, close to Lanark and knowing his concerns for the king,
consulted Lilly on Thursday evening, 11 November, unaware that the king
was just then fleeing Hampton Court.

> The citizens of London were very unruly ... and wholly devoted to His Majesty
> [so they planned] a design to get him among them, settle him in parliament
> house and so conclude a peace. [However] the cabal of Parliamentary officers
> sitting at Putney, made [Charles] think of an escape, if he could well know to
> what place he could go. Jane Whorwood, knowing this, she went to William
> Lilly the astrologer, living in the Strand.

Her communication with the king was eased by father and brother-in-law, and
she approached Lilly on Charles's behalf with evident urgency. The Scots had
advised the king not to trust Cromwell or the army, knowing, with the moderate Presbyterian MPs and City merchants, that an alliance between king and
army could only work to their (and eventually the king's) disadvantage.[20]

Elias Ashmole was reminded in 1668 by Lilly, a friend since 1646, that they
both knew Jane Whorwood. Lilly was justifying himself to his Royalist friend
after the Restoration.

> [The king] was at Hampton Court when my house was visited with the plague.
> *Upon the king's intention to escape, and with his consent* [author's italics], Madame
> Whorwood, whom you [Elias Ashmole] know very well, came to receive my
> judgement, viz, in what quarter of this nation he might be most safe and not
> be discovered until he himself pleased. When she came to my door, I told her
> I would not let her come into my house, for I had buried a maid servant of the
> plague very lately.

Lilly later claimed to have buried *two* servants and to have been house-bound
by plague for seven weeks, during which he compiled his *Almanack* for 1648.
It was late, dark and he recognised his strong-willed visitor, probably cloaked
and hooded against the cold from the river down which she had come. Plague
or no, he had seen four clients already that day. He was probably irritated at
being disturbed again.

'I fear not the Plague, but the Pox', Jane retorted, in an earthy riposte suggesting venereal (great) pox, and which Lilly remembered years later as a
bravada refusal to take no for an answer, perhaps using her visible small pocks
as her authority for risking any plague threat. Years later she confided in Lilly

about her marriage crisis. A Restoration satire (its chronology impossibly confused) also lampooned Brome for having caught a venereal infection from an actress and passing it on to his wife.[21]

Lilly continued:

> So up[stairs] we went. After the erecting of my figure [astrological chart] I told her that about 20 miles or thereabouts from London, and in Essex, I was certain the king might continue undiscovered. She liked my judgement very well and being herself of a sharp judgement, remembered a place in Essex about that distance, where was an excellent house and all conveniences for his reception. Away she went, early next morning, into Hampton Court to acquaint His Majesty, but he, either guided by his own approaching hard fate, or misguided by Ashburnham, went away in the night time westward to Titchfield in Hampshire and surrendered himself [at the Countess of Southampton's home there], to Colonel Robert Hammond, governor of the Isle of Wight.

Jane Whorwood had already passed money to the king for an escape. Lilly recorded for Ashmole (and later confirmed to Anthony Wood) that 'whilst the king was at Hampton Court, Alderman [Thomas] Adams sent him one thousand pounds in gold, five hundred whereof [the king] gave to Madame Whorwood. I believe I had twenty pieces [£20] of that very gold [clarifying to Wood] for my share for this and other judgements.' The claim has no other confirmation, but Adams was in the Tower from September 1647 to May 1648, the senior of the City moderates, including merchant aldermen Langham, Bunce and Gayre, imprisoned by army and City radicals to prevent their dealing with the king. Jane was in and out of the Tower, a veritable school for conspirators led by Dyve and Adams. To collect nine kilos of gold on Adams' bond was nothing compared to the many hundreds of kilos she had smuggled to Oxford. She had also colluded with Adams in corrupting Lord Howard.

The place 'she remembered about 20 miles from London, in Essex' could have been Alderman Adams' own manor at Elsenham, or Blomfield, home to Ann Manwood, her mother's gentlewoman attendant. Eliab Harvey, syndicate merchant, brother of William Harvey the physician and close to Jane's parents, had a home at Hempsted, not much more than twenty miles out, and Robert Abbott, banker to the Royalists, had Barringtons at Chigwell. However, the most likely place she had in mind was the Maynard house at Little Easton, where Dorothy, daughter of Sir Robert Banastre, had married into the family. Lilly's advice came too late. The headstrong, frightened and indecisive king blew everything. Months later, before another escape attempt, Jane noted that whatever she organised, the king could destroy his chances: 'nothing but himself can let [hinder] it.'

Lilly's notes bear out his memories of 11 November. Five unnamed clients visited that day, one around 5.15 p.m., at least one asking about the king,

De Rege Committ (the king's confinement). Dates and times of enquiry were more important than birthdays in Lilly's horary astrology, and afforded quicker results. On 12 November he added to his notes of the 11th that '5.35' was the '*tempus regis euntis a Hampton Court* [time of the king's going from H.C.]'. By then, the London grapevine knew that the bird had flown the pound. Two more people consulted Lilly '*De Rege* [about the king]' on 12 November and another came on 15 November to enquire whether the king '*an incarceratu-rus* [were to be imprisoned]'. Charts were drawn up, words exchanged, and sessions cost fees. Perhaps Jane made a second visit, frustrated and confused by the king's ill-planned move. Over several years she became increasingly, even recklessly reliant on Lilly, ignoring his hostility to the king and his Parliamentarian sympathy. For now, the king had pre-empted everything and his small band on the road to the Isle of Wight ferry was *incommunicado*.

When Jane returned upriver to Hampton early on Friday morning, 12 November, she found her father among the servants 'standing gazing at one another, the master being gone, the diet [wages and rations] ceased, so as with sad hearts they all went to their respective homes'. The confusion of the guard company was even more marked. Cromwell, alerted immediately at Putney on 11 November, went over the escape route with Colonel Whalley, writing his report to the Commons by midnight candle. He estimated that Charles had fled at about 9 p.m. (it was nearer 6 p.m.) by the cellar, backstairs and over the garden to the river and then south into Surrey and Hampshire. Hesitant officers had delayed searching Charles's rooms for two hours when he failed to appear for supper. There they found three letters, one for Parliament, one for Cromwell, and one thanking Whalley, asking him to look after some possessions and a dog.

Whalley appeared before the Commons on 13 November. He handed over the letter Cromwell had sent him on 11 November warning him of 'rumours abroad of some intended attempt on his Majesty's person. Therefore I pray you have a care of your guards. It would be accounted a most horrid act.' Putney radicals had called Charles the 'Chief Delinquent' and the biblical 'Man of Blood'. Cromwell really may have feared for the king and for what his murder might do to a country concussed by the War and the collapse of traditional frameworks. He admitted, too, that his junior consul, Henry Ireton, was inflexible.

Ashburnham, Berkeley, attendant courtiers, with Governor Hammond and Deputy Lieutenant John Oglander on Wight, all left accounts of the next few days. Whalley praised Ashburnham's integrity, and his fear that the king's circle was 'so much scottifyed' – Maxwell, Lanark and Whorwood among others – 'there would be workings to get the king away'. As they walked the footpath by the Thames out of earshot, Ashburnham complained to Whalley that 'no other language is spoken in the court but Scotch'. He ranked the Scots as low as the army's Agitators and Levellers. Whalley defended his own role: 'It was impossible for me to keep the king, he having such liberty and such Bedchamber men about him, his ancient servants', including James Maxwell. Thomas Adams in the Tower suspected 'juggling in the king's being found at the Isle of Wight' and condemned it immediately in a pamphlet. The fugitives stopped briefly with the dowager countess of Southampton, Lady Wriothesley, at Titchfield; her son, Lord Wriothesley, had visited Charles on the day before the escape. Ashburnham crossed to Wight, persuaded Hammond to return with him to Titchfield and the king duly crossed with them both to Cowes, probably from Hill Head, late on Saturday 13 November. He was tired and in mental turmoil, 'after a day and night riding [but he] saw not well whither else to go'. He reached Newport on Sunday before dawn, where Governor Hammond lodged him in Carisbrooke Castle, the official residence. Hammond wrote to Parliament the next day.[22]

The king was a vacillator, his escape as miscalculated and indecisive as that from Oxford, and it increased his enemies' mistrust of him. He had already tried to escape the Scots at Newcastle in December 1646. The Isle of Wight was isolated, war-weary, more dead end than escape route, 'just like other parts of England, a melancholy, dejected, sad place, no company, no rents, no neighbours seeing one of the other'. Ashburnham claimed to have pressed the king to get Henrietta Maria to send a French ship to Southampton, coordinated through the Pitts and the La Motts of the Royalist merchant oligarchy there. This was 'discreetly performed', said Ashburnham later, but the ship was eventually dismissed. Again the king had vacillated. Sir John Berkeley had warned for some time that escape required 'three or four ships in several ports', and his collaboration in the aimless escape was obtained only by the king's personal demand for his unquestioning obedience. Berkeley thought Cromwell genuinely concerned for the king, 'sometimes wishing that he, the king was more frank, and less tied to narrow maxims; sometimes complaining of his son[-in-law] Ireton's slowness in perfecting the proposals and his not accommodating more to His Majesty's senses'.

Ashburnham claimed that he had advised 'concealment at Sir John Oglander's house until the king had gained experience of the governor's inclination to serve him', but Oglander was not consulted.

His Majesty came into our island on Sunday November 14th to my great astonishment ... He could not have come into a worse place for himself. [That] Sunday morning at church I heard a rumour that the king was that night [13–14] landed at Cowes. Governor Hammond commanded me [as deputy lieutenant] and my [eldest] son [William], as all the gentlemen of the island, to meet him at Newport the next day [Monday 15th] by nine in the morning.

Hammond pledged the king's safety to the assembled gentry, but hinted strongly that they might contribute food. At the castle after lunch the king explained himself: 'I was forced from Hampton Court by Levellers resolved of my death. I have put myself in this place to be secured till some happy accommodation may be made.' Three days later he rode to Oglander's house seven miles away. Oglander was discreet, '[He] dined with me at Nunwell and during the time he lived in our island he went to no gentleman's house besides. In the Parlour Chamber I had some speech with him which I shall forbear to discover.'[23]

Loyal, but not blind to Royalist failings, Oglander knew the Crown's shortcomings and that informers watched. He was discretion personified, putting little in writing about the War and less about the royal captivity. He visited the king at Carisbrooke even after the close-guard was imposed in January. 'I went most commonly to see him once a week and I seldom went but His Majesty would talk with me sometimes almost a quarter of an hour together, but all, since his close imprisonment, openly [not alone].' Jane Whorwood would have had a roof at Nunwell when she first visited Wight. Through Eleanor Brome of Holton, Lady Ursula's aunt who married first Richard Lewknor of Chichester and then John Oglander's father, Jane was Sir John's step-cousin. The families had stayed in touch for over half a century. The Lewknors were also cousins to John Ashburnham, at the centre of every twist and turn of the royal escape attempts and Jane's constant shadow.

Notes

1. TNA PROB 11/239, 21 February 1647, probate 10 February 1654.

2. Clayton Mss, LSE Archive, Box 6, WI–WE, 22/4/6, miscellaneous folder, marked *Brome Whorwood Defendant*, probably written *c*.1658.

3. CSP Venetian, XXVII, 1643–7, 458, ambassador in Turkey to the Doge that the 'merchants rejoice greatly' at Constantinople, at Bendish's nomination being preferred to that of Bernard; *Remonstrance or Manifest of Sir Thomas Bendish to Charles II* (1662), Bodleian Library copy with petition handwritten on flyleaf: 'Your petitioner sent £3000 to His majesty in Newcastle which was all out of his own purse ... [he was also] imprisoned in the Tower 22 months for serving His [late] Majesty ... in which time his estate was sequestered'; Nicholas Papers I, 1646–52, Camden Society, 1886, NS 40, 73–80; 'Sir Thomas Bendish', *ODNB*, 2004; John Ashburnham, *Narrative* (1830), appendix, *Accompt*, 1642–3, xxiv; CCC, II, 847; Alfred Wood, *The Levant Company* (1935), 89–94.

4. Harry Tibbutt, ed. 'The Tower Letterbook of Sir Lewis Dyve', *Bedfordshire Historical Record Society*, XXXVIII (1958), 53–4, Letter 2, 3 January 1647; Nicholas Papers I, *op.cit.*, 1886, 80; Charles I in 1646, Camden Society, OS 63, 1856, 63, 64, 76, 99. The king wrote frequently from Oxford and Newcastle to his wife in Paris.

5. Nicholas Papers, I, *op.cit.*, 73, Endymion Porter to Edward Nicholas from Paris, 19 January 1647; King Charles in 1646, *Camden Miscellany*, Camden

Society, OS 43, 1856, 63, Charles I from Newcastle to Henrietta Maria in Paris, 31 August 1646; also, 64, 76 and appendix, 99. Alfred Wood, *The Levant Company*, PhD thesis, Oxford, 1934, Bodleian Library, 127, 142 n.

6. Nicholas Papers I, *op.cit.*, 74–5, Nicholas Oudart to Edward Nicholas, 18 February 1647; ibid., 77–8. Edward Andrews, Surrey landowner and of Grays Inn, was also a correspondent of Jane Whorwood, see Chapter 8.

7. TNA, C3/467/115, May 1658.

8. Bodleian Library, Ashmole Ms, 1141, Edward Andrews '337' in Edward Nicholas's cipher list; Nicholas Papers I, *op.cit.*, 79–80, Nicholas Oudart to Edward Nicholas, 4 March 1647. On Elizabeth Hamilton's networking, Montreuil Correspondence, 1645–8, *Scottish Historical Society*, XXX (1899), II, 83, 30 March/9 April 1647.

9. Bodleian Library, Rawlinson Ms, B225, 2, Library, the king to Dowcett, 19 January 1648.

10. Nicholas Papers, I, *op.cit.*, 80.

11. George Baker, *History of Northamptonshire* (1832), I, 204–5; III, 189–95; HLJ, IX, 189b, 13 May 1647, letter from Holdenby, 12 May. Pauline Gregg mistakenly identified the woman who helped Mistress Cave as 'most likely' Jane Whorwood, but Jane was by then in London (see notes 12 and 17 below), *King Charles I* (1981), 412; *Perfect Weekly Account*, 20, 12–19 May 1647, Thomason 62:E.388 [9]; HLJ, IX, 202b, 203a; Parliamentary Records, House of Lords Mss, Braye 57, 46–8.

12. TNA SP 19 162: 92–6, 98, 103, 105, for the detailed enquiry of June 1651 into the events at Haberdashers Hall in May 1647; CCAM, II, 601–3; CCC, III, 1671–3; O. Brown and C. Roberts, *Passenham, History of a Forest Village* (1973), 53–64, 101. Banastre was known for corruption, violence and fraud, even withholding his daughter's and granddaughter's dowries, and his second wife's portion: for his will, see TNA PROB 11/210, 1649.

13. Antonia Fraser, *Weaker Vessel* (1984), 249–68; TNA SP 19 162: 103 for the use of the mocking, but revealing 'Chairwoman', in line with the attempts of some freeholder women to vote for the Long Parliament in 1640 and the women's petitions to and demonstrations outside the Commons during the 1640s; Anthony Wood, 'Life of Wood' in *Life and Times of Anthony Wood*, I, xxviii–xxix (ed. Clark, 1891).

14. Sir Thomas Herbert, *Memoirs*, British Library, Harleian Ms, 4705, 34 (1678); British Library, Additional Ms, 42118, f. 32–52, Herbert to Dugdale (1681); Ashmole Ms 1141, Bodleian Library; reproduced in Anthony Wood, *Athenae Oxonienses*, IV, 15–42; for the house search, Rawlinson Ms B225, f. 6, Bodleian Library, Letter from George Payne of Abingdon to Major General Browne, 29 April 1647.

15. 'The Tower Letterbook of Sir Lewis Dyve', *op.cit.*, 49–96. Nicholas Papers I, *op.cit.*, 81. Dyve and fellow Royalists in the Tower were sent venison by the king in August 1647.

16. 'The Tower Letterbook of Sir Lewis Dyve', *op.cit.*, 76, 83, 92; Harry Tibbutt, 'Life and Letters of Sir Lewis Dyve', *Bedfordshire Historical Record Society*, XXVII

(1948), 103, letter from Dyve in the Tower to the king at Hampton Court, 16 September 1647; ibid., 83. Adams joined Dyve in the Tower on 24 September, with Aldermen Gayre, Langham, Bunce and others; Dyve was transferred to King's Bench Prison in November 1647.

17. William Lilly, *History of His Life and Times* (1668), 109; Bodleian Library, Ashmole Ms 184, 'Lilly Notes and Appointments', I, 1644–5; Ashmole Ms 178, 'Lilly Notes and Appointments', II, 1645–6; Ashmole Ms 185, 'Lilly Notes and Appointments', III, 17 August 1646 – 4 May 1647; Ashmole Ms 420, 'Lilly Notes and Appointments', IV, April 1647 – September 1648; *op.cit.*, III, 520, 276, 281(v); a 'Mr Adams consulted'; *op.cit.*, I, 184, 30; Anthony Wood, 'Life of Wood' in *Life and Times of Anthony Wood*, I, xxix–xxx (ed. Clark, 1891).

18. Sir Thomas Herbert, *op.cit.*, British Library, 19.

19. British Library, Additional Ms 42118, 35; Gilbert Burnet, *Memoirs of the Dukes of Hamilton*, V, 316, 323–4, 329 (1673); Allan Fea, *Memories of the Martyr King* (1905), Appendix I, 259ff, for Whalley's letter to the Speaker, 15 November, following his oral report of 13 November.

20. Anthony Wood, *op.cit.* (n. 17), xxviii–xxix, and 226–7, drawing on Lilly's memoirs; William Lilly, *History etc, op.cit.*, 86–91; Sir John Berkeley, *Memoirs* (1699), 149; Bodleian Library, Ashmole Ms 420, 83, 88, 126–9. A professional astrologer might glean much for historians from Lilly's arcane charts in the Ashmole Mss.

21. British Library, Harleian Ms 7319, 237, anti-Whig satire, *c.*1682, which date would exclude Jane, but not Kate Allen, his mistress. Jane accused Kate in 1657 of 'defiling' Brome, see Chapter 11. Kate and Charlotte Butler, an actress linked with Brome, were described by hostile contemporaries as respectively 'famous strumpet' and 'termagent strumpet'.

22. Herbert's memoirs quoted in Fea, *op.cit.*, 93; John Ashburnham, *Narrative and Vindication* (1830), 108, 120, 292; Ashburnham's Letter to the Speaker of the Commons, 30 November 1647, Thomason E418 (4), 3; Thomas Adams, *Plain Dealing*, 16 November 1647, 2–3.

23. Sir John Oglander, *A Royalist's Notebook* (1936), 112–28; Berkeley, *op.cit.*, 163–4, 168. See also, *Nunwell Symphony*, Cecil Aspinall-Oglander (1945).

8

November 1647–June 1648: '715' and a Frightened King

Mistress Whorwood is aboard the ship. She stays to wait upon the king.
Derby House to Colonel Hammond, 1648

You may freely trust Whorwood in anything that concerns my service, for I have had perfect trial of her friendship to me. I cannot be more confident of any.
King Charles I to William Hopkins, 1648

Colonel Robert Hammond, governor of Wight and captain of Carisbrooke Castle, was at the eye of a storm, under orders from Parliament's executive committee at Derby House, and under pressure from Cromwell and Ireton. At twenty-five, a respected field officer, he became governor of Exeter in 1646. His family was seriously divided by the War: his grandfather had been doctor to James I; an uncle, Henry, was King Charles's closest chaplain, mostly barred between 1646–9 from the king's presence; another uncle, Thomas, was among those who helped judge the king in 1649. William Temple, Hammond's cousin, visited Wight early in 1648 and, after public audience with the king, impulsively etched a Biblical curse on Hammond ('Haman') with his ring-diamond on an inn window. He was brought before the governor, but Dorothy Osborne, his then travelling companion, took the blame to free both cousins from the hook. She and Temple later married.

Jane Whorwood may have appeared in December 1647, when the king still moved freely on the island and when brother-in-law Lanark attended as a Scots commissioner. She had relayed communications for the king in several directions over many months and now extended her courier network across the Solent.[1] Her father, Maxwell, although approved by Parliament to serve at Carisbrooke, retired pleading age and ill-health, and could no longer help her from inside.[2] Cousin Oglander may have offered her a roof, but the Nunwell recipe advising burnt cork three times a week to darken red hair was not yet needed. The Bromes, the Lewknors and the Oglanders were still close after seventy years: Sir Christopher Brome left Sir Richard Lewknor £100 as his executor in 1589; 'sister Eleanor Oglander' was left a signet ring in George Brome's will of 1605 (proved 1613), when her stepson John Oglander was at Balliol College; William Oglander, John's father and Eleanor's second husband, left bequests to 'brother Brome and sister Brome'. Sir Christopher Lewknor, recorder of Chichester, executed Sir Thomas Whorwood's will in 1634, after Jane's disastrous wedding, 'with £10 of plate to remember me by'. Nine Oglander children were step-siblings to 'divers [Lewknor] children', but despite Eleanor's wealth, it was 'an unfortunate match. No man living could have had a better wife than his [father's] first, [but] his last wife was clean contrary.' In 1642 Sir Christopher Lewknor joined the king at Oxford; Sir John Oglander suffered prison, sequestration, and the deaths of his wife and of 'a most loving brother, most violent for the Parliament cause'. His diplomacy masked a turmoil. 'Would I could write or be permitted to write the history of these times when brother killed brother, cousin killed cousin, friend killed friend, gentry made slaves to commonwealth, and avarice and plunder.'[3]

William, Lord Lanark, was part of his sister-in-law's network, and she part of his. Montrose, the Scottish arch-Royalist, gave Lanark an apt cipher, 'Peter Juggler', since he juggled divided Scots with divided English loyalties, but never balanced them. He was close to his father-in-law, Maxwell, yet as he had borne arms against the Crown, the king never fully trusted him. At Hampton Court, Lanark made firm an offer he had made tentatively several times that year, to prepare an invasion by Scots loyalists in 1648, led by his brother James and himself, but the king doubted they could achieve it. In December at Carisbrooke he repeated the offer, negotiating there in parallel with, but separately from, English commissioners in attendance. The cousins signed, sealed and buried their secret 'Engagement' encased in lead. It promised an invasion and the king conceded a three-year trial of Presbyterianism in England. The juggling only divided the Scots further. Parliament soon learned about it and about an aborted escape by the king near the end of December – the wind changed unexpectedly as he was about to dash for a ship, just after he had agreed the 'Engagement' and rejected the English envoys' terms. A tumult (the favoured word for an uprising) also broke out in Newport, and its instigator was executed. On Governor Hammond's advice, all private communication and audience with the king was banned by Parliament and he was confined to the castle early in January, 'No Addresses' permitted. Charles's deceit and tactical stalling were becoming royal policy. His servants were changed and reduced in number; his coach specially shipped from London lay idle; hunting and visiting were banned and his furniture and library brought from Hampton Court became the lining of a cage. Even his chaplains were dismissed, leaving him 'chaplain to himself'.

Cromwell was Hammond's cousin through Hammond's marriage to John Hampden's daughter, and he ordered him on 3 January to 'search out and let us know of any juggling [by the king]', the day Parliament ordered the close guard. 'Juggling' was an apt and repeated metaphor for the events of 1648. Ireton, Hammond's old field commander and now cousin-in-law, rebuked him for seeking 'ease and quiet' on the island, despite Hammond's proven battle courage and the real vulnerability of Wight to attack from abroad. Hammond was naively open, which Ireton may have considered a weakness: 'I have often asked that if [the king] be not thought safe here he may be removed, which is the thing most desirable to me.' Cromwell was terse but tactful: 'Some of us think the king well with you.' Ireton pulled rank, age and heaven: the guarding of Carisbrooke was 'God's charge'. Both knew Hammond was as God-fearing as they, but his tendency to question himself was not Ireton's idea of strength.[4]

In Edinburgh, the Estates did not discuss the invasion plan until March, when they demanded the king's release. Lanark left London with the other commissioners late in January 1648, but stayed in touch with Jane Whorwood between then and April when Firebrace took over the clearing of loyalist correspondence. Jane's first known cipher, '409' (to Lanark's '410'), was used on 1 February in response to a letter from him after he arrived back in Edinburgh.[5] They were obviously close. 'Your expressions highly endear and might if possible make me more yours. The General [Cromwell] dines this day at the Tower where I believe will be some results about the City; what, you shall know by my next.' Dyve had been transferred to another prison, but Adams remained Jane's contact in the Tower; John Lilburne, after breaking bail conditions with a Leveller meeting, had just been returned to his cell there and both might have been Cromwell's guests. The king later gave Jane similarly consecutive ciphers, '390' (to his '391'), and 'N' (to Henrietta Maria's 'M'). They marked as much the work she was taking on as any growing closeness.[6]

Jane was evidently still in touch with the City as well as the Tower, from which Alderman Adams had protested in print in November, 'Is there not juggling in the king's being found in the Island? Juggling hath been with the Army since its beginning. Doth any man know what to make of the Army now?'[7] Accordingly, Jane indicated to Lanark in her opaque courtly way that her responsibility was the king's escape, which they had discussed in confidence before Lanark left.

> The business we whispered about, I am in hope may succeed. I sent a messenger thereabout [to Wight], with probable [well-considered] instructions for the accomplishment and I conceive it well takes as to the project and desire the continued conjunction of your prayers as to the success … so little of consequence

to write at present, I shall refer my enlargement [on] it to the next opportunity, against when I shall doubtless be furnished with abundance of pleasing news (if expectations with eminent wishes fail not).

As she folded the letter, 'my messenger [from Wight] brought this enclosed [from the king] and assurances things go well in the whispered business, but not a word thereof for your love's sake. I had another [letter] which I delivered to your wife [Jane's sister Elizabeth, nearby in London with a sick child and trying to raise formal French support for the Engagement] concerning my father [Maxwell, also sick and probably in London].'

Other Royalists corresponded with Lanark, while the king remained sceptical about the Engagement.[8] James Fenne, East India merchant, son of a Company director and son-in-law to Henry Andrews, merchant and alderman, wrote regularly. Edward Edgar, Jane's Maxwell cousin, to whose brother Sir Robert had tried to bequeath the office of Commons Serjeant, was a member of the Estates and provost of Edinburgh; he corresponded with Fenne, Lanark and Jane. Edward Andrews, neighbour of the Maxwells at Guildford, an Oxford garrison veteran who had brazenly seized back his confiscated estate at Wanbrough, kept Nicholas Oudart informed in Holland and corresponded with Edgar, threatening a 'Surrey Association' ready to rise. James Fenne cautioned him against wild talk, 'never foment a war if it can be avoided'. Lord Digby, half-brother to Lewis Dyve and no stranger to conspiracy, begged Lanark's forgiveness for 'the part I was necessitated to bear [against] you and your noble brother [before and during the War] now that we are united in public interests'. Colonel Mungo Murray of Blebow, late aide to the Scots commissioners and a bedchamber colleague of Maxwell, had been caught at Newcastle trying to slip a letter to the king as he kissed his hand. He advised Lanark that in planning the Engagement, even if Kent and other counties were to rise 'and do the business without you, it will not be well for you if you have no hand in it'. Jane's communications net served them all, but it had its glitches as Andrews observed. 'PS. the enclosed came from the king hither [London] last week whilst I was in the country [Surrey], but not to my hands until this evening. I was not sure it was for you [Lanark]. It not being mentioned in mine who it was for till Mr[s] Whorwood informed me.' Overall, Andrews commended Jane's network to Lanark: 'my way to the king is yet sure, and I think the only one remaining.'[9]

Elizabeth Hamilton buried her three-year-old son James in an alien rite in Westminster Abbey on 12 March and left for Scotland a week later. She had consulted Lilly about the child in January and stayed after her husband returned to Scotland. In Edinburgh she encouraged her husband's invasion preparations and worked on the French ambassador. Her sister Diana spent the War in Hertfordshire, where her husband, Viscount Cranborne, was Parliamentarian MP. He and his father, Lord Salisbury, sat on the Derby House committee from which someone, allegedly, was informing Royalists. Jane also had Lord Howard of Escrick at her beck as chair of the Committee for the Advance of Money. He too joined Derby House in May 1648.

The 'whispered business' was not the 'Engagement'. Jane played little or no part in military or diplomatic affairs, and lacked her sister Lanark's rank and influence to do so, yet '409's' surviving two letters reveal a closeness to her brother-in-law and a willingness to help in any way. She had known him from Charing since at least 1632. William Lilly mistakenly linked Charles's escape with the southern uprising, and both as if synchronised to greet the Engagement, 'that he might be at the head of an army in Kent and thence to march immediately to London where thousands there would have armed for him'. In reality, the county risings of the summer of 1648 were headless, premature 'tumults'; the Scots with their own internal jugglings came too few, too late, and the king sought to escape towards Holland, not to join his followers at home. Jane's 'whispered business' was the first of these escape attempts (or gestures) by the king. As in her previous letter to Lanark, her words to him in confidence show she was the escape attempt manager, 'he will be with you before you can hope … so well have I ordered the business', but her leading role was never acknowledged in 1660. Lanark's plea to Charles at Hampton Court in November to head for Berwick had not been heeded; escape was even more difficult now that Hammond's guard had 'narrowed', but Berwick was still considered an alternative destination should the king attempt an escape.

A handful of letters from the king to Abraham Dowcett, clerk of the kitchen, and his wife, in January and February 1648, with three letters from the king to Mary (? Lee), sub-laundress, are the earliest surviving correspondence from Carisbrooke. Charles promised Dowcett he would not 'needlessly employ' him, yet he accorded the couple ciphers. Special favour became regular service, a letter 'once a week to [the queen] my wife' through Mrs Dowcett who routinely visited Windsor. Edward Worsley, a local squire, was similarly drawn in when he smuggled a gift from a third party to Charles. 'Assure all my friends,' promised the king, 'that I will neither be cheated nor frightened from my grounds.'[10] Mary and he exchanged letters by hiding them under the carpet of his chamber when she brought his linen, and through her he seems to have tried to communicate with Henrietta Maria in France, but Mary was dismissed after being caught with a letter in February.

On 20 January, Derby House, 'to whom you may safely communicate [by cipher]', advised Hammond 'there are plottings and contrivances in hand to convey away the king'. Berkeley and Ashburnham, expelled by Hammond, lurked on the mainland at Netley Abbey, home of the Marquess of Hertford, where 'the king's party makes continual resort about some such purpose'. Hertford later praised Jane Whorwood's role above all of that 'king's party'. Derby House persisted: 'The king hath constant intelligence given him [from Netley and elsewhere] which he receives by a woman [Mary] when she bringeth his clean linen.' Jane Whorwood was despatcher and clearer, Elizabeth Wheeler, laundress from Oxford smuggling days, and Mary, her assistant, were courier and go-between, while Hertford provided a clearing house. Three days later, the committee warned again about Wheeler, and she was easily watched: her home on fashionable Cannon Row, Westminster, was six doors from Derby House.[11]

The king's staff was reduced to thirty and the king's goods sold to pay their wages. Hammond could hire or fire on their perceived loyalty to Parliament. Thomas Herbert, Anthony Mildmay and Captain Silius Titus were taken on as groom of the bedchamber, gentleman usher and equerry respectively in January. Mildmay slept across the king's chamber door each night and was impervious to the king's charm or aura. He warned his courtier brother, Henry: 'The king is the most perfidious man that ever lived and will hang you.' Henry Firebrace was a closet Royalist appointed across from the Earl of Denbigh's entourage at Newcastle, before the War Maxwell's junior colleague of the bedchamber. Carisbrooke staff made uneasy bedfellows – loyal Royalist indiscernible from respectful Parliamentarian and secret informer. Revealingly, Sir John Oglander remembered how 'the Governor himself told me he would not inform against me if I saw the king [alone], but some gentlemen of the House would'.[12] Supporters outside the walls were no less uneasy with each other. John Loe, the merchant coordinating and providing escape ships, was suspected by Jane and others of informing Derby House. Lucy Hay, Countess of Carlisle and a glamorous chatterbox, was mistrusted for her tongue – her brother Northumberland sat at Derby House and signed their warnings to Hammond. The conspirators adopted a policy of informing only those who needed to know, a sign at least of increasing professionalism during 1648. The king could still receive in semi-public audience, and confer the 'touch', but never alone. Governor Hammond thoughtfully turfed a bowling green for him, complete with gilded pavilion to shelter him from cloudbursts, on the castle drill ground.

Again, on 8 February, Derby House warned, 'the king's escape is designed [whereby] he is to be drawn up out of his bedchamber into the room over it, the ceiling whereof is to be broken, then conveyed from one to another, till he be past all the [guarded] rooms'. Such detail came from an insider, but by mid-March the committee was no wiser. 'There is some design in agitation concerning the king's escape, who is to be carried into France. Two of those now attending the king [will be] effecting the escape.'[13] Jane kept Lanark at Holyrood informed of the 'whispered business'. Meanwhile, detachments of Hammond's own regiment, followed by money enough to pay them, and (worn) cannon, were delivered to allay Hammond's fears of a seaborne attack. Earlier, Charles had asked Dowcett about 'artechokes' (a French invasion), and 'fresh asparagus from London' (a popular revolt), requesting hand signals in

1. Charing Cross, 2009. Charles I's statue (1633) marks the site of the medieval Cross and of the regicide executions in 1660; *near right*, Royal Bank of Scotland on the site of the Ryder/Maxwell house (*c.*1610–59); *far left*, before the trees, the Banqueting House (1622), sole remaining wing of Whitehall Palace and place of Charles I's execution. *(Author)*

2. James Maxwell, Earl of Dirleton (c. 1580–1650), Jane Whorwood's stepfather in old age, by Lely or Tyssens. Maxwell's last attendant service was at Hampton Court, autumn 1647, when Lely was drawing and painting there. This portrait belonged to Diana, Viscountess Cranborne, Jane's half-sister. *(Marquess of Salisbury, Hatfield House)*

3. Old St Paul's and London Bridge. *As the sun encircles the earth, so the King enlightens the City*, Return from Scotland Medal, 1633. Jane and Brome married in the crypt church of St Faith-under-St Paul's. Anti-Scots prejudice sneered at 'the sunrise in the North', unwittingly depicted here. *(Author)*

4. Holton House, *c.*1785, watercolour by Richard Corbould, whereabouts unknown. By the drawbridge, *near left*, Brome took a whip to Joan Miller, the dairymaid, for her defence of Jane whose chamber in 1656 was at the top of the medieval Tower, *distant left*. An eighteenth century 'gothick' façade, *far right*, fronts the south-west service wing. Deer inhabit the Park beyond the palisade. *(Kevin Heritage/Nigel Philips, Wheatley Park School Archive)*

5a. Holton House site today. A fixed bridge replaces the drawbridge. *(Author)*

5b. The filled-in basement remains of the south-west wing, beyond which a bridge connected the rear courtyard to the Park. *(Author)*

6. Diana, Viscountess Cranborne, *née* Maxwell (1622–75), Jane Whorwood's half-sister, marriage portrait by Lely *c.*1645–55. The pearls in her reddish hair, the heavy pearl necklace, the collet and the pyramid-cut breast jewel may have been among the £4,600 worth of jewels her father gave with her marriage. *(Marquess of Salisbury, Hatfield House)*

7. Oxford, 1644 (Crown coin). The viewpoint is debated, but St Mary's spire, the wartime earth bastions and the pallisades are clear, while the square tower may be Magdalen College. *(Author)*

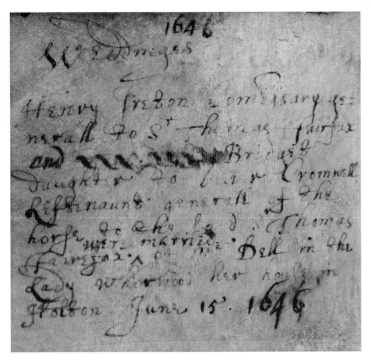

8. Holton St Bartholomew's Church Register, 15 June 1646, the marriage of Bridget Cromwell to General Henry Ireton. Alban Eales, Rector of Holton, made the entry and his nerves may have made the mistakes. *(Holton Churchwardens and Mike Oxlade)*

9. The Holton Cromwell Portrait, now Oxford University's official picture of its chancellor, 1650–8 'A contemporary or near-contemporary Walker', it was bought for the University by public subscription in 1913. The Biscoe family (descended from Colonel John Biscoe, regicide) claimed it was found 'in a lumber room' when they bought Holton House in 1801. Whatever its link with the Naseby wedding at Holton, it is the most plausible of several 'relics'. *(Bodleian Library, University of Oxford)*

10. Carisbrooke Castle Courtyard and Gatehouse from the bedchamber window of the king's first lodging. Charles failed to squeeze between a vertical bar and the side frame on 20 March 1648. *(Author, facility English Heritage, and Carisbrooke Museum Trust)*

11. Carisbrooke Castle Courtyard and the king's first lodging, seen through the Gatehouse doorway. The castle doors are original; the ten-light window of the King's Chamber, *centre*, is a Victorian replacement for the original two-light window. *(Author, facility English Heritage)*

12. Carisbrooke Castle Courtyard, from the battlements. The king's first bedchamber, November 1647–April 1648, is behind the Victorian ten-light window, *right*. At the end of April he was moved to rooms in the Tudor governor's lodging, now ruined, *left*, within the curtain wall. *(Author, facility English Heritage)*

13. Carisbrooke Castle from the approach road. The king was trying to remove a vertical bar from the window on the left around midnight on 29 May 1648, when Governor Hammond entered the room. *(Author)*

14. Commonwealth Silver Coins: a 1649 sixpence (25mm diameter) and two undated halfpennies (10mm diameter). Two weeks after the king's execution in 1649, Parliament ordered new (headless) coin designs, with the conjoined shields of 'George' and the Irish harp. The twinned shields, reminiscent of outmoded Jacobean breeches, were mocked as 'silver pantaloons to cover the Rump [Parliament]'. During the Commonwealth period, Jane's husband declared that her life was not worth a halfpenny. *(Author)*

15. St Bartholomew's church, Holton, where Jane, Brome, three of their four children, Brome's mistress Kate Allen, and their child 'cousin Thomas' were buried. Victorian renovation obliterated the graves so that only those of Sir Thomas Whorwood (d. 1634, on Jane's wedding day), and his daughter Elizabeth (d. 1633) remain marked. *(Author)*

reply; 'Dutch pinks' (a *pinck* was a sea-going sail barge) stood for his hope of an invasion. Naval intervention from France, Holland or Ireland, or even an island uprising, was a constant hope (or threat) in the game of freeing (or constraining) the king. Charles was 'weary with deciphering' when he approved a plan to spirit the Duke of York down the Thames from St James's Palace in April, lest he too become a hostage.

Dowcett brought one letter which excited Charles's curiosity on 27 February.[14] He responded immediately: 'I know not your [written] hand but I find by your good sense that you are one of my good friends and that you judge rightly of those people in whose care I now am and who yet have made no address of me.' The correspondent had shared some evaluation of Parliament's order for close-confinement and no-addresses. The king then added:

> I believe you and I are not made alike below the girdle [author's italics, censored by Cordell Firebrace] … Neither mistrust my discretion nor secrecy [and do] not let me be long ignorant to whom I owe this timely warning and good advice. Besides, I [wish] by this safe way to ask you some questions, if I knew by which of my friends you were trusted. I have burned your letter.

Family tradition held that the writer was Dowcett's wife, but Charles knew Mrs Dowcett and her cipher from previous correspondence. The destroyed letter may have been his first sight of Jane Whorwood's handwriting, but no direct correspondence between them is known before the end of April 1648. It could even have been from the countess of Lanark in London. On the previous day, Charles had thanked Mary, the laundress, for attempting to pass a letter from him to her 'Cornish acquaintance', possibly code for the queen, or possibly a real Cornish courtier. Two weeks previously he had sent a letter to another unidentified lady through Mary, who was ordered to say only that it was from the lady's 'best Platonick lover or servant'.

Lanark was far away and silent, as '409' reminded '410' on 7 March, the day the Estates in Edinburgh issued their ultimatum to Westminster to release the king, and the day '409' visited Lilly about 'lord Lanark, sick of a cold'. Jane rebuked Lanark: 'I fear you forget you have a servant in these parts, or take not me for one, otherwise I [would have] been made happy with a more frequent receipt of your letters. Yours to the king I have sent and shall send you an answer shortly.' She reported on the escape plan, assuming that the king would head north and aware that he could destroy her planning by his indecision, 'so well have I ordered the business, as nothing but himself can let [hinder] it'. Another correspondent confirmed on 11 April that the king would head either for Berwick or Holland. Although the Engagement itself, the strategic priority, was not Jane's concern, she was willing to be involved.

[Let me know what] service I may do you, for I shall hold a constant correspondence with him [Charles], but as faithful with you. Let me know by the
impose [-ing of trust] how much I have attained the ambition of being Your
Lordship's acknowledged servant. 409[15]

The escape failed on 20 March. The king lodged between the bar and frame
of his bedchamber window on the first floor. He was to have lowered himself the one storey, ten feet, on a silk cord (easier to coil and conceal than
a hempen rope). Once across the unguarded courtyard and onto the south
curtain wall, he would be lowered about fifteen feet to the steep slope down
to the outer bastion, from which the drop was short. Carisbrooke on its hill
is dry-moated. Cromwell revealed to Hammond on 6 April that 'a very considerable person of Parliament' had learned that the king had tried to escape
'with a cord of silk on a dark night about a fortnight ago, but ... the bars
would not give him passage. A gentleman with you [Firebrace] led the way
and slipped down. The guards that night had some quantity of wine with
them. The same party assures *aqua fortis* [nitric acid to degrade the bar metal]
has gone down from London.'[16] Firebrace supplied the detail:

> His majesty, sticking fast between his breast and shoulders, [was] not able to get
> forwards or backwards, [but] by means of [the] cord tied to a bar of the window
> he forced himself back. I heard him groan [and] to let me see the design was
> broken he set a candle in the window.

Firebrace flung stones from the battlement down over the bastion to warn
the others and they fled. 'After this I sent for *aqua fortis* from London, and
files. Hammond did pump me, and so he did others, and when he could make
no discovery he told me the reason.' Firebrace, on notice from Hammond
to leave the isle, reported Hammond's suspicions to the king, warning him
against 'constant intelligence from his friends', which must have been Jane's
correspondents. He re-routed all the king's mail through himself, which
explains why so few letters survive from May when the next escape attempt
was made. 'In my absence,' Firebrace noted, 'another attempt was made, but it
was unhappily discovered in the execution.' Lilly outside and Mildmay inside
may have been the informants; Salisbury, Cranborne, Northumberland (and
later, Howard of Escrick) were 'considerable persons of Parliament' on the
Derby House committee, and William Fiennes, Lord Saye, was rumoured to
have visited the king in March.

Charles asked Titus, his equerry, how to improvise 'a forcer' out of 'the fire
shovel and tongs' to bend the window bar. *Incommunicado* behind deference
and bars, his notes were his only link with the world, but each required a day
to encipher or decipher. It made for nervous exhaustion, paralysis behind a
controlled composure. He believed Loe and the postmaster were reading his

letters. If one went missing, especially if a cipher were involved, he fretted. He had too little to do and feared the worst, including the army radicals. Several times since 1646 he had spoken of preferring a death sentence to going against his conscience, or being kept in an undignified political limbo. The execution of 1649 was in the air and at the back of minds unspoken three years before it happened.

Charles suggested they corrupt the guards and walk across the courtyard out through the gatehouse. After the experience of 20 March, 'the ease or difficulty of removing the [vertical window] bar will cast the scales between the two ways'. He refused to wear a false beard, remembering his undignified scuttle from Oxford, and he fussed about every detail. An inability to trust or to delegate dogged his reign and explains the 'promiscuous frequency' of his letters of which so few survive. Writing also gave the feeling of doing, as he admitted to Titus: 'I importune you with papers having little to say.' Four letters of his to Titus on four consecutive days in April repeated anxieties about filing a bar. April was wasted. Loe wanted him to go to London, but Titus and the king 'earnestly and particularly recommend the providing of a ship [to go abroad]. I pray you have more assurance [for me] than bare confidence in having a ship ready.' He asked again 'whither you intend I should go, after I am over the [Solent] water'. Berwick or any other destination ceased to be mentioned. Some time in April, Jane Whorwood approached Lilly in London. 'The Lady Whorwood again came to me and acquainted me with the matter. I got G. Farmer, a most ingenious locksmith in Bow Lane, to make a saw to cut the iron bars asunder and *aqua fortis* [nitric acid] besides.' In later years both Sir Thomas Herbert and Henry Firebrace claimed to have sent for the files and nitric acid, but neither mentioned Jane, nor did they accuse Lilly of informing for Parliament. Jane was not the only conspirator to confide in him.[17]

She was now '715' in the king's cipher list, and chartered a ship. Charles reassured Titus, 'you are not mistaken, for I am confident that she will not deceive your trust'. He asked Titus to reassure her that 'I am in no ways disgusted with anything I heard concerning her', possibly a reference to her 'applying herself' to Lord Howard, or others. From her London base she must have been privy to the escape of the Duke of York downriver on a barge provided by the Loes on 20 April. It rendezvoused with a *pinck* which had stood two weeks off Gravesend. Meanwhile, Derby House had alerted Hammond on 15 April to 'a new design to take away the king'. John Burroughs, Harbinger or travel master to the king (as Jane's father had been), was arranging horses in Sussex, 'to lie ready there at a place appointed. Firebrace and Titus have gone to make ready a boat of four oars to bring off the king [from Wight]. The king has a bodkin to raise the lead in which the severed bar sits to put in *aqua fortis*. He will cast himself off from the bowling alley [green] over the [outer] Works.' (Plan B was to set alight a great heap of charcoal near the king's courtyard lodging as a distraction. 'Upon that tumult he will make his escape.') Concern at Derby House was such that 'the Committee not sitting, some of its members came in and commanded this be signified to you.' Someone (not Jane) also wrote to Lanark on 11 April, indiscreetly, of 'four servants about the king ... to assist in this attempt ... an engine made to pull out the bar of his chamber window and so to get over the wall. I hope your Lordship will not communicate this *to any but your best friends* [author's italics].' Security was a folorn hope.

Three days later Derby House confirmed,

> if you do but examine whether the king hath not lately had a relation or journal of all the proceedings of Sir Thomas Bendish at Constantinople and by whom he received it, as also whether he hath not lately written letters to the Muscovite [Company] in favour of merchants trading thither and by whom these letters were procured.

In mid-April Jane brought the king an advance copy of an account of Bendish's stormy arrival in Constantinople, *News from Turkey: A True Relation of the Passages of Sir Thomas Bendish*, published in London in May 1648. The book was presumably annotated in citrus juice or minuscule, with escape plan details or intelligence from London, or both.[18] Jane ensured Firebrace understood the book's importance and the king dutifully maintained appearances by writing to Bendish to commend his 'discreet and sound behaviour' on behalf of merchants' interests.

He also wrote to the Muscovy, or Russia Company, which traded with Persia, through Russia, close to routes within the sphere of the Levant and East India companies from which its membership was drawn. By the 1630s it was under the older companies' control, all three companies enjoying their royal monopolies to the chagrin of Parliamentarians in the absence of Parliament, and to the benefit of the Privy Purse. Now as a prisoner, Charles could still confirm monopolies, even if he could not enforce them. The Russia Company came naturally in the same breath as Bendish's report, and Jane Whorwood was in her element acting between king and the City. He also wrote or included something else under the cover of his Muscovy correspondence.

Jane knew that she was being watched. Her cipher with Firebrace, as with the king, was currently 'N' and she advised Firebrace on 20 April to

> [pretend] the opinion of the nullity of our design, for none is worthy of that high trust but ourselves. I could wish I had an hour's discourse with you to discover to you the villainies I have lately met with. When the party [king] hath read the [Bendish] book, beg a sight of it and I shall hereafter inform you more ... in despite of treachery we will [bring] our desires to pass.[19]

She was talking about betrayal and Firebrace was faltering, but she steeled him: 'take my counsel and act it with resolution.' Firebrace warned the king on 23 April that Derby House had sent a letter of his 'in characters' to Hammond: 'you keep intelligence with somebody that betrays you.' The anonymous writer of 11 April assured Lanark that he (or she) had Hammond's ear and could bend it to the Scots Royalist cause. The committee warned that about a third of a packet of fifteen of the king's letters had been read and that 'a hacker [hacksaw] is due to be collected … at Newport on Saturday morning 29th April. The intention is that the king should go to the house of a gentle-man at Lewes, a Parliament man [Sir Edward Alford MP, at Hamsey].' The saw would be carried by fishermen from Portsmouth to Wight. 'The king will also send letters to Scotland [to the Hamiltons] by Portsmouth; they are to be intercepted and brought here. A porter who takes coal to the king's room, it is planned, will take the king's place while he comes down and escapes during supper.' Hammond, naively open and self-questioning as ever, told the Speaker on 22 April the responsibility was 'exceedingly too weighty for me'.[20]

On 27 April Charles passed a last note to Firebrace through the cracked panel of his great chamber, just before Hammond expelled the courtier. The king explained the 'villainies [Jane] mentions, she suspects Loe for … As I told you yester night, upon my word, you may trust N and I believe you will find her industrious in and useful to my service.' That day two people visited William Lilly on Strand Lane: an unnamed *mulier de viro in Turkey* (woman about a man in Turkey) and *Dominus Loe, mercator* (Mr Loe, merchant).[21]

By now the boat was out, literally, and Derby House watched it.

A ship is fallen down from London to Queenborough on Sunday [30 April] where she rides to waft him into Holland. Mistress Whorwood is aboard the ship, a tall well-fashioned and well-languaged gentlewoman with a round visage and with pock holes in her face. She stays to wait upon the king.

Hammond took immediate precautions, moving the king to new quarters in the domestic wing of the Tudor governor's mansion against the north curtain wall. It was more secure, further from the gatehouse and nearer the keep in the event of any attempt to free the king by force. Hammond found some pretext for the move which aroused no suspicion.

Derby House alerted him with more detail on 2 May that

a merchant had gone from London to tell the king all is ready. Four horses in or near Portsmouth to take him by or near Arundel, and thence to Queenborough. A Parliament man [Alford MP] near Arundel is to be his guide. The king is to get out of a low room window. Have a special care … lest he escape under the cover of bowling … they will have a ladder up against the wall against the bowling alley [green] and horses and a boat ready.

The king had files, replenished *aqua fortis* – the first batch had spilt en route from London – and stockings to muffle his footsteps. Derby House expected a breakout on or around 1 May. However, Charles was now behind a different barred window high in the castle wall, double the ten-foot (three-metre) drop from his previous apartment window, and well away from the paved courtyard on which the stockings were meant to have silenced his tread.

He passed the time fretting, writing to the queen and to N. 'I desire you,' he told Firebrace, on Sunday 30 April, 'to deliver that to N with your own hands and always let her know when you send to me, that I may by you receive her letters.' He had already sent her two notes on 26 April 'of some concernment and [I] demand an answer'. From the closing days of April, Jane Whorwood, the courier 'for whose fidelity I [Charles] will answer', formally became the king's correspondent, although of the known fifty-four letters between them from that date, only one indirectly from her (to Hopkins, for the king's eyes) and two from him survive.

The king was disconcerted by his new quarters. He complained (3 May) that escape was 'impossible to be done'. One window was too small, another reachable only by ladder, the third barred. The next night he declared, 'It is absolutely impossible to do anything at night', as the moon was only just on the wane. Jane Whorwood's boat, probably a *pinck* – sturdy at anything from fifteen to fifty tons displacement – was anchored off Queenborough on the Medway estuary. Dutch vessels poaching oysters to sell abroad stood out in the closed season when local dredging ceased. It became increasingly hard for Jane and her companion, John Browne, Ashburnham's man, to pretend to be waiting for a favourable wind when one was blowing across the anchorage. After embarking at the end of April, Jane wrote three letters to the king explaining the situation, but he only received them on 14 May. Despite a backlog of delayed letters to be answered, he found time to write three letters back to her, to 'encourage and thank her because she hath assisted you [Titus] in providing the ship'. On 13 May Jane wrote to Firebrace, presumably upriver in London:

> I am happily arrived at the place appointed [Queenborough], and wait the good hour of meeting with our friends (to my grief and wonder not yet come) what news you have concerning them or what may concern your friend, quickly despatch to [me greatly longing for] letters from you.

She sealed it with an oval stone cut with shield, helmet and wyvern, one of three she carried, all 'male' oddments and including her husband's signet.

Twenty-four hours later, on the night of 14 May, the king instructed Titus:

> begin to wait for me on Monday next [15th] and so after, every night for a week together, because one night may be fail … and it being both troublesome and

dangerous to send often to you … it is my chamber window by which I must descend, the other being so watched it cannot be cut, wherefore I must first go to bed so that my time of coming from my chamber may be about eleven at night.

The letter was taken by Edward Worsley to Titus staying at an inn run by Mistress Pitt of the Southampton merchant family. John Ashburnham, meanwhile, was arrested on the mainland on 19 May and taken to London, along with evidence for the escape plan found in a search of Lord Hertford's home at Netley.[22]

On Monday 22 May the king advised Titus 'Wednesday [24th] next may be the first night I shall endeavour to escape but … assure me that you will be ready … and send me a password, which yet you have not done … remember to order things so that I shall need no stop until I go to the ship'. The climate itself was against him: Sir John Oglander noted three dry days without rain and cold wind between May and August. Charles also 'thought it necessary to write this to 715 [Whorwood] that I stay [delay] not for the ship, therefore pray you send it speedily to her'. On the Wednesday he did delay, but

by the help of fate I shall try to escape upon Sunday night next [28th] … we could not do it this night because the course [rosters] of the guards are altered, for our men have it settled so that their turn comes … on Sunday night next, and … that Mistress Whorwood may wait for me with as much patience, as I know you would … I pray you send this enclosed speedily to her hand.

Violence broke out across Kent and in the fleet, making it doubtful whether any of his letters reached her at Queenborough.

The name of the vessel carrying Jane Whorwood and John Browne is not recorded, nor that of its master, although it had some link with John Loe. Jane had organised it, presumably with minimal crew. When the Loes helped the Duke of York escape down the Thames to Gravesend in April they gave him £150 for the journey. Charles instructed his close circle to take any money Loe offered, but not to trust him.[23] Whorwood and Browne marked time in the tidal mudflats of the Swale for five weeks, largely uninformed of events on Wight or in Sussex. Two days after her first letter to Firebrace, perhaps unwell due to Queenborough's limited hospitality, a rogue oyster (the month had no 'r'), or simply the sea, Jane countersigned and postscripted briefly a six-inch square letter written by Browne, again to Firebrace. Browne had been arrested and imprisoned twice by town mayors at Hull and Northampton in 1647, and was wary of a third confinement.

He wrote with the confidence of a gentleman, addressing Firebrace as 'Sir' and signing 'friend', as Jane herself addressed him, but his tone was urgent and direct.

We do very much wonder that in all this week we have heard nothing from you. All the time past we have been in a readiness to depart, but now lie under a contrary wind and [under] some suspicion having neglected a fair wind. Therefore we could not omit to give you notice that we intend to remove into Margarett Roade [Margate roadstead] and therefore have sent up the bearer hereof that if they be not come out before this arrives [to] you, you may let them know it, so they come to the Reculvers or Birchington where I shall not fail to meet them. But in case they should be come forth before you receive this, then I shall lie at one ferry coming into this island [King's Ferry crossed the Swale to Sheppey below Queenborough] and the bearer at his return at another [Elmsley Ferry, Sittingbourne], so to prevent their coming hither and to guide them to the other place [Thanet and Margate] ... I entreat that you fail not to send word punctually how your business stands and what [their] speed hath been since their departure, by this bearer who is faithful and honest and will be [returning] here tomorrow night ... Your true friend, J. Browne.

He did not qualify for a cipher. 'N desires you to send what news you can and remember her to you.'[24]

Two days later Jane replied to one from Firebrace. She may still have been sick, she was certainly anxious; the letter is smudged, written with a blunt quill, and its lines slope, possibly written on her lap on board, or in a cramped inn. Loe had been asking questions 'to sift [quiz]' Firebrace, so Jane trailed a false scent in a letter to her husband through the same courier, perhaps telling him she was heading for Holland alone and that sickness was delaying her. 'I left a letter for [my] bedfellow sufficient to satisfy [Loe]. In what state we have been, are and shall be (in relation to our present business) Browne will inform you. I shall only lay an importunity on you of hastening on the business.' Browne was her aide and escort, but his other letters have not survived. Mistress Whorwood was bred to expect more than Queenborough could offer. A Parliamentary borough with a mayor and a small oyster industry, its hospitality was limited to two high street inns. John Taylor claimed to have arrived there in 1619 in a papier mâché boat with two oars made of dried giant flatfish which the population, festive on bread, oysters and beer doles for the feast of St James the Oyster Fisher, understandably vandalised. The mayor hosted him for the night during which 'cheer upon cheer, wine upon wine' appears to have inspired more verse. Seventy years later Defoe found a 'miserable dirty fishing town [of] alehouse keepers and oyster catchers'.

Jane hinted genteelly at Queenborough's limitations. 'I am grown high into the favour of the Corporation here and doubt not to have all the civilities the place is capable to show. The wind being contrary hath much befriended us, but if it should chance to change (to avoid suspicion) we shall be enforced abroad [to Margate].' A senior naval officer boarded her boat on instructions from Derby House and was evidently helpful while conscientious. William Cooke was acting captain of the forty-two-gun *Henrietta* on 'Thames and Medway guard' against smugglers of fullers earth, gunpowder, illegal oyster hauls and treasonable correspondence hidden in coal barges. He held the substantive rank of principal master, or master attendant, at Chatham, akin to a senior captain or king's harbourmaster, responsible directly to the admiral. By 1648, after more than forty years in the navy, much of it on Medway patrol, he was struggling with conflicting loyalties, as were many in Kent and in his fleet.

Firebrace, clearing the king's correspondence through London, had offered Jane official passes for any passengers who might join her. 'The passes,' she replied, 'may happen to be very useful, for upon our late contest [encounter] with Captain Cooke, it was resolved that our captain might without opposition take any with [passes] into his ship for their passage.' Cooke was the expert on the rules governing cargo, passengers and papers in his Medway and Thames estuaries. A black market existed for passes, supplied by corrupt officials or simply forged. A pass had to be judged on the spot, whether at a Kent port or an Oxfordshire roadblock, as there was no means of verifying it. Once issued, only blanket revocation could invalidate it.

Jane requested the passes, 'let not, if to be compassed, such a put off, if any occasion should require it, be wanting to us'. She was not short of money, despite harbour dues and civic hospitality 'at very great charge'. Whatever it cost in couriers, horses, lodging and presumably bribes, she insisted 'no money you shall disburse but shall with thanks by myself be repaid you'. A similar promissory note from her through Firebrace to someone in London had 'booked no more effect', hence her need to reassure.[25] Protracted play-acting in a hostile environment was the problem, not the cost. 'Pray make all the speed you can, for I lie at very great charge and am in more discontents and fears through this prolongation. On your part and be confident of no fail in N.' She was in control of her part of the plan, but Derby House saw the wider picture. Walter Frost kept Hammond posted on Tuesday 23 May, 'the design still goes on. The ship still lies in the Isle of Sheppey. I have written again to Colonel [Vice-Admiral] Rainsborough of it. The time is to be Thursday, Friday or Saturday next [25th, 26th, 27th], or about 4th June, if opportunity serve them right.'[26]

Queenborough held a snap election which Jane and Browne could not have avoided. Sir Edward Hales, Royalist MP for twenty-five years, had been expelled from the Commons and imprisoned. At two weeks notice Parliament ordered a by-election. On 26 May Augustine Garland, staunch republican and minor landowner in Queenborough, was returned for the town. He sat in judgement on the king in 1649 and was accused at his own trial in 1660 of spitting in the king's face. The voting freeholders, anyway, would have descended on the town with other concerns in mind. That week the Kent 'tumult and disorder', as Derby House called it, broke out, headed by

Hale's grandson. While Jane Whorwood and John Browne worried about the wind ruining their cover story, they were in more danger than they knew. Jane did not mention election or uprising in her letters, but she delayed the ship at Queenborough into the first week of June. The emergency plan to sail away to stand off Margate, a depressed, harbourless village where they would have been less conspicuous, had to be dropped as the 'tumult' around the Medway trapped her and as the king's escape bid was continually postponed.

Colonel Rainsborough, admiral of the Parliament Ships, formerly the Royal Navy, was due to check Jane's ship again.

[It] lies still at Sheppey waiting for the king's escape ... You formerly had notice from [Secretary] Frost of a ship lying at Queenborough for the king's escape. We hear since that the right ship has been visited by you [*per* Cooke], that it still lies about the Isle of Sheppey, that the design continues still and that the escape will be attempted about Thursday or Friday night next [25th or 26th], therefore if you could send some ship thither on Friday next [26th] to visit it again you might perhaps discover something. We have given notice to Colonel Hammond.

Friday the 26th was election day. Rainsborough had two blockade ships 'riding at the mouth of the Medway near Sheerness to visit and intercept all vessels on that river'; for some years *Henrietta* and the much larger *James* had been on this deployment, one or other frequently under William Cooke covering for a shortage of captains. Given the urgency (and *kudos*) of taking the king, Rainsborough, a radical, may have considered boarding Jane's ship in person, but mutiny overtook him. London was placed on full alert. A dozen ships, one in four of the fleet, mutinied ('a distemper' Derby House called it) on the day Jane's ship was due to be boarded, and the mutineers literally beached Rainsborough in Essex. On 27 May Sir Nicholas Crispe and Sir Thomas Adams, key Royalists, were ordered to report to Derby House; on 1 June Silius Titus and Francis Cressett of the king's household were also summoned.[27]

Lord General Fairfax, ordered to 'take care of Kent', moved rapidly to quell the 'tumult'. He encircled Maidstone on 31 May, the day Jane wrote her last letter from Queenborough, twenty miles away. Two days later, Maidstone fell. Captain Cooke, who may have searched Jane's ship a second time, had himself to consider. He seems to have been the highest ranking mutineer sent into 'safe custody' in London in June for examination by the Navy Committee.[28] Evidently he shared the widespread hostility towards Rainsborough who had taken Vice-Admiral Batten's place. Rochester and Sittingbourne were held by the rebels, the Scots did not cross the border for another month and the king fantasised on Wight about 'Dutch *pincks*'. Jane wrote to Firebrace on the Wednesday Fairfax surrounded Maidstone:

I received the 29th instant a note from W [Titus] that he would that day be with me (he and as I fain would have understood the other parties being at the despatch thereof at Tunbridge in Kent), but his fail thereof hath put me into great perplexities. Pray send this enclosed away instantly and inform me of all occurrents in relation to our Master, more particularly what you conceive to be the occasion of this delay, for longer than one week more [to 7 June] it will not be possible ... to abide here ... despatch me [any news] by this bearer and so in haste [I] rest your assured friend N.

She sealed the letter with a winged griffin and torce.

Jane knew nothing of the king's failed escape attempt on 29 May, two days before her letter, or that Tunbridge had been merely a warning order: Titus in Southampton only *planned* to be in position there Sunday and Monday to re-horse the king. Charles had applied the nitric acid to the base of the bar and two sentries agreed to turn a blind eye. At the last moment they informed Hammond, who timed his entry into the chamber to midnight when the king was working on the bar. He offered to 'take leave of Your Majesty, for I hear you are going away' and reputedly the king laughed, from relief. The guards failed to catch the conspirators waiting below the bastion beyond the bowling green. Pursued by musket fire they hid in the woods and eventually escaped from the island. Even had Charles taken their boat across the Solent to catch the horse relay from Portsmouth to Queenborough through Arundel, Lewes, Tonbridge and Maidstone, he would have been blocked by Fairfax's army. His presence in Kent could not have made a chaotic rising less so, nor could it hasten the Scots. The naval mutineers 'no more listened than if a dog had sent them' to pleas to rescue him from Wight. The king was sidelined and embarrassed. From his eyrie he tried to monitor the 'tumult' and urge on the Scots by wishing. Beyond his barred window, according to Thomas Coke interrogated in 1651, 'young [William] Oglander and most of the gentlemen in the Island were engaged in the design of the surprise of Carisbrooke Castle and the late king's escape and blamed very much the revolted ships for not appearing before the island to give them an opportunity to rise'.

Weary from weeks of vigil at anchorages and horse stages, the frustrated conspirators regrouped in London. A correspondence silence descended. Titus consulted William Lilly on 24 June in what may have been yet another indiscretion.[29] On Saturday 1 July the king replied eagerly to a letter from him:

I know not whether my astonishment or my joy were the greater, for indeed I did despair of hearing any more from you or any other of my friends. Commend me heartily to the rest, particularly to 715 [Jane] ... I hope she knows before this how it was not my fault that I did not wait on her according to my promise, for which you may assure 715 that I was and am very much grieved.

Wight was vulnerable, as Hammond reported, 'only one ship guarding the island and that about to re-victual'. He requested a company to guard mainland and island shores, and a majority for Rolph, his regimental second-in-command. Welcome farce was afforded by a Surrey doctor, 'an agent of malignants there', who arrived unannounced, fainted, then told of verbal orders from Fairfax to take the king to Portsmouth. A fleet, he said, was ready in the Solent to escort. Eventually he admitted he wanted the king's commission to lead the Surrey gentry in an uprising.[30] Derby House, meanwhile, reassured Hammond that ships were being sent and that the fleet mutiny had been contained.

Belatedly, James, Duke of Hamilton, finally 'Engaged', with brother Lanark at his side, leading a Scots army south on 8 July. By then Kent had been subdued, leading Royalists were trapped across the Thames estuary at Colchester, and the bulk of the Navy, which had remained loyal to Parliament, held Chatham, the Medway and the Thames. Two weeks later the Commons voted a battalion of 500 to the Isle of Wight, the order signed by Lord Howard of Escrick, Jane's old prey. Hammond was still apprehensive. 'I feel revolting ships will still bring troops to the island and islanders may be forced to join them … I hear rumours of troops arriving and nothing comes.' The committee also heard of ships under Lord Willoughby, rebel vice-admiral, coming via Calais with 1,000 troops. Mushrooms in the dark were well nourished with improbable tales.

The committee even heard that admiral, the Earl of Warwick, was at Carisbrooke with the king despite the rules, pretending 'to be touched [for the evil]', but in reality to treat about the Surrey 'army of desperados under Lord Holland [his brother]', Captain William Whorwood and Edward Andrews among them. Small troops of horse amounting to 500 men secretly rendezvoused at Kingston, among them 'many persons of great quality', rumoured to be heading for Reigate and ultimately for Wight. 'Stay boats on your side to prevent their landing', Derby House ordered Hammond, but it was just another 'tumult', over in three days. When on 15 July the committee warned that the Scots had invaded and that ships were heading for Wight, they did not then know that the invasion was already faltering, or that the 'tumults' were over. At the end of July, instructions from the deskbound in London to the 'Hampshire and Isle of Wight Committee of Safety' bordered on farce, even asking 'is there such a thing?'

The announcement by Parliament at the end of July of treaty talks to be held with the king was a surprise change of face; they hoped to pre-empt a military coup with a political coup, while the army was distracted with 'tumults' and invasion. Moderates tried to pull the rug from under radicals. Charles would soon be allowed to meet freely, talk privately and write openly. Under the truce terms, the inner circle could emerge from hiding to visit him on Wight – save for the legally unpardonable John Ashburnham.

The negotiation, however, was agreed only on the Speaker's casting vote after a Commons deadlock, a sign that fewer were ready to trust the king. Once the army had restored peace it would inevitably vent its anger on Parliament, and perhaps the king with it. Army, King, Parliament, English, Scot, Presbyterian, Independent and Leveller, all shorthand labels rather than analytic descriptions, were wary of each other, if not downright resentful. Strange bedfellows played for time to play off one another. They juggled and the polarities of the War were reversed. In the end, neither Parliament nor King had the power to deliver any treaty or compromise without the army's assent.

Notes

1. Correspondence sources for Chapters 8–10: British Library, Egerton Ms, 1788, thirty-three letters and a memorandum from the king to Henry Firebrace, two from Firebrace to the king, seven from Jane Whorwood to Firebrace, two from the king to Jane Whorwood, and one from Lady Newburgh (d'Aubigny) to Firebrace, all 1648. Royal Library at Windsor, Hopkins Correspondence, Royal Collection Inventory No. 1080413, printed inaccurately in Thomas Wagstaffe, *Vindication of King Charles the Martyr* (1711), appendix, including sixty-two letters from the king to William Hopkins of Newport, one from the king to the Prince of Wales in Jersey, and one from Jane Whorwood ('Hellen' overwritten on 'N') to Hopkins to be shown to the king, all 1648. Carisbrooke Castle Museum Trust own two letters from Charles to Edward Worsley of Appuldurcombe, both 1648. Bodleian Library, Rawlinson Ms B 225 contains nine letters from Charles to Abraham Dowcett, clerk to the kitchen, all 1648. British Library, Egerton Ms, 1533, fifteen letters from Charles to Silius Titus, all 1648. Cambridge University Library, Additional Ms 7311, three letters from Charles to Mary (? Lee), laundress, all 1648. No letters from Jane Whorwood direct to the king survive, the last probably destroyed when he burned his papers before execution. Two more letters in Jane Whorwood's handwriting as '409', previously attributed to Firebrace, to her brother-in-law, William Hamilton, February and March 1648, GD406/1/2205 and GD406/1/2228 in the NAS, were published in Hamilton Papers Addenda, Camden Miscellany IX, NS 53, 1893, 3 and 21. Cordell Firebrace in *Honest Harry* (1932), reproduced much of the above material, although with inaccuracies and unpardonable censoring. *Letters Between Colonel Hammond and the Committee at Derby House* (1764) preserves transcripts of twenty-five letters made before they were destroyed by fire in the eighteenth century; they overlap with and should be read alongside the rest of the Derby House records in CSP 1648–9, DXVI. The French ambassador in Edinburgh worked closely with the Lanarks, but was aware he was being manipulated: Montreuil Correspondence, 1645–8, *Scottish Historical Society*, volumes 29 and 30 (1898, 1899).

2. HLJ, IX, 22 November and 21 December 1647.

3. TNA PROB 11/74; TNA PROB 11/122; Sir John Oglander, *A Royalist's Notebook* (1936), 173–6; *Visitation of Sussex*, Harleian Society, LIII (1905), 27.

4. Hamilton Papers Addenda, Camden Society Miscellany IX, NS 53, 3–4, (ed. S.R. Gardiner, 1893), originals in NAS, see note 1, is in Jane Whorwood's hand, as is a second from '409', ibid., 21, 7 March. She also refers to 'father' and 'sister'.

5. *Derby House Letter*, 2; 3; Clarke Papers I, 420.

6. Several apparently undeciphered letters to Lanark from the south still sit in the NAS. Lanark was in close touch with the king and his supporters, including Jane, during 1648. See also, Gilbert Burnet, *Memoirs of the Dukes of Hamilton* (1673), 332.

7. Thomas Adams, *Plain Dealing*, 17 November 1647.

8. See published Hamilton papers in Hamilton Papers, Camden Society, NS 27, 1880 (ed. S.R. Gardiner, 1880), Letters 1 (p.1), 5 (p.5), 9 (p.10), and Letters 10, 12, 13. Also, Nicholas Papers I, Oudart to Nicholas, 18 February, 74–5, Camden Society, NS 40, 78.

9. Letter 106 and 107, Hamilton Papers, *op.cit.*, 168–9; for Fenn and Andrews, see CCAM, I, 54; III, 1129; *Westminster Abbey Registers*, Harleian Society Register Series, X (1875), 141.

10. Bodleian Library, Rawlinson Ms B 225, Dowcett Letters, 2; *Reliquiae* (1889), III. Mary (? Lee's) letter originals in Cambridge University Library, Additional Ms 7311, are published in Jack Jones, *The Royal Prisoner* (1965), Appendix A, 141–3.

11. *Derby House Letters*, 4 & 5. Lilly was consulted on 22 January 1648 'of a plot', Bodleian Library, Ashmole Ms 420: 176.

12. Sir John Oglander, *A Royalist's Notebook* (1936), 117.

13. *Derby House Letters*, 8, 9, 11.

14. Rawlinson Ms, *op.cit.*, f. 2, words in italic suppressed by Cordell Firebrace in *Honest Harry* (1932), 264. See also Chapter 7, n. 9.

15. Bodleian Library, Ashmole Ms 420, 216; for letter of 11 April, Hamilton Papers, Camden Society, *op.cit.*, Letter 114.

16. *Derby House Letters*, 14.

17. Charles Carleton, *Charles I, The Personal Monarch* (1983), 330; king to Titus, 13 April.

18. *News from Turkie*, by W.L., pub. 9 May 1648, by Henry Blunden of Cornhill, London, Thomason E.441 (10).

19. *Firebrace Letters*, 9, 20 April 1648, Whorwood to Firebrace.

20. Henry Cary, *Memorials of the Civil War in England* (1842), 387–9, Hammond to Speaker Lenthall, 22 April 1648.

21. Ashmole Ms 420, 264v and 264.

22. Charles to Worsley, 16 May, with enclosed for Titus: 'Also advise with him where I shall take the boat and where land and the watchword as soon as you can.' For Ashburnham's arrest at Winchester Park, 19 May, and the Netley evidence, see John Ashburnham, *Narrative*, 223, and *Vindication*, 123, 128 (1830). He oversaw

the plan from Hertford's house at Netley, a horse stage in the relay plan, and from his own home at Battle, another stage on the road to Queenborough; a barque was also held at Hastings to take the king to France, but this was discharged in the summer. The king reinterpreted the discharge unfairly as 'some persons near him having refused to serve him in his escape'.

23. HMC, XIII, 1891, Portland Mss, Appendix 1, 578, Coke's confession, April 1651; *Firebrace Letters*, 38, 1 August, king to Firebrace, in third person.

24. 'Our captain' of Jane's letter of 17 May was not Browne, despite this assumption by Cordell Firebrace and Jack Jones. John Browne, 'gentleman and servant to John Ashburnham since 24 November 1642' (Ashburnham's Oxford *Accompt*, xxxvii) knew Jane from her gold-smuggling days. He escaped from Oxford ahead of the king early in April 1646. After the king's escape later that month, Hudson, the escape leader, wrote to a Mr Browne at Lincoln's Inn (Henry Cary, *Memorials of the Civil War in England* (1842), I, 109, which may explain Browne's being called 'an ex-innkeeper': Francis Peak, *Desiderata Curiosa* (1779), ed. IX, 352): 'Mr Ashburnham did employ him and promised to do him some courtesy.' Browne was arrested both at Hull and Holdenby for bringing messages from Holland to the king. In 1648 at Newport the king allegedly promised Browne the post of Solicitor General (see Chapter 9). Ashburnham was so intent on justifying himself after the Restoration that he gave no credit to agents like Browne and Whorwood. John Loe, son of Lawrence Loe, surgeon royal in the Scots War, was regarded as a Presbyterian activist, turning the king against the Army, see John Loftis and Paul Hardacre, *Colonel Bamfield's Apology* (1993), 29, and called 'a reputed knave' by Anne Fanshaw (*Memoirs*, ed. John Loftis, 1979, 121). See also Earl of Clarendon, *History of the Rebellion* (1674), II, 65. A John Browne of Lincoln's Inn died in 1668, from Kirkby, Lincoln, son of a former gentleman of the privy chamber to James I, see TNA PROB 11/181; *Lincolnshire Pedigrees*, Harleian Society L, 1902, 181. Jane's sister Lanark was meanwhile urging her husband into the Engagement and the French into a formal alliance with the prisoner king: Montereuil Correspondence, *op.cit.*, II, 486, 16/26 May; 518, 27 June/6 July 1648.

25. Mutilated receipt from Jane to the king for £100, British Library, Egerton Ms, 35, cited by Firebrace, *Honest Harry* (1932), 293.

26. Cordell Firebrace assumed that the ship went to lie off Margate, *Honest Harry*, 111–12, but between tumult and mutiny that journey became impossible. Derby House on 23 May (Letter 21) was clear that the ship was still in the Swale. The returning Royalist courier on 16 or 17 May would have brought instructions to the effect, 'Stay – We are coming'. CSP 1648–9, DXVI, 74, 23 May, Derby House 'desire Colonel Thomas Rainsborough to visit it about Friday next …'.

27. CSP 1648–9, DXVI, 74, 75, 77, Derby House Proceedings, 23–26 May 1648.

28. HCJ, V, 1646–8, 606, 19 June 1648. Gunnery officers, boatswains, a chaplain and even the mariner Mayor of Rochester, all men in authority, were arrested as mutineers. Cooke was the most senior, and unlike the others his ship was not

named as he took on only acting commands by virtue of his post. At Chatham he managed all ships in harbour; he was nominated in 1637 to command the newly built, but oversized, *Sovereign of the Seas*, after commanding large new capital ships on estuary blockade. While Jane was on the Medway, it was said that his command, *Henrietta*, was in danger of being boarded by mutineers for its ordinance, and perhaps because of Cooke's known sympathies, CSP 1648–9, Navy Papers, 142; bail was requested for the prisoners to be examined by the Kent committee on 'their activities in the insurrection', HCJ, V, 659, 3 August 1648; in March 1649 several were reinstated, when Cooke evidently retired unscathed to his home in Gillingham and died there in 1655. He left his silver naval whistle to his mariner son, TNA PROB 11/281; CSP 1633, CCXXXIII, 1 March 1633; CSP 1634–5, CCLXXXII, 19; CCLXXXII, 29; 1636–7, CCCLXX, 4; 1644–5, DIX, 34, 46; 1648–9, DXVIII, 142; TNA PROB 11/281. See also Rodger Nam, *A Naval History of Britain, I, 660–1649* (1997), 379–46, 482–3.

29. Bodleian Library, Ashmole Ms, 420, 314v.
30. Derby House Letters, 20.

9

June – November 1648:
'Sweet 390 … Your Most Loving 391'

Had the rest done their parts as carefully as Whorwood, the king would have been at large.
Marquess of Hertford to Jane's brother-in-law, Lord Lanark, 1648

Jane Ryder, an exceeding loyal woman, understanding and of good judgement.
Anthony Wood, Oxford, c.1670

The burning of letters by the king and his circle often creates 'silences' when correspondents were actually in touch. Dowcett burned twenty letters on his dismissal from Wight. The king reportedly tussled with Hammond after finding him searching his desk, and threw crucial letters onto the fire. Hours before his execution in 1649 he 'burned all his papers and his several clevises [cipher keys]'. In June 1648, however, everyone really did lie low to weather the Kent rising and to await the Scots. Depressed and exhausted after the failure of the escape attempts, they simply stopped writing. The Marquess of Hertford, whose house at Netley had sheltered the conspirators, explained the silence to 'my dear Lanark' and singled out Lanark's sister-in-law for special mention. The king 'is not averse to answer you, but his friends are too watchful over him [and] I have been so indisposed to sickness. Had the rest done their parts as carefully as Wharwood [*sic*], the king [would have] been at large.'[1] The king was relieved when supporters did renew contact early in July, and elated when the Hamiltons invaded that same week. Their campaign ended six weeks later at Preston, with James Hamilton taken prisoner and William fleeing back home. James was remanded to Windsor castle, charged with treason under his English title, Duke of Cambridge.

The king at least escaped into writing and prayer. He composed poetry and wrote to unseen correspondents; chess and 'gough' no longer happened, let alone hunting or riding. The castle, he complained, was 'a base imprisonment, cooped up' with only the view of Carisbrooke village through his barred windows. Walking the battlements he could see Newport a mile away, watch the seasons change in the surrounding countryside and, in good weather, glimpse the tantalising grey-blue pencil line of the mainland. He renewed contact with Jane ('715') through Titus on 1 July, apologising for the Medway fiasco. Meanwhile, the Surrey 'tumult' collapsed. On 10 July he wrote again to Titus (confusingly in both second and third person). 'On the occasion of some discourse before some ladies I heard the king say that the Governor [Hammond] never offered any personal incivility to him nor did he ever expect hurt from him in the way of treachery.' Hammond was accused by Royalist London broadsheets of exposing the king to poison and to Major Rolph, his second-in-command, who tended to wave pistols and shout. The king also assured his correspondents that although the governor 'pumped' and 'screwed out an examination from [him] concerning his pretended escape', he gave nothing away. More important, he ordered Titus to pass on two letters, one to Lady Carlisle, the other to '715'.

Bizarrely, despite escape attempts, risings, a mutiny and an invasion all in his name and with his connivance, Charles was invited to the negotiating table by Parliament. He was allowed open communication with William Hopkins and his wife at Newport, by letter and visit, although private discussion was still forbidden and they kept to their ciphers. The Hopkins' identity is uncertain, as are the locations of their house and of the negotiations, but they were to host the king during the talks. Knowing the feeling in town Hopkins immediately suggested a local rising to overpower the garrison and prepare the way for an invasion, despite the failure of the mutineer navy ships to appear. Charles responded blandly on 10 July. 'I can give you no opinion concerning the feasibility of it, nor [advise] you … I shall do my part and will let slip no opportunity.' It was a diplomatic cough and he knew the island garrison was being reinforced. When Hopkins ventured more detail, the king advised, 'unless you seize Hammond, the seizing of all the rest of the Horse will not in my opinion do the work because he will sooner get help, than you will be able to force [me] out of his hands'. Charles suggested they take Hammond and the island simultaneously, or at least take Hammond as the king embarked: 'one [boat] will do it as well as a thousand.' He wrote out of cipher, but so tortuously to hide his meaning that he worried lest 'my brevity make me obscure'.

Mistress Hopkins took his other mail (in cipher) to London. Jane's first letter to him since the Medway arrived on 15 July, to which he replied three days later in a packet of letters through Firebrace in London. Two more from Jane arrived on 19 July together with one from the queen, from whom he had last heard in May, and one from the countess of Carlisle. By then it appears that Jane had arrived at Newport. After promising replies to all, he ran out of sealing wax and asked for Mistress Hopkins. 'Tell her I am sure the Queen would not be displeased at, much less forbid her private conferences with me and that (if she will not forbid me) I will try if I can make [her] procure me freedom of conference.' Hammond stuck to the letter of his orders and refused Mistress Hopkins any unwitnessed discussion; even whispering in public audience, forbidden since January, remained so until clear new instructions came from Parliament. Charles's only private contact was the emptier of his stool pan, 'who gives all the despatches to me and receives all from me. She can neither write nor read.' Someone from Parliament was also sounding him out through Jane, but 'I can say nothing to the proposition of a personal treaty from my Little Officer of the Parliament Side, until you [Jane] tell me whom you mean'. Most likely it was Lord Saye, the 'old Fox', conveying his 'proposition' anonymously in Jane's two letters which arrived on the 19th and which are now lost. Saye was rumoured to have been on the island in the spring and was alleged, for his own ambitious ends, to have pressed the king to delay agreeing with Parliament as long as he could; Saye preened himself that his own influence with the army could secure a more successful outcome and Black Rod's daughter was as good a courier as any; his son James was married to a Cecil, sister-in-law to Diana Cranborne, Jane's sister.

Charles was overcautious to the point of carelessness. He sent one messenger with letters to Firebrace to clear in London, but received by another courier. Ciphers were 'most tedious and much subject to error, three letters have taken up so much time that I am unwilling to stay this despatch any longer', yet he fretted about his tortuous writing out of cipher. On 21 July he shared a rare chuckle with Hopkins 'that Hammond fell flat on his back walking by me on Wednesday last ... a punishment for his incivility to [Mistress Hopkins] and equivocating to me'. Charles still toyed with an uprising. 'Can you master this place? How long can you make good the Island?' News of Parliament's proposed talks was spreading, which allowed Charles to distance himself from Hopkins' coup: 'I believe it will not fall out.' Pettily, he relished Hammond's stumble a second time, with Firebrace, 'which we royalists take for a good omen, not at all disordering the king's pace, [except] by laughing at the fall'.

At least his mood was improving, as his earthy response to Jane's three (lost) letters of 19 and 23 July showed. She proposed something, or was misinterpreted. He mixed first and third person and changed her cipher yet again, to run consecutively with his own.

Sweete 390, your two letters of 19th of this month I received late yesternight [23rd] and ... I cannot give you a greater compliment than ... to satisfy your desires, I must tell you that without any difficulty you may see the king [me]

and speak to him [me] too, [as long as] you do not offer to whisper, but you
will not get leave to speak privately with him [me] unless you had a recom-
mendation from Derby House so to do. Yet I imagine there is one way possible
you may get *a swyving* from me.[2] You must excuse my plain expressions ... get
acquaintance with the new [stoolpan] woman (who conveys all my letters) and
by her means you may be conveyed into the stool room (which is within my
bedchamber) while I am at dinner ... I shall have 3 hours to embrace and nip
you, for every day after dinner I shut myself up alone for so long and while I go
a walking she can relieve you. When however this should prove impossible (as I
hold it will not) ... this new woman can convey to me what letters you would
give her.

More immediate business then took over. 'Here enclosed you will receive
the bill [receipt] signed by the king as you desired, but as for the Memorial
ye sent for my own use, it will need an inter ...' A receipt was enclosed in the
letter, but both are now mutilated. The king did sign for £100 on 20 May
during the Queenborough episode. 'Will: Wi ...' had sent money earlier by
courier presumably for his escape.[3] Jane's 'Memorial' (memo) to Charles has
not survived.

He conveyed another 'urgent' letter to Jane through Firebrace, now back
in Newport, on 26 July. 'In case N be gone out of town before this packet
come into your hands, send it speedily after her, because it may assist her in
her journey.' It may have been money, or listed tasks, but she was not away
long. Charles acknowledged hers of 23 July. 'Sweete 390, yours of 23rd of this
month to my contentment came this morning [26th] to my hands ... Now
all that I can add to my former is that if you like not or find/fear impossible
the way that I have set you down for a passage to me, all I count on is that you
invite yourself to dine to Captain Mildmay's chamber (which is next door to
mine) where I will surprise you and between jest and earnest *get you alone in
to my chamber* and smother Jane Whorwood with embraces/kisses which to
be doing is made long by your most loving 391 [Charles].'[4] Mildmay was a
dangerously hostile player to enlist.

In fact, Jane was still in Newport. Firebrace, *alias* 'David Griffin', gave her
the letter. She replied immediately, confiding in a covering note to Firebrace,
not through her host William Hopkins, perhaps because of the sensitive content. Her loyalty was under strain and her feelings mixed.

As to the satisfaction of him in the contents of it, I could not so suddenly challenge [produce] an answer, I was willing to decline it [the visit] but having
in some sort acquired the means to do it [the stoolroom plan, or a key from
Hopkins], I have now written and entreat your speediest convey thereof. I must
not likewise be denied the favour to speak with you [Firebrace] this evening,
how late so ever it be before you can come, for tomorrow I shall go out of town

and there is a necessity of some conference with you first. Wherefore as you respect me (or that greatest engagement) [the ongoing Scots invasion] I fail you not to fulfill this request of your affectionate friend.

She sealed it with the Whorwood–Ryder impaled arms, on an oval signet. The king pursued Firebrace two days later (29th) with 'the thinnest despatch you have yet had from me': he was sick of ciphers. Titus, he believed, was due to visit him. Jane 'is gone to see a friend', perhaps Sir John Oglander, as she was only away three days. An overdue note was also enclosed for Lucy Carlisle, lower on the king's list of dependable helpers, although not for disloyalty.

Letters came to the king on the evening of the 29th, from the queen and Lady Carlisle, but nothing from Jane. Charles replied to his cousin Lady d'Aubigny (now Newburgh, newly married) at Bagshot. Jane reappeared at Carisbrooke on 3 August with Mistress Hopkins, and the king's renewed optimism showed in his letter to Hopkins that night,

> having this day been visited by a friend with whom I had not time to speak. Deliver this enclosed note unto her ... you may freely trust her in anything that concerns my service for I have had perfect trial of her friendship to me. The speedy delivery of this to Mistress Whorwood (who is this friend I mentioned) will be no small courtesy. Tell her that I expect an answer, either by word or writing.[39].

Twelve hours later, he asked Hopkins to deliver another 'enclosed note unto the same party [Whorwood] to whom I sent you one yesternight, which is occasioned upon a discourse I had this morning with 50 [Hammond].' That evening Hopkins brought him one from Jane to which he replied immediately with 'this enclosed for the same Friend which my two last were, in answer to what I received within yours tonight'. Twenty-four hours later he sent another to her by Hopkins, 'this enclosed being to the same friend my last was'. He was grateful

> for the staying of my Friend so long in this Isle, who as you say may be of excellent use for our Great business [the island uprising and his escape] and therefore by this enclosed I have desired her to have a little more patience. I entreat you to deal freely with her; tell her particularly how her stay may be useful to me, as to the securing of Hammond.

Parliament formally proposed the personal treaty on 3 August to which Charles responded on 8 August, asking for the 'same state of freedom as his last at Hampton Court'.

If Hammond was to be 'secured', was Charles asking Jane to honeytrap the twenty-seven-year-old as part of the islanders' coup, or alluding to the governor's increasingly obvious torn loyalty? He had written cryptically to Hopkins on 26 July of 'laying a train for 50 [Hammond]', like the drag-decoys of his favourite sport. The hope of taking Carisbrooke and Hammond with it to enable an escape to France was still in Charles's mind, even as he began talks with Parliament: the duplicity led directly to his death, although he saw it as the royal cause justifying any deception. His mind in its isolation was fermenting with possibilities; increasingly he leaned on Jane (now 'N' again), telling Hopkins 'I long to have an answer to this for I have written very freely to my friend'. When, as usual, he retired to write after supper on Monday evening, 7 August, he had letters from London and another

> from my friend N to which this enclosed [to Hopkins] is an answer. And [I] am well satisfied with those Hints she hath given me … for advice from my friends may do me good, but never harm. I pray you give my friend N a copy of all those names and figures [the cipher list] I have with you.

The coming treaty talks were the main subject of her 'hints', 'arguments' and 'advice'.

A new cipher, '64', stood for 'Treaty'. The preparatory commission came and went, and the king responded. He had a daily routine, rising early, 'walks about the Castle from 7–9 then returns to about 11 and stays two hours at dinner, then returns to write and then to bowls with the Governor with whom he is very familiar'.[5] Hammond thought Charles 'approves beyond expectation and intends a very fair answer'.[6] It afforded the king time and space to scheme, but it also drained him, as treaty papers came and went, lengthy considered replies had to be composed and advisers consulted, while his hope was really to cut through it all with an escape, an invasion or a coup. 'Tell N that what she desired concerning the City of London is already done in my last despatch' was obviously his reply to the merchants' letters from London of 7 August. Hopkins' merchant son George provided an added link with 'London friends'. Preparing his responses to Parliament, Charles told Lucy Carlisle, 'hath cost me so much pains [that] you must excuse me to all the rest of my friends for not writing to them at this time', although he found time for Jane. On Sunday 13 August, a reading and reflection day in default of the banned *Common Prayer*, Charles received letters from Hopkins and Jane, along with London pamphlets, 'very welcome in divers respects, telling me some good news of which I heard not before, and confirming others to me'. Thanks to pursuing Jane, as much as to the treaty and the arrival of his old barber, Charles 'clipped his beard and asked the Governor if he saw a new reformation in him'.[7]

> Tell N when you give this enclosed to her that is it is now the best caudle [medicinal broth] I can send her, but if she would have a better she must come

to fetch it herself … her Platonick Way doth much spoil the taste in my mind, and if she would leave me to my free Cookery, I should think to make her confess so herself.

The double entendre was loud, and 'Platonick Way' – he had called himself 'best Platonick lover' in an anonymous letter to an unidentified lady in February – smacked of masqued and repressed courtly romancing. Jane was also sounding Hammond. Twelve hours later, Charles told Hopkins: 'tell N that 50 [Hammond] spoke to me this morning about her business, but I told him that if she came to me herself I would give her an answer, but to nobody else.' The king was openly referring to the coming negotiations, to the stance of his City friends with whom Jane was his customary link, and to Lord Saye's secret lobbying using Jane as a go-between. Still close-guarded with 'no addresses' allowed, he was unable to discuss business with her in private.

A day later and another letter to Jane via Hopkins: 'this enclosed [is] an answer to N and tell her that she neither dated the last nor gave a full answer to mine. But I lay the fault on Hammond's doggedness to her and no want of civility to me.' He was in messianic mode, 'when [the king] keeps house again, there will be those who shall think themselves then happy, and yet sit lower at the table than [William Hopkins]'. After supper that day he wrote yet again to Hopkins,

> commend my service to all my feminine friends and tell Mistress Hopkins [I merely wanted] the conversation of such honest persons as herself. Tell N when you deliver this enclosed that I see she will in time learn to answer letters, but yet she mistakes dates, for she called this the 14th, and that I expect an answer to this.

Jane had in fact written that day. Twenty-four hours later Hopkins took another letter back to her with instructions, 'when you deliver this enclosed to N, I pray you tell her I will be in much impatience until I receive an answer'. Less than twelve hours later Charles sent another, '[tell] N that I expect an answer to this enclosed and desire her well to mark the Postscript'. Letters and postscript are lost.

Hammond, escape, the treaty, the City and Lord Saye were enough to preoccupy anyone, but Charles was also flirting, frantically talking-with-nothing-to-say to Jane. That was in the morning. After supper the same day (17th), he sat and wrote: 'My haste this day to return N a speedy answer made me slip something which since I have remembered, and therefore again I put you [Hopkins] to this trouble hoping that by the morrow at night I shall have answer from her of both together.' The flurrying notes were addictive. On Friday afternoon he bade Hopkins, 'thank N for the good news she sent me, deliver this enclosed and desire her to remember her promise'. He followed with another that night, 'deliver as soon as you can if, before it comes to you, she be not gone to a visit, in that case keep it until her return' (18th). If Jane did travel it was within Wight, and the 'good news' was evidently her promise to visit him. He replied again to one of hers on 20 August, a Saturday afternoon, warning Hopkins in mock annoyance that 'against [Jane] and your wife I have a quarrel for being here yesterday and not seeing me, but an easy satisfaction will content me, though some I must have. For news I refer you to N expecting an answer both from you and her, by tomorrow morning before Noon.' Jane's letter came at the same time as 'a voluminous despatch from London'. Life was taking on a new hue. That night, on a practical after-thought, he sent Jane another note by Hopkins, 'desiring N not to send her horseman [courier] until I send you my packet for London'.

Jane now corresponded out of cipher with Firebrace who acted as post-master clearing letters in London:

> Many thanks for your late convey of my letters, pray continue that favour in the despatch of these. I wonder the king's condescension to treat is not made public, since when nothing of moment here. The messenger is in such haste for my letters that I cannot enlarge … your civilities shall find a faithful remembrancer in your real friend, J.W.

A garrison officer wrote to Colonel Rich: 'the king told the Commissioners that if Parliament would but walk towards peace, he would run.' Jane obvi-ously failed to persuade Hammond to bend his rules. Charles cursed him roundly to Hopkins on 21 August, 'a pox on Hammond, the devil cannot out-go him neither in malice nor cunning, but believe before this comes to you, you will hear more of his praise [ironic] from N to whom when you deliver this enclosed, desire her to return an answer as soon as she may'. The following night, 22 August, he 'sent N some fresh news this day come from London, which she will shew you'. Jane replied with a tale of woe ('praise') on 23 August: N's sad story. Seriously I could not have believed that so much barbarity [discourtesy] could have been in anybody that pretended to be a gentleman, and therefore in charity I thought myself obliged to return her a consolatory letter herewith.' He needed no such excuse, but in a letter later that day he expanded, 'certainly all sort of barbarity is to be expected from Hammond and it is some little consolation that in spite of him I con-verse with those friends with whom he debars to speak with'. Hammond had shown similar 'incivility' in July at Mistress Hopkins' request for private access, but the pressure on him and within him was now mounting.[8]

The tempo of the king's letters quickened. On Thursday morning, 24 August, 'N had reason indeed to desire a speedy answer and I hope by this enclosed she hath it to her contentment, and it was reason she should have it, for hers to me gave me much'. Letters became oblique, perhaps sensitive, rather than obscure

– but still torrential. That afternoon he wrote again: 'Herewith I send to N that which I promised her by my letter this morning expecting an account of that other business which she hath put me in hope of.' Some misunderstanding filtered through on 25 August, and he forgave

> slight mistakings upon relations cannot make me chide my friends ... it being little or no shame (especially nowadays) *mendacium dicere* [to tell a lie] for it would too much hinder conversation strictly to be tied to tell nothing but truths: I mean as to reports. Wherefore I leave N to your chiding and desire a speedy answer from her to this enclosed and particularly to the Postscript.

The postscript is missing, but his justifying of deception, 'especially nowadays', spoke volumes on the eve of talks. Coyness and anticipation now replaced discretion and prudence, and even treaty considerations.

That afternoon he wrote another to Hopkins and Whorwood, 'my second to you this day ... I would not so much as seem lazy to my friends, and you know repetitions especially to some sort are very grateful. Tell N that notwithstanding her often writing, yet she is in my debt as to punctual answering.' Something from the London moderates made him observe to Hopkins on the 26th, 'I can well distinguish between gentlemen and merchants' humours, the shifting of the one shall not make me mistake the other ... tell N she shall have no more pardons without answering more punctually to my letters, beginning with this enclosed'. Jane however had two letters of his to answer for every one she wrote.

Suddenly, Governor Hammond relaxed. He had confided in his friend Colonel Rich that he had been 'impatient of my load and sought ease, but found none'. Free in principle since July to allow the king open access, he stuck to the letter until he had detailed instructions. In real life outside 'Avalon', as one news sheet called Carisbrooke, the Hamiltons were roundly defeated at Preston on 24 August and Colchester fell on the 27th without quarter given. The king's personal parole was essential to his temporary release, but many doubted its worth. On the 27th Hammond bluntly asked Speaker Lenthall to clarify the king's new freedom. Did it extend to 'horses and riding abroad'? Was Charles to be allowed 'letters or any [person] whatever to come to him'? He, Hammond, only had others' word for the extent of the king's liberty at Hampton Court which he was now ordered to restore, but with no idea himself of how it was: 'I was not there.' The day he wrote he accepted the king's parole giving 'absolute freedom accordingly', in front of Sir Peter Killgrew, a visiting commissioner. 'His majesty is now at liberty from his restraint.'[9] Two days later, 29 August, Charles sent another packet of letters to London by George Hopkins, and one to Jane, at the Hopkins house, asking her host, 'when you deliver [it] to N thank her for the visit she stole upon me yesternight [28th], for seriously I scarce believed my own eyes when I saw her'. What the Hopkins' made of their lodger's (or their monarch's) tryst is not recorded.

That the king 'embraced and nipped', and even 'swyved' Jane Whorwood, within twenty-four hours of Hammond's freeing him, seems clear. She too had written of her own need to 'satisfy desires'. He was a demanding king and used to his way. His expectation of loyal friendship was 'forsaking oneself' for him. 'Sweet', as in modern use of 'Dear', when addressing the Inland Revenue, was a convention (it lacked today's sugar coat): Clarendon and Berkeley used it to each other as friends, as did royal princes; 'Sweet Saviour' was used in prayer, but was still not the 'Sweet Heart' or 'Dear Heart' of Charles's letters to the queen; the 'eternally thine' he signed himself to her eclipsed the distant 'you' with which he addressed Jane Whorwood.[10] 'Caudle', on the other hand, between two Scots, was a homely version of the French *medecin*, which king and queen used of their sexual love. On 13 November Jane asked Hopkins to 'present my affectionate love ... to my dear friend, 391' (see Chapter 10).

Charles's enemies made his private life a public issue. He was accused of 'uxoriousness' when they failed to find evidence to compare him with his sexually nomadic father. His dependence on his wife, they scorned as unnatural, against patriarchal order. Anecdotes of royal immorality were spread to dull royal halos – *Mercurius Britannicus* called the queen 'our sovereign she-saint', the liberated recusant lady incarnate. With humbug innuendo, Lilly wrote: '[Charles] rarely frequented illicit beds ... [he was] cautious and secretive [and] prostituted his affections only to those of exquisite persons or parts, as the Queen well knew ... he rarely forgot [his marriage] ... when he did wander it was with much caution or secrecy.'[11] Before execution in 1649 Charles asked his daughter to tell the queen his thoughts had not strayed from her since they parted at Abingdon as she left Oxford in 1644: she remained what schoolmen would have called his 'fundamental option' and he carried her miniature concealed in his jewelled Garter George.

In the year Lilly wrote, Sir Edward Peyton spewed fifty years of venom about the morals of the royal family, even questioning their proxy wedding in 1625.[12] He accused the king of courting 'a very great lady, now alive' at Oxford, in the queen's absence in 1643, after sending the lady's husband abroad – an uncanny echo of the Whorwoods. John Milton, the icon-breaker, relished the 'whispers in court of the king's bad actions ... polluted with Arcadias and Romances'. As runt of the Stuart litter, Charles was always vulnerable to accusations of undue dependence on women; governess and nurses around the 'spindly small and stuttering' junior prince in Scotland had to make up for a long-absent mother gone south to be queen in 1603.

On Thursday evening, 31 August, the king planned to visit the Hopkins' openly at Newport, but only 'when Hammond send you word of it, for yet I have not told him'. The previous evening, Charles instructed Hopkins: 'tell N that I shall be willing to see her tomorrow [31st] her own way and so after dinner shall expect your key.' It was evening, Hopkins' key was involved and sentries were stood down. Hammond hovered in and around his lodging in the castle courtyard, but no longer theatened. 'I could wish that [he] would stay at home, but cannot hope it.' Jane saw the king formally at the Hopkins' house, and had open access to him at the castle where they met privately more than once. On Saturday 2 September he told Hopkins:

> The friend you sent me this day gave me a chiding and yet I will not complain, for there was more justice than malice in it. It was because I did not look kind enough on [your son George] on Thursday last at your house. I had so many things that day in my head, [I wonder not that] everyone [felt] that I looked doggedly on them.

Through Jane he sent an oral message back to Hopkins. 'I desired N to make a proposition to you in my name ... I pray your opinion of it. Remember N to send me back what I lent her this day.' The item loaned is unknown, but a day later he explained the 'proposition' as another escape plan, in spite of parole and the pending talks. 'What I proposed to you by N is yet but in embryo and well to be thought on before resolved ... this enclosed to N is my opinion concerning her journey and that is *quod dubitas ne feceris* [when in doubt, don't].'[13] Shortly afterwards she was approached on Charles's behalf to see William Lilly and others in London, for advice about the Treaty, Lord Saye and the political horizon beyond.

Charles drove – the royal coach was dusted down for the talks – through the late summer hedges to Newport on 5 September, in preparation for the last political negotiation of his life, and asked Hopkins 'to give N a short answer to the long wise discourse she sent me'. The lost 'discourse' might have been advice about Lord Saye, or the proposed escape, but from this point Charles preoccupied himself with the talks, a free monarch with all trappings conceded, holding court at a private house. He held formal audience at the Hopkins' house on 6 September, but Jane did not appear. A last 'enclosed' was conveyed to her by Hopkins after the visitors had gone home. 'I could not choose but give a chiding to N ... for not giving me a visit with the rest of the Ladies this night, to which at least I expect an answer.' She was already on her way to London. The king passed his following week at Newport, prior to the talks, enjoying his new-found freedom to ride around the island.

The king's and Parliament's commissioners arrived on Friday 15 September and Newport filled with high and low life from both sides. Tavern resentment inevitably grew between Royalists on safe conducts and Parliamentarians barking top dog. Once again, Court faces familiar to Jane from Charing and from the Oxford garrison appeared: Sir Thomas Gardiner from Cuddesdon with his legal team; George Kirke, her old neighbour from Charing, the king's longest serving servant and her father's oldest colleague; and even John Browne, her Medway escort. John Taylor, to be found wherever water flowed, came later to pay respects, 'to get some silver in this iron age'. It took him four hours to cross Southampton Water to Cowes, arriving at Newport by horse, 'embroidered all over with mire and mud'. His king was 'heroic and unconquered, expects a happy deliverance [and spends] twice a day on his knees in public prayer. [Despite] those buzzards of incredulity, he hath cured many.' The touch for the king's evil had been banned over and again by Parliament, but people still begged it. Taylor, who once described Hammond as 'coarse, rigid and barbarous' towards the king, found a changed man, relaxed and off duty, 'a gentleman of quality [with] the humbleness of dutiful service'.

Taylor's king nevertheless said one thing and planned another. The fulsome prayers of his own composing (*Common Prayer* was banned, although he would have known it by heart), which he led each day at the start of talks, may have irritated those who already considered him deceitful. He withdrew his parole in a mental reservation, and some development in Newport or in London, or fatigue from pretending, made him approach Hopkins on 7 October:

> where I shall take the boat? Spare not my walking in respect of security. Then how the die falls out? Or whether in case the wind do serve, it be necessary to look to the tides? What winds are fair? and what are contrary? Consider also if a pass from Hammond may not be useful. How soon all will be ready and what the impediments are which rest … By what I have heard, a few days will make that impossible which is now feasible [a reference to the autumn tides, the extra troops due on Wight and worsening rumours from London].

Next day, 8 October, he admitted to Hopkins he was stalling for time, meant none of his promises in the talks, and had run out of deceptions.

> Go on cheerfully with your preparations, for I cannot make good what I now put them in hope of, only I durst not dissemble in point of conscience, which they care so little for, that I hope they will not break with me for it … Haste the work I have set you upon … Lose no time. I am so careful to keep this business secret.

The following night (9th) he wrote yet again to Hopkins 'notwithstanding my too great concessions made, I know that unless I shall make yet others which will directly make me no king, I shall be at best a perpetual prisoner'. This was at the end of ten days discussion of church issues, closest to his heart. He refused to pretend to concede church reform, 'from which I cannot depart, no not in shew [pretence]', but

> the great concession I made this day was merely in order to my escape. Now they believe that I dare deny them nothing, they be so less careful of their guards. Let us despatch this business as soon as we can without expecting news from [Jane in] London. If I were once abroad and under sail I would willingly

hazard the three pinnaces [guard ships off shore]. I am lost if I do not escape, which I shall not be able to do if I stay for further demonstrations.

He kept the escape plans from Jane Whorwood, 'not out of mistrust, for I cannot be more confident of any, but to keep my rule of not putting more upon such a great secret ... than is of absolute necessity'. She was more use sounding out London than taking up a scarce billet in Newport. Francis Cressett, royal treasurer, gave her £300 in front of Under-Secretary Nicholas Oudart, evidently for her expenses.[14] Cressett was not named to the king's attendance until 2 September, and Oudart did not arrive on Wight until 30 September, therefore the money was paid either on her return from London in November or, more likely, in an unrecorded return to the island in the intervening weeks in early October. It was not paid from the £8,000 expenses voted to Cressett, but from his own purse.

Jane tested feeling in the capital and wrote at least once in early October to the king out of cipher: the letter is lost and she may have written it in Newport. Charles was too distracted and weary to respond immediately. Alderman Adams, released without trial in May, and Pindar and Crispe, with other merchants, were still key City players, but Charles was now more preoccupied with escaping, or the gesture of it. 'I pray you [Hopkins] to be quick and diligent in freeing of me. Tell N that I cannot answer that letter before tomorrow' (9 October), which suggests she had returned to Newport temporarily. 'The procuring of a Dutch *pinck* would make all sure' (10th). The prince of Orange, despite promises, failed to deliver a rescue force, and a week later the strain of continually pretending in conference told on Charles. 'I shall hold out as long as I possibly may, but it cannot be long. I cannot promise you a week, therefore lose no time' (16th). He was fraught. 'Excuse my impatience that I desire an account of where the business [of escaping] sticks. I shall have but a few days free to act my part' (17th). By then, he had composed an open letter to 'all my people' in which he contrasted conditions at Carisbrooke and Newport with those of Hampton Court. 'Since therefore none of the conditions are kept to me upon which I gave my word, I cannot truly be said to break it.' Hammond, he claimed, removed open sentries, but kept secret ones in Newport, so breaching the terms of the talks.[15] Meanwhile, Ashburnham on the mainland, with others, spent 'near a quarter of a year's attendance in the nights up on the seashore and the great part thereof in the winter season [September–November]'.

There was no party without Lilly. Jane's first stop when she left Newport for London early in September was an appointment with the astrologer, days after Colchester fell. It was a worrying time. Her brother-in-law, Captain William Whorwood, had been confined in Peterhouse prison along with Sir Joseph Wagstaffe for rebellion; James Maxwell was also being questioned with Lord Salisbury, Diana Cranborne's father-in-law, by the Parliamentary Committee for the Advance of Money, over their financial links with Lord Lanark, now a delinquent since his and his brother's defeat at Preston. Jane joined a growing anxious Royalist queue 'of ladies that creep by twilight ... [to dance] attendance on Lilly at the *Fleur de Lys*'. Lilly told the story years later to Anthony Wood and Elias Ashmole, but Sir Edward Walker, the king's secretary, whose loyalty Charles equated with Jane Whorwood's, dismissed it.[16] 'These things Anthony Wood had from William Lilly, who told him, and so he [Wood] afterwards found it among some of his notes, that the said Jane Whorwood came to [Lilly] again, upon the direction, as he thought, of William [Fiennes], Lord Saye.' Saye, a Parliament commissioner at Newport and a conservative or Royalist-inclined Independent, was ready to compromise with the Crown, along with Lord Salisbury and Lord Howard of Escrick. He had been accused in 1645 of secretly negotiating with Royalists in Oxford without reference to the Scots or to Parliament, and in March 1648 of visiting the king secretly on Wight. A friendship with Cromwell inflated Saye's belief in his own influence over the army.

Before the king left Hampton Court in November 1647, Saye was 'in continual motion' with the army at Putney, and from there kept the king informed. However, the more the Army mistrusted Charles, the weaker Saye's mediation became, whoever his contacts. At Newport, when the Army was spread thin mopping up Scots invaders and policing the last of the English rebels, Saye tried to steer the king. Newport was a negotiation between king and moderate politicians, both looking over their shoulders. Ultimately, Parliament legislated only with army approval. The king's dilemma was whether to sign immediately, go to London to make his peace on Parliament's terms, thereby pre-empting the army radicals (which made him 'no king'), or as Saye pressed him to do, to go through the charade of wringing from Parliament's commissioners every last concession (and they from him), while looking to a real and better compromise with the army which Saye would eventually deliver.[17] The king's favoured alternative – escape – went unspoken to all parties, and he played for time.

About September the Parliament sent their commissioners ... into the Isle of Wight, the Lord William Saye being one. The Lady [*sic*] Whorwood comes again unto me upon [His Majesty's direction] or by his consent to be directed, whether his Majesty should sign the propositions sent to him by the Parliament so soon as they were read. To which William Lilly consenting, and that it was his [the king's] only way so to do, which by her or her letters, were communicated to His Majesty. After perusal of my figure [astrological chart] I told her the Commissioners would be there such a day [15 September]. I elected a day and an hour [for the king] to receive the Commissioners and propositions, and as soon as the propositions were read, to sign them and make haste with all speed to come up with the Commissioners to London, the army being then far distant from London and the City enraged stoutly against them. [The king] promised he would do so.

Lord Saye, however, worked on him. If Lilly was right, Jane wrote or reported back in person to the king *before* 15 September.

> That night [15 September] the Commissioners came and old Saye and His Majesty had private conference till one in the morning. The king acquaints Saye with his intention [to sign], who clearly dissuaded him from signing the propositions, telling him they were not fit for him to sign, that he Saye had many friends in the House of Lords and some in the House of Commons; that he would procure more, and then they would frame more easy propositions.[18]

Lilly expressed regret. 'This flattery of this unfortunate lord occasioned His Majesty to waive the advice I and some others had given ... The Army, having notice hereof from one of the Commissioners [? Sir Henry Vane] who had an eye on old Saye, hastened to London.'[19]

Interrogated in the Tower in 1651 and in fear of torture, Thomas Coke, the Royalist agent who sat as a legal adviser at Newport, confirmed that

> Lord Saye was of all the Parliamentary Commissioners the most inward with the king and undertook most on his behalf with his interest in the Houses. The Duke of Richmond [a king's commissioner and gentleman of the bedchamber] and he were very intimate and by him Saye contrived to convey his intelligence to the king ... [Saye] was so confident of the success of the Treaty that he had bespoken himself to be Lord Treasurer and places likewise for his sons and kindred ... the king was often in conference how he should dispose offices to please them all. Mr Holles was intimate with the Earl of Lindsey [a king's commissioner] and by him conveyed opinions and proposals to the king.[20]

Coke had heard Oudart boast of 'good intelligence from Derby House ... but from whom he had never heard him speak'. Saye ranked as high a suspect as Howard, Salisbury or Cranborne – all, perhaps coincidentally, linked with Jane Whorwood. That Saye was a manipulator is undeniable, but his sway over the king was denied outright by Sir Edward Walker. 'If the Lord [Saye] had ever been privately with His Majesty or given him that counsel, I should have known it. How treacherous and backsliding the Lord Saye has been to the king and your party, you know.' Others, not just Charles, were pretending at Newport, and the negotiation was doomed from the outset by bad faith on all sides.

Jane Whorwood had performed almost her last service to the king and, like much of her previous labour, it ended in failure. The king played for time as he was still, ostensibly, bent on escaping. John Ashburnham, banned from Wight, stayed near Hastings, where

being at my own house [I] held intelligence with [the king] and returned commands from him to provide a barque at Hastings [near Sir Edward Ford] in
readiness to carry him to France and to send horses again to Netley and lay
others between there and my house. Within 20 days he asked us to discharge the
barque and horses.

It was the Medway failure repeated. At least in the reckless promising of
confetti promotions at Newport, John Browne of the Oxford *Accompt* and
the Medway mudflats 'had good opinion there with the late king and was
designed for Solicitor [General] or such other place of advantage'.

Notes

1. Hamilton Papers, Camden Society, NS 27 (1880), 224. The familiar address and
   tone are of social equals; the signature 'H' is a monogram, not a cipher, below an
   open letter; the writer has an overview of the conspirators and Hertford knew
   Jane from Oxford.
2. Sarah Poynting, 'Decyphering the King: Charles I's Letters to Jane Whorwood',
   Seventeenth Century, 21, 1, 2006, 128–40, an analysis of the surviving two enciphered letters from the king to Jane: British Library, Egerton Ms, 1788, 34 and
   37. 'Swyving' is obscene and obscure, but Andrew Marvell accused Charles II
   of 'swyving' (as Nero fiddled), while the Navy burned. Cordell Firebrace in
   1932 deciphered it as 'answering', *Honest Harry*, 291. Poynting notes modestly
   that Firebrace, for all his mistakes, did pioneer the deciphering of the various
   Carisbrooke correspondences. Whether the king intended to smother Jane with
   'kisses' or 'embraces' is now unclear, but to the recipient they were certainly
   'plain expressions'.
3. A William Williamson, merchant, was former treasurer of the Levant Company;
   his father had been a governor of the East India Company.
4. '*[G]et you alone into my chamber*' (author's italics) was suppressed by Cordell
   Firebrace (*Honest Harry*, 294), though he left the cipher version intact. Similarly,
   he suppressed '*we are made differently below the belt*' in reproducing the Dowcett
   correspondence (*Honest Harry*, 264; Bodleian Library, Rawlinson Ms B225,
   Letter 6). Firebrace accepted that there was a sexual liaison between Charles
   and Jane, but that a wartime brief encounter did not lessen the king's propriety.
   Sarah Poynting notes that Charles addressed Henrietta Maria with the familiar
   'thou', while Jane Whorwood was always 'you' in a relationship 'more obsession
   than romance'. She speaks of 'the intimacy of the shared plight or cause' and
   of 'terror sex', a momentary delusion of security amid wild instability. On the
   same emotional see-saw, the king's renewed optimism in August may explain
   revived libido. 'Carpe diem' and 'brief encounter' come to mind. Women, as
   Poynting reminds, rarely let him down: men did.

5. HMC 70 (1911), Pepys Mss, 223–4, 9 August, anonymous officer commanding a troop at Carisbrooke to Colonel Nathan Rich.

6. Ibid., 222–3, Hammond to Colonel Nathan Rich, 9 August.

7. Ibid.

8. 'Barbarity' did not denote atrocity; it was the opposite of civility, courtliness or courtesy, more like 'ungentlemanly behaviour'.

9. Henry Cary, *Memorials of the Civil War in England* (1842), II, 5–10, Hammond to Speaker Lenthall, 27 August 1648; HMC 8, 1907, pt 1, Section 1, App. 28, 217 (b), reporting the king's parole to Parliament.

10. Poynting, *op.cit.*, 138.

11. William Lilly, *Observations on the Life and Death of King Charles I* (1651), 185.

12. Sir Edward Peyton, *The Catastrophe of the House of Stuart* (1657, 1731 ed.), 27, 33, 69–73; John Milton, *Eikonoklastes* (1650), 2, 10, 74.

13. Pliny the Younger, *Letters*, I, 18, 5, with thanks to Professor Jasper Griffin and John Prest of Balliol College for locating and translating this precept of caution.

14. Firebrace, *op.cit.*, 207, but I cannot trace Francis Cressett's original petition of 1661, certified by Lord Newburgh. Cressett was given £1,000 in August 1647 to cover the expense of meetings with the Scots commissioners at Hampton Court, HLJ, IX, 532, 3 August 1647; Parliament voted £8,000 to him to cover expenses at Newport, HLJ, X, 5 and HCJ, VI, 29, 25 September 1648, of which £4,000 was raised from City merchants, HLJ, X, 584, 10 November 1648. See also Francis Peck, *Desiderata Curiosa*, IX, 51 and Lib X, 2, for lists of those approved to attend at Newport and for Nicholas Oudart's diary of his attendance at Newport from 30 September.

15. Bodleian Library, Ashmole Ms 800, Art XXXVI; John Ashburnham, *Narrative and Vindication* (1830), 126, 128.

16. Lilly's appointment notes for this period are missing. The text combines the Lilly and Wood versions. For the queues to consult Lilly, *Mercurius Elencticus*, 42, 6–13 September 1648; for William Whorwood and Sir Joseph Wagstaffe, CSP 1648–9, 261, 263, 268, September–November 1648, and TNA SP 16 DXVI, 116, 25 November 1648; CCC, III, 1596; for Maxwell's interrogation, see CCAM, II, 954 – Salisbury and Cranborne were close to Saye; Sir Edward Walker, *Historical Discourses* (1707), 287; *Letter to Lilly on his Confused Mix of Observations* (1652). 'Lily kept a sort of correspondence with the king by means of Mrs Whorwood': John Oldmixon, *History of England during the Reign of the House of Stuart* (1730), 354.

17. John Adamson, 'The English Nobility and the Proposed Settlement of 1647', *Historical Journal*, XXX, 3, 1987, 567–602, describes Ashburnham as a bridge between Saye and the king from July 1647; Valerie Pearl, 'London Puritans and Scotch Fifth Columnists', *Studies in London History*, eds Hollaender and Kellaway, 1969, 317–34; Valerie Pearl, 'The Royal Independents in the English Civil War', *RHS Transactions*, 5th ser., XVIII, 1968, 69–86; 'William Fiennes', *ODNB*, 2004, for Saye's rumoured visit to Wight in March 1648, and his lobbying the Army early in November.

18. Anthony Wood, 'Life of Wood' in *Life and Times of Anthony Wood*, I, xxix (ed. Clark, 1891).

19. Of the Parliamentarian commissioners at Newport, Sir Henry Vane was possibly the closest to Cromwell; at one stage John Lilburne paired the two as 'sons of Macchiavelli'. William Pierrepoint, Denzil Holles, Lord Wenman, and the Earls of Middlesex, Salisbury, Pembroke, and the Duke of Northumberland, were the others.

20. Thomas Coke's confessions, HMC XIII, Portland Mss, 1891, I, 593, April 1651; for Coke's place in Sir Thomas Gardiner's legal team, HCJ, V, 693–5, 31 August 1648.

10

November 1648–June 1651:
The End of Service

That Mistress Whorwood do pay £600, to such use as Parliament shall appoint, and that she stand committed [to prison] until she pay the same. Resolved that the said sum be paid to the Treasury for sick and maimed soldiers.
House of Commons motion, carried 25 June 1651

On Monday 13 November Jane sent her courier from London with an express warning to the king to escape from Newport. She had arrived in the capital only that morning on a flying visit from Wight. Since September she had been to and fro between Wight and London, seeing Lilly, the City and her inform-ants, and writing occasionally from London to the king. In mid-November, the Army was deliberating on the king's arrest, and William Levett, a royal house-hold servant, had returned from London on Saturday 11th, presumably with worrying news. Leaving Newport for Cowes and the ferry to Hill Head, Jane would cover the sixty-five miles to London via Alton and Guildford (and her parents' estate). John Taylor had returned that way only two weeks before. John Barwick, the ordained spy, who visited Newport during the talks, claimed to have covered the route and back in a day, 'without being tired'. Jane arrived around 10 a.m., rested briefly, then confirmed the rumours before writing post-haste to Hopkins and the king in one letter. The Hopkins' house was now the king's court in limbo, as talks were reaching stalemate. The king's parole still stood and the commissioners still sat at the treaty venue. Hopkins was to pass Jane's letter 'to my dear friend, 391 [the king], who I know will lend you his key' and to confirm 'by return, assurance of this convoy'. She had been given the cipher key on 7 August (see Chapter 9) before Newport, for just such an emergency. She also called herself 'Hellen'.

Her writing was as firm as were her instructions, and the seven by ten-inch sheet was folded securely into sixteen.[1]

> I shall give you no accompt of my travails ... the variety of accidents (and especially dangers) that may more become a Romance than [a] letter, but wearied with a bad journey I safely concluded it about 10 of the clock this morning, since when I have bestirred myself in some[thing] satisfactory concerning the present occurrents; and have discovered that an absolute comply[ance] is insisted upon ... from the king, and without it no acquiesce[nce] on the Parliament's part.

The army had prepared its *Remonstrance* to present to Parliament, a demand framed by Ireton for a political settlement, echoing Parliament's *Grand Remonstrance* of 1641 against royal misrule. It was news before it was publicised. After defeating the Scots and suppressing the 'tumults', the army was in no mood to meet Charles halfway. The *Remonstrance* demanded a representative Parliament, a monarchy subject to law and that Charles be tried, with his sons, for waging War on the people. Lilburne saw ambition behind it, calling Cromwell and Ireton 'dissembling, juggling knaves'. 'Hellen' did not wait for its presentation as the army had a clear intent, 'a notable design to which are agreed the army and Parliament, to which end an express is sent to Cromwell to dispose of his Majesty'. Two weeks after her warning, the king was indeed arrested. Ireton handed the *Remonstrance* to Parliament on 20 November and the army moved headquarters to Windsor.

'Many here wish,' Jane continued, 'for [the king's] friends in the City are numerous, that the king would thoroughly concede ... But I fear, if good be not intended him, and any such design be hansomely [carefully] laid, no condescending of his can abort it.' She mistook any agreement between the army and Parliament. Three weeks later, after her brother-in-law Cranborne, with others, had secured Parliament's vote for Newport to be accepted as basis for a settlement, Colonel Pride arrested or excluded about seventy moderate MPs (about as many absented themselves) to secure a majority vote for a royal trial: the moderate Long Parliament was reduced by force to its radical Rump. However, Jane's belief that the king was to be arrested was correct. Derby House warned Hammond that the king planned to flee on 16 or 17 November and make for Gosport. On 17 November Ireton took the initiative as 'junior consul' in the absence of Fairfax and Cromwell, ordering Hammond to 'secure the king from escaping, by returning him to Carisbrooke or such other way'. His promise of a confirming order from Fairfax was cosmetic since 'it has pleased God miraculously to dispose the Army to interpose in this Treaty'.

Jane had discussed escape with the king previously, and her letter to Hopkins was to 'advance [her] overtures'. She insisted Charles escape 'on Thursday or Friday next [16/17 November] out of some door and not from the top of the House' and involve only Hopkins' son, George, and William Levett. The coincidence of her proposed dates of escape with those known to Derby House was certainly due to leaked intelligence. She also had come to know Governor Hammond better at Newport. 'I have such grounds of the Governor's indisgust of [non-aversion to] His Majesty's escape, as shall never bring you [Hopkins] into any examination, or trouble.' She asked no risk of Hopkins, 'I would not be so peremptory as to cash your discretion'. A typical Whorwood courtly appeal rounded off her letter, part mannered flourish, part the words of a strong and warm personality.

> I shall not torment you with long compliments, but if by your return I receive reassurance of this convoy, I shall be ready in this or any kind of command to show how really I am, your most affectionate, Hellen ['H' heavily overwritten on 'N']. *Present my affectionate love to the party I named to you last.*

Hopkins used her 'N' cipher in corresponding with the king but Jane had second thoughts about using it, probably concerned she was being watched. 'Hellen' may have been a privately understood play on the Scots 'N'[ell] or 'Ellen', or even the heroine of Kirkconnell who protected a forbidden suitor with her life. Helen of Troy was a favourite target of the late rector of Carisbrooke, Alexander Ross, as an archetypal, ungodly, pre-Christian strumpet. Jane had spent that summer with the Hopkins' who would remember Ross and his strictures well.

The window for escape closed; Charles was drained and resigned. Ireton reminded Hammond that Parliament and the army were 'a higher and more public end' than the Crown which had commissioned him. Cromwell went one higher: 'did not God find you out there?', justifying the arrest of the king, the ending of talks and rule by 'God's people, now called the Saints, by providence, having arms'. However christened, it was a military coup. On 25 November the king took formal leave of the commissioners at Newport with the warning: 'In my fall and ruin you may see your own.' He had heard Jane's and Hopkins' pleas – by then she was back at Newport – and knew that Firebrace was still in town, with a waiting boat 'always ready'. On the mainland Ashburnham had horse relays ready from Netley to Hastings for the barque to the Continent.[2] Charles, however, no longer dreamed of 'Dutch *pincks*' in his exhaustion, and pleas to escape passed over his head. He submitted to what 'God shall be pleased to suffer men to do to me' and accordingly God's Saints arrested him. Hammond was relieved of his command and sent back to London; Ashburnham and Firebrace stood themselves down to await another opportunity.

It was an unambiguous end to thirty months ambiguity since Oxford fell. Charles was taken immediately from Newport to Yarmouth without returning to Carisbrooke, and from there by boat to Hurst on the mainland, a dismal shore fort from which a shingle causeway projected into the sea. They held him there for three weeks before escorting him to London for trial. Despite the odds, talk of escape persisted.

On 5 December Elizabeth Wheeler, the laundress, now 'Lady' since her husband's knighthood at Newport, took letters from Hurst to Firebrace and Oudart, and conveyed greetings to Jane Whorwood in London. Charles had nothing to say, but 'like poor men's gifts to great persons to gain by giving, for this one letter I hope to gain many ... I pray you commend me to Mistress Whorwood [and others] how they may write to me. Excuse me to them for having written to none of them at this time.' He wrote to Hopkins more urgently, signing himself 'I'. 'Commend me to N [Whorwood] ... to correspond with me speedily and often. I have all my ciphers wherefore you and N may write freely to me. Let me hear from both of you as soon as you can.' Jane wrote to him four days later [9th], but he had not received it by 17 December when he asked Firebrace, 'not to be behind hand with her in civility, deliver her this enclosed from me and put her in mind to answer it'. The king needed human contact more than escape plans. Lord Newburgh, twenty-seven, groom of the bedchamber at Newport, whose father had been a groom with James Maxwell, offered to abduct the king as he exercised along the causeway, but the king was transferred to Windsor without notice on 19 December. From Winchester, en route, Charles wrote to Oudart, 'I am of your mind concerning my escape and like well the instruments you name, but you at London must lay the design. I can only expect it.' Evidently something, if not quite a plan, was being tabled in the capital. He rested some hours at Bagshot Park, where the resourceful Newburghs – Kate d'Aubigny was the new Lady Newburgh – planned another escape bid, providing a fast horse for a dash through woods the king knew well from hunting. A wary escort colonel with 1,200 cavalrymen was too alert, and the selected horse fell lame. Just before the former feast of Christmas, they confined Charles at Windsor, the nation's chief castle and now army headquarters.

The Thames froze; the battlements were cold when Charles walked them with Colonel Wychcott, his last jailer and, as at Carisbrooke in 1647, Christmas festivity was banned, otherwise it would have been embarrassing. One unpaid soldier of the garrison tasked the king over his diet of £15 a day, addressing him as 'Stroker', a sneer at touching for the king's evil. The king, who had his 'usual bedchamber', at least dressed for the day, and others thought of him: Jane Whorwood and Kate Newburgh wrote on 25 December. He told Firebrace, his postmaster, that he had received 'two letters from N, to which this enclosed is an answer [and] for news I refer you to N to whom I have written all that I know'. (The letters from both sides are lost, probably among the papers burned by the king at St James's Palace on the eve of his execution.) Jane sent him another through Hopkins (by then in London) to which he returned 'this enclosed as an answer' on 30 December. It was their last known contact, although Lady Wheeler, 'this trusty messenger', took him a letter from the queen.[3]

More escape attempts were feared by the authorities who ordered Wychcott to dismiss suspect royal servants; four days later, worried about the 'easy possibility of escape', Parliament required of Cromwell 'speedy care of the close securing of the king's person and preventing of recourse to him'. Robert Monteith related that the Newburghs even conveyed a master key to the king affording him passage to the river and a waiting boat, but it was discovered on his person. Oaths not to assist an escape were then demanded of those around the king. Charles was taken down-river to Westminster on 19 January and lodged overnight in 'James' Palace' (saints, like kings, were forbidden their titles). From there the following day he was taken to Whitehall, then by river to Westminster, where he stayed variously at Cotton House, Whitehall and St James's in the eleven days remaining him.

The execution may have been as inevitable as winter. Fairfax was a sick man with a low profile, increasingly overshadowed by Cromwell who, finally exasperated with the king, had felt 'necessitated to consent' to Ireton's *Remonstrance*. One hostile observer noted that while the army had 'but one general [Fairfax], things were so much out of frame in the Commons House and the Army that there were many Commanders'.[4] No court could try a king, but an unprecedented 'High Court of Justice' with 135 commissioners was given a month's authority from 'Parliament and People' to do so. Even bad Old Testament kings were not tried (although they were murdered), and Cromwell reminded publicly that David had refrained from killing Saul. Lawyers like Ireton knew that the king would pose one question: 'By what authority do you judge me?' Question and answer would have to be public, or silenced by procedure. Hugh Peter, the appropriately rowdy artillery chaplain, leafed through Lilly's latest *Almanack* looking for divine confirmation through the stars, but Lilly later denied that his forecast of 'justice against offenders' for 1649 influenced the verdict.[5]

Optimism about liberating the king was still high, or so the inner circle claimed later. Parliament assessed the risk as high. John Ashburnham, who spent later years clearing his name of connivance with Cromwell, stated solemnly that escape was envisaged up to the eve of the king's execution:

> I laid the design of his escape from St James [Charles's last two nights were spent there] and had attempted it had he not been so close restrained that very day it was to be put into execution, of which there are three persons of honour yet living who were to have had dutiful shares in that action, but man proposeth and God disposeth.

It tallied with the king's note to Oudart from Winchester, 'you at London must lay the design'. One anti-Royalist news sheet reported the king's 'much pressing' to have use of the 'horn room', next to his bedroom, on Sunday 28 January, the last day he lay at Whitehall. 'Upon a strict search a trapdoor was found in the said room at which he intended to escape.'[6]

At Colonel Hacker's trial for regicide in 1660, Colonel Tomlinson, known and pardoned for his chivalry towards the king, testified: 'It was observed by some that there was too great an access of people admitted to the king.' A party of halberdiers was therefore added to the guard, under Hacker, to whom Tomlinson had to hand over the king at Sir Robert Cotton's house each evening of the abbreviated trial. The same halberdiers escorted Charles to Whitehall through St James's Park on execution day, Tomlinson by the king's side as his personal bodyguard. Any attempt to free Charles by Royalists, or to assassinate him by extremists was out of the question, but it was on everyone's mind. At the trial of the regicide Colonel Harvey, a witness vouched to have heard him reply when his Royalist merchant partner, Alderman Sleigh, asked about the king's escaping, 'he would do what lay in his power that he might not come to have sentence pass'. That was before sentence on 27 January.[7]

Sir Purbeck Temple's evidence was so highly embroidered it even had to be curbed by the judges of the regicides in 1660. At Henry Marten's trial he testified: 'When that horrid murder was being contrived in Town, there came persons of honour, servants to the late king, to my father [in-law]'s house, Sir Edward Partridge [Partheriche, MP for Sandwich], to engage me to join with them to attempt the king's escape.' He used Ashburnham's phrase, 'persons of honour', and may have been describing Ashburnham's circle, including Whorwood. Temple claimed to have eavesdropped from behind an arras on the Council of War the day before the trial 'to discover their counsels, that the king and those that were to attempt his escape might have notice'. As the council debated its response to the crucial question, 'By what authority?' the king landed at the river stairs below the chamber and councillors rushed to the window, Cromwell 'white as the wall'. Marten then proposed the court's authority be from 'The Commons in Parliament Assembled and All the Good People of England'.[8]

A persistent whisper of last-minute rescue plans suggests more than mere compensating for the memory of helplessness. 'A cabal of papists and anabaptists [including Lilly, Rushworth and Lord Baltimore] met at Wandesford's house in the City of London to discuss about the king's execution ... to set him on his throne again [if he took] on himself the guilt of all the bloodshed in the War.' Fairfax was said to have been pushed to rescue the king from St James's the night of 29 January, after spending a morning trying to delay the execution. He was reportedly promised 20,000 volunteers to back him. Henry Hammond, the favourite royal chaplain, and forty-seven 'ministers of the Gospel of the Provinces of London', in an ecumenical coalition of goodwill, had already approached the Army on 15 January, praying 'that God would modify your hearts towards the king … or else interpose his hand to rescue his royal person out of your power'. There was even talk of revenge, an informer 'troubled in conscience' supposedly warning Parliament that 'some have entered into an oath, taken the Secret and entered into an Engagement with their blood to murder the Commissioners that judged the king'.[9]

Charles was found guilty and Fairfax, sick and ashamed, did not attend court; army officers, 'act all things without Fairfax's privity'. In this aftershock of the Reformation, the ordained monarch (crowned, they said, with 'the superstitious trumpery of the time of Popery [with] oil poured down his neck and upon his skin') was judged by his subjects.[10] Both sides claimed divine authority: God's anointed was disposed of by God's elect; bishops had gone and kings could go too without leaving a vacuum. The king denied the right of the court to judge; the court denied the king his right of address; he kept his hat on and restricted his authority to the controlling of face and emotions. On the opening day of the trial, 20 January, Lady Anne Fairfax remonstrated from the gallery that Cromwell was a traitor and that her husband, still commander-in-chief, would take no part. 'Shoot the whores', Purbeck Temple heard Colonel Hacker order the guards, which Hacker explained at his own trial: 'If a lady will talk impertinently, it is no treason to bid her hold her tongue.' Undeterred, she spoke out another day. After sentence on Saturday 27 January, the king too was silenced and hurried away in a sedan chair along King Street, 'as they carry such as have the plague', noted Temple.

According to Sir Thomas Herbert (nearly forty years later) the king was in shock and was seriously insulted on his way back to Cotton House. After dark he was transferred to Whitehall Palace. He asked for a transcript of what had just happened and decreed that only his children be allowed to visit him. Sunday brought a welcome service of prayer with Bishop Juxon, and late in the afternoon Charles was transferred to his old home at St James's Palace for his last two nights, out of earshot of the scaffold-building. 'That evening,' remembered Herbert, 'the king took a ring from his finger which had an emerald set between two diamonds and delivered it to Mr Herbert and bade him, late as it was, to go with it presently from St James to a lady living then in Channel Row [*sic*] and give it to her without saying anything'.[11] Derby House was on Cannon Row, six doors away from Sir William Wheeler and his wife Elizabeth, the royal laundress and courier. Sir William, newly knighted at Newport, was one of the MPs purged by Colonel Pride on 5 December and may still have been smarting.

Herbert, a colonel himself, had the passwords from Colonel Tomlinson and was treated civilly by the sentries manning the park and King Street to Cannon Row. The night was bitter and few would have been around.

Being arrived at the lady's house he delivered her the ring [presumably in its box]. 'Sir,' said she, 'give me leave to show you the way into [my] the parlour', where she desired him to stay until she returned, which in a little time she did, and gave him a little cabinet which was closed with three seals, two of them being the king's arms ... praying him to deliver it to the same hand that [had] sent the ring, which was left with her.[12]

On the Monday morning after prayers with Bishop Juxon, 'His Majesty broke the seals open and shewed them what was contained in it'. There were diamonds and jewels, most part-broken Georges and Garters. 'You see,' said he, 'all the wealth now in my power to give my two children.' Even damaged they were valuable bullion and he wrote for Herbert a testimonial for his services. The king then distributed 'all his jewels except the George he wore' to his children when they visited him to bid farewell. Twice, on the orders of the court, William Dell with other chaplains visited the king, but their insensitive zeal was rejected: 'those who have prayed against me shall not in my Agony pray with me. They may pray for me if they please.' The king that day 'burnt all his papers and his several *clevises* to the private letters sent to him', probably Jane's later letters among them.

Thomas Herbert has never been trusted by historians for his memory, his accuracy or his truthfulness as a Parliamentarian recreating himself after the Restoration. He pleaded 'dizzy moments' when he copied out his *Memoir* for Sir William Dugdale in 1678, and 'notes I then took are lost or mislaid', but he did annotate that the lady on Cannon Row was 'the wife of Brome Whorwood, Esq, daughter to James Maxwell's wife by Rider, her former husband', an oblique description also used by Firebrace in 1675, as if to demean Jane by associating her with Brome. Herbert was close to Anthony Wood of Oxford and his letters, manuscript and conversation led the Oxford chronicler also to believe that Jane, whom he knew, was the lady involved. In 1681 Herbert would have heard from Wood, a staunch Tory, of the growing suspicions of treason against Brome. Wood, who lived until 1695, never revised his identification of the lady of Cannon Row, and Ashburnham believed 'his authority is not to be made light of'.[13]

In November 1681 Herbert wrote to Dugdale that he had 'nothing to add to the manuscript, save that it was *not* Mistress Jane Whorwood to whom I gave the ring His Majesty sent by me, as you find related in my short narrative of some occurrences. She was wife to a knight and if it be desired I will give you her name and shall satisfy you herein.' He identified Lady Wheeler, 'the king's lavander'. His afterthought is puzzling. He may not have wanted Jane linked amorously with a king who by 1681 was the martyr saint of the *Book of Common Prayer*, or the Whorwood surname hallowed at all, given her husband's Whig 'sedition' against Charles II. In March 1681 Brome had lost his seat in the Commons and was being closely watched, and both Wheelers were dead, unable to counter Herbert's claim. Accordingly, Dugdale scored out Herbert's earlier marginal note about Jane in the *Memoirs* manuscript with eleven quill strokes, to insert 'wife to Sir William Wheeler, the king's laundress'.

The Wheelers, however, owned *two* houses on fashionable Cannon Row: 'Rogers' house', their own home, and 'Weldon's house' next door, home to a tenant, Lady Anne Everard, widow, who lived there alone. She had been disinherited by her husband, Sir Anthony, in 1614, and may have been eccentric, with her musical box and her vision of heaven as 'my bed of feathers'. Her estranged daughter, who inherited all the family property, married William, Baron Maynard of Little Easton, Essex. Their son married Dorothy Banastre, only daughter of Sir Robert and Lady Margaret Banastre of Passenham. Lady Margaret, Jane's distant Holton cousin, was close to her son-in-law. It is possible that the Banastres, as well as the Wheelers, led Jane to Lady Everard's spare room.

Herbert was *equally* categoric about *both* Jane and Elizabeth being the lady of Cannon Row, although the king apparently did not name her. Both women had collaborated since the end of 1642 and Herbert knew the houses and people of his own elite parish of St Margaret's, to Parliament what St Martin-in-the-Fields was to the Crown. On 19 April 1648 the Commons had challenged Elizabeth Wheeler about an ivory cabinet delivered to her on the king's order. A committee examined 'what contents, papers or other matters of value have been delivered, by what authority, to whom and by whose hands, and to confer with Mistress Wheeler on this business; to take an inventory of what cabinets, furs or other matters of value are remaining and to take some good course for the possessing thereof and report to the House'. She was then attending at Carisbrooke. Her ivory cabinet of April 1648 cannot be identified with the jewels passed to Ashburnham and Jane at Oxford, nor can it, or the Ashburnham jewels, be identified with those in the 'little cabinet' held on Cannon Row, which must all have added to Herbert's confusion in 1681. The box was 'little', wooden, and with drawers, but whether veneered with ivory, metal or stumpwork was not stated. The royal children who received its contents would hardly have stuffed their pockets, and presumably took the box with them.

Jane Whorwood had been stranded at Oxford when the king fled in April 1646. Her stepfather was Garter Usher and long trusted by the king with jewels and unofficial revenue, but left Oxford in 1643, and Sir Edward Roe, Garter Chancellor, had died there in 1644. Jane had proved herself Maxwell's daughter in her gold running and intelligencing, and the Cannon Row jewels were largely Garter property. Jane, while close to the king at Carisbrooke in 1646 was just one of several valued couriers from Oxford, while Lady Wheeler was a royal official, trusted by Parliament and king alike, with passes to every successive royal residence, and openly scrutinised. Much points to her and not Jane's having the jewels in 1649, though conceivably with Jane lodging next door. Herbert's lady did disappear briefly (? next door) as soon as he arrived, to collect the cabinet. No servant or husband was present and the ring was instantly recognised. It would have been substantial, not a bauble, and any signal it sent would have been pre-arranged, by letter, at an intimate moment, or through emerald green being an agreed match for a certain complexion and hair. Elizabeth Wheeler could easily have brought the jewels away from Oxford in 1646 (if the Cannon Row jewels were indeed the Ashburnham jewels) in her soap barrels when she left on safe conduct after the surrender. If she did take them, however, it was odd that she did not return them to the king during the 'halcyon' autumn of 1647 at Hampton Court.

A tantalising new shred of evidence emerges. Cordell Firebrace concluded in 1932, 'no proof is possible, for the subsequent history of this ring has never been traced'. In 1684, after Brome died, an inventory was made of Holton House. Jane was in her last days, possibly ending them there with her daughter. The elderly William Pokins guarded the jewellery of the lady of the house in his role as butler. A jewel box within another box in his room held several rings which were listed in 1684, but not valued as they were not Brome's to bequeath; among them was 'a ring box with an emerald ring and two diamonds'. It may have been passed by Jane to her daughter, Diana Master, married since 1677 and lady of Holton, when Jane had fled the house in 1657, but between Lady Ursula's death in 1653 and Jane's flight, Jane was mistress of Holton and Pokins her butler. The ring may have been in his care since Jane first came home after imprisonment in 1651, the only jewel recorded there with its box. The king would have had cases for all his jewellery and changed rings several times a day. Had Lady Wheeler been the ring's recipient in 1649, it would have featured in her will: her husband, who predeceased her, proudly left 'the sword wherewith the late king of glorious memory knighted me' at Newport, and left Charles II a jewelled miniature. Jane Whorwood left no will.[14]

30 January 1649 was bitter, the Thames still frozen and the king wore two shirts on the scaffold lest he shiver. Years later, Fairfax shuddered at the memory: 'O let that day from time be blotted out.' The *esprit* of the Naseby wedding had long evaporated. Charles was guarded within his rooms, not just at the doors, and allowed no privacy when with his children, or when simply functioning. As he strode briskly, 'marching apace' to the scaffold across St James's Park, every step was watched. Sympathisers strode with him: Bishop Juxon, Thomas Herbert and Colonel Tomlinson; halberdiers under Colonel Hacker surrounded them and Whitehall was guarded against demonstration or rescue attempt by infantry companies marching to and fro between Charing and the Banqueting House. Herbert described the procession through St James's Park as 'uneventful'; other sources say the king's dog Rogue was taken away and that a joiner from the scaffold builders harassed the king. A tale has also persisted in modern times of how 'the faithful red haired figure of Jane Whorwood stepped forward to greet him as he left [St James's Palace] for Whitehall, thus inevitably reviving the rumours that

they had been lovers at Carisbrooke'. So many compared the king's journey to the block in Westminster with Christ's *Via Dolorosa* through Jerusalem: soldiers mocking and spitting, ducks flying from St James's Palace lake to darken the sky, and particularly women grieving. In the same vein as comparing heaven to 'God's Whitehall', the Garter Order to a 'royal priesthood' and St James's Park to 'Eden or Paradise', a Scots Veronica embracing and soothing the king would not have been out of place. However, no evidence for the tale exists.[15]

Hostile news sheets would have been as eager as Lilly or Milton to publish the episode for its innuendo. Royalty stories sold and were made to order, then as now. The anecdote may in fact have been some later neo-Royalist, even Victorian attempt to neutralise a scurrilous tale relayed by *The Moderate* in the week of the execution.

> A gentlewoman, big with child, some days before the king's execution, persuaded [the guard] she longed to kiss the king's hand, which after some denials of the officers who attended him, was at last (considering her condition, though contrary to instructions) admitted. After she had greedily kissed his hand His Majesty as eagerly saluted her lips, three or four times. This gentlewoman is reported by some that then knew her to be formerly the black [haired], handsome maid that waited on him at the Isle of Wight.[16]

The 'gentlewoman' might suggest Jane Whorwood, but she was well known, and only burnt cork and padding, liberally applied, could have made her 'dark and big with child'. The innuendo, however, was unmistakeable: the baby had been conceived on Wight in the summer of 1648, and king and gentlewoman were intimate enough to kiss 'eagerly' on the lips.

Sir Purbeck Temple claimed that after the execution, 'I received an importunate command from a lady of great honour (a servant of His Majesty's) that I would find out where the body of the Martyred king then was at Whitehall and give her an account. After *two or three score* [author's italics] entreaties I was denied', whereupon he gave a sentry half a crown and saw the open coffin under guard in the king's lodging in Whitehall. A modern author suggests Temple was acting for Jane Whorwood, who could certainly be 'importunate', yet might hesitate to 'command' a knight, unlike Kate Newburgh or Lucy Carlisle.[17] Others did escape when London was distracted by the execution. Sir Lewis Dyve dropped into the Thames through a privy sump up to his neck in sewage, leaving his enemies a vivid metaphor for the depths of the Hell they felt he deserved. James, Duke of Hamilton, the king's cousin and Lanark's brother, escaped from Windsor Castle. Accused as a traitor he expected no quarter at his trial and had nothing to lose. They caught him hammering at a door in Southwark in the early hours. Lord Capel, who had also escaped, was caught in Lambeth. Both were taken back and executed in March.

Once the king was dead, Jane Whorwood's service ended and she looked to herself. She may have been based at Cannon Row, or at the Charing house in its ghost parish where many homes had been confiscated. She may have rationed time between the children at Holton and her parents at Guildford Park. James Maxwell was sick and retired, his service ending with the king's flight from Hampton Court. Elizabeth Lanark had gone to Holyrood and Dirleton Castle in March 1648, but William had to flee to Holland early in 1649 to avoid arrest by his countrymen, or the English. Diana Cecil's husband sat safe at Derby House with his father Lord Salisbury until the committee was disbanded in March 1649; Diana spent time – and money she did not have – between Hatfield, London and the repairing of Cranborne House in Wiltshire. Lady Anne Bowyer had assisted her stepfather by taking his goods into her family's protection at Leighthorne in Sussex, but the Bowyers themselves remained under a sequestration order. Maxwell's goods there were confiscated, then returned.

Jane may have been involved in the release of her brother-in-law, William Whorwood, arrested in September 1648 with Sir Joseph Wagstaffe for insurrection, probably in the futile Surrey tumult. He was released late in November, on £500 bond and the surety of his lawyer brother Thomas, to report to Derby House at twenty days notice. Pindar died bankrupt in 1650 and Bendish remained in Turkey until 1662. On 6 April 1649 in the Scillies, where Prince Charles took refuge, Secretary Robert Long noted:

> Authority [is] given to Mistress Whorwood that the King of the Scots [Charles II] would not dispose of the place she moved him for during the space of six or seven weeks after this date, in which time I may receive any proposition the Company [? Levant or East India] shall make me concerning it, which I authorise you [Jane] to receive and convey.[18]

Long knew her from Oxford, as did Colonel Blagge, formerly groom of the bedchamber with her father, and ex-governor of Wallingford, who knew she was house-hunting before Long did. Charles, however, was so short of money that Thomas Coke alleged during interrogation he was planning to sell the Scilly Isles to the Dutch. He could offer Jane no more security than his late father had done.

The Parliamentarian cause was sealed, the monarchy abolished, and in March 1649 the House of Lords disappeared; three peers crossed into the Commons, one of them Lord Howard of Escrick. The Earl of Dirleton, without influence or immunity, was arrested by the sheriff of Middlesex on 4 April, and held liable for the late king's entire eight-year East India pepper debt.[19] The Company, still firmly Parliamentarian, pressed its suit, but Maxwell's lawyer argued that it was harsh to hold Maxwell alone of ten underwriters responsible for the total £60–70,000, nor was his health up to a trial. He needed to tend his estate in Scotland which was in some trouble and belonged to the Earl of Lanark, 'therefore he entered a course of physick [medicine] for his better performance of the journey and if he could not be permitted to go home, he would not live three months, especially as he is an aged and unwieldy man'. A similar exacting journey to Scotland had killed Jane's father in 1617. Maxwell was allowed house arrest with his lawyer to avoid the privations of King's Bench prison.

Two days later, his lawyer asserted that Maxwell had already loaned Parliament £12,000, and that his estate was mostly in Scotland where he was also still owed half of the £8,000 (sterling) he had loaned the Scots in 1645. Maxwell offered £5,000 cash to cover his share of the pepper debt, or £7,000 to include the balance owed him on the Scots loan. The Company rejected it, pressing for £100,000. In July the Court of King's Bench ruled that the East India Company might charge his 'body or his estate' if they could find any estate; in October the Company governor agreed to accept Maxwell's original limited liability of £4,000, which Eliab Harvey, the family's merchant friend, promptly deposited on bond. Singed fingers were a light injury; Guildford Park remained intact, Maxwell free and his City friends had come to his aid.

Maxwell travelled north, lodging variously at Dirleton Castle, his palatial home at Innerwick and his chambers at Holyrood. His son-in-law William's 'trouble' was that he was now Duke of Hamilton after his brother's execution in March and the Hamilton estate was forfeit. James had inherited their father's debts and added to them; by the 1630s he was at the heart of Whitehall life, master of horse, gentleman of the bedchamber and tenant of Wallingford House which he filled with artworks. His execution in 1649 affected his younger brother's mind, driving him to make a new will in favour of James's children, but detrimental to his own. Maxwell's help and advice was sorely needed. Jane may have drifted between London, Holton and Sandwell. Lady Ursula kept Holton going and Brome occupied himself with his servant mistress. Alban Eales, now 'minister' at Holton, tempered the impact of rapid change to some extent, conforming while condoning, like an old church papist. Perhaps the War mementoes in the great 'Red Trunk', the family's heirloom depository, were deposited by Jane, with the gilt George salt and the gilded plates. Someone certainly added 'a sealed gold ring in a leather comb case, and a little diamond ring; King Charles the First's picture enamelled; a gold whistle [and] in a leather spring purse, 3 Oxford [War mint gold] £3 pieces'. In the jewel box held by Mr Pokins the butler, along with the cased emerald and diamond ring, were 'two small silver medals', perhaps loyalty medals from the Wartime Oxford mint.[20]

Countess Dirleton had to defend Guildford Park against trespassers and legal intruders after her husband died at Holyrood in April 1650. He left her a 'life interest' in the park with reversion to his daughter Elizabeth, by then second duchess of Hamilton, his way of helping his daughter after her husband's bizarre will. Diana Cranborne, whose husband eventually fled abroad to escape their creditors, accused both her mother and sister of 'combination [conspiracy]', objecting to Elizabeth's eventual right to Guildford. Once Worcester was fought and lost in 1651, and William Hamilton killed in the field, Diana, the Parliamentarian Cecil, gave no quarter to her Royalist duchess sister. She denied their father ever left a will, and insisted that 'in Scotland in April [1650], he promised [legacies] to Diana and Elizabeth, wife of William Hamilton ['Duke' deleted by an irritated scribe] of Hamilton, but now Lady [Elizabeth] Hamilton is unable to take her moieties because of the delinquency of her late husband' in invading England. His property too was now forfeit. Significantly, her enemies accused Diana of living 'in a Scottish mist between light and darkness'.[21]

The countess explained that Guildford Park had been held for her in trust by merchant and banker friends of her husband, returnable on repayment of a deposit they had given Maxwell. In May 1649, she alleged, her husband, before leaving for Scotland, conveyed the park to John Prestwood and Henry Pratt, Royalist East India men, and Heneage Finch, lawyer. They became trustees for it through Robert Abbott, banker, just when Maxwell was contesting his pepper liability in court against the East India Company. His trustees gave him a paper transaction deposit of £2,500 which was recorded in Chancery and would be repaid in November 1649, ending their entrustment of the park. Prestwood insisted that the trustees had no financial interest, citing Maxwell's will requiring that the property be held by them for the countess. This was confirmed by Eliab Harvey, East India merchant, and Thomas Woodford, lawyer, whom Maxwell informed of this intention before his death. (Prestwood and Pratt also oversaw Harvey's will.) Prestwood denied that the Cranbornes had been defrauded. It was, in fact, Maxwell's last evasive financial scheme to hinder any attempt by the East India Company to distrain on Guildford Park. In law they could not 'find' his estate.

Diana Cranborne had card-table habits to feed and loved money. She and Viscount Charles accused Lady Dirleton, Sir John Scott of Scotsarvet, Eliab Harvey [*and* Jane Whorwood *interposed*], William Weston and Thomas Woodford of pretending that Maxwell had left Guildford to a trust for his wife and Elizabeth Hamilton. He had promised it, said the Cranbornes, to Heneage Finch, but Lady Dirleton and Elizabeth Hamilton 'refused to contribute to redeeming' a £2,500 *mortgage* put on it by Maxwell. The Cranbornes demanded that the two share in the redemption 'if the house really were in mortgage', and the countess, Finch [*and* Jane Whorwood *interposed*] should be subpoenaed to declare 'what means [they] have to pay towards it'. Jane's name was interposed by the same irritated republican who scored out and replaced '*Duke of* Hamilton' with '*William Hamilton*', and '*Duchess of* Hamilton' with '*Mrs Duke* Hamilton'! Eliab Harvey testified that Maxwell did offer the house as security for a loan from Finch and two others, but denied that he bequeathed it to them and confirmed that no repayment had ever been made. Finch testified that he knew nothing of any conveyance 'if any such were made', he never talked with the Duke of Hamilton and 'disclaims all claim on the estate'. Finally Abbott, banker to them all, admitted to hearing of a conveyance, but had no evidence of it.

In February 1651 the countess explained afresh how a dower of £2,500 was made upon her by Maxwell in May 1649, by bargaining the land to the trustees as a security worth £1,500 p.a; the money was never paid to him, but held in trust, based on £2,500 he had borrowed from Weston on another manor. He did convey Guildford to her for life. Her daughters, she accepted, were all entitled to the eventual reversion, but they were refusing to convey to her; the Cranbornes and Hamiltons actually held the deeds and had already entered upon the premises.

The four daughters were polarised when they most needed each other. Diana was greedy and profligate, Elizabeth increasingly tragic, bereft of her Hamilton men and with her children dying around her; Jane was a maverick with her own family problems, and only Anne Bowyer in Sussex stayed buoyant to help. At such moments hairlines become fissures. Jane, the eldest, remained closest to her mother, although in later years, Anne was appointed the countess's executrix when domestic violence affected Jane's health. The countess in her will expressed fear of her daughters' quarrelling; her husband had this in mind when he left everything to his wife, insisting that the girls' marriage settlements were proof enough of their mother's love. A marriage portion was a de facto bequest in advance. Jane received a small fortune in trust from her mother, who treated all the sisters well. However, they predeceased Jane and excluded her from their wills.

Dirleton Castle was not a family home and by the end of 1650 it was a ruin. Months before Maxwell's death it echoed to the cries of witches awaiting execution. Countess Elizabeth paid for a new aisle or side chapel in Dirleton kirk to house James's grave, but the intended marble monument from London never materialised. The very month Maxwell died, April 1650, Jane's sleight of hand in Sir Robert Banastre's case came back to haunt her. She had claimed 'public faith' for most of Banastre's Wartime debt, produced a witness, but deposited no receipts as evidence. When in May 1647 the Committee for the Advance of Money at Haberdashers Hall discharged Banastre, Martin Dallison, its clerk, was absent. On return he was suspicious, annotating the register as 'signed in my name, but not by my order'.

The courier to whom Sir Robert had refused £14 expenses was sick and in debt. Banastre, with 'cholerick', had referred him to Mistress

'Chairwoman' Whorwood, who had taken £40 expenses on top of £600. Jane had received another £600 from Alderman Adams on 17 May 1647 and the matter closed when Banastre died in 1649. However, Lord Howard of Escrick, chairing the committee, had long been suspected of corruption. Parliament swooped in 1650 (the day after Howard acquired Wallingford House, his dream property), and summonsed Alderman Adams to explain Banastre's discharge without documentary evidence. Adams admitted paying Jane £600 and produced her letter promising the discharge and to account for over £2,000 supposedly owed to Banastre on public faith. (Another person had offered to do the job for £100, but let Adams down.) He produced the signed discharge Jane had obtained, and denied any 'indirect practice by which Sir Robert and many others escaped payments'.[22]

Howard had undermined Dallison in 1647 by intercepting the clerk's summons to Jane and by paying off the courier. Between May 1650 and June 1651 Parliament investigated Howard on two specimen charges of corruption, one of which was the Banastre-Whorwood case. On oath Dallison admitted he was not present when Mistress Whorwood obtained Banastre's discharge,

> but there was a general rumour that my Lord Howard was instrumental in that business. [In fact,] Lord Howard was examined by this [Haberdashers Hall] Committee and not able to name particular persons. [Dallison] said that [when Jane was summonsed] it was perceived by this examinant and by other officers that [she] had applied herself to Lord Howard.

How she 'applied herself' was left unsaid.

Dallison was 'so scandalised by the carriage of business concerning Sir Robert Banastre, he was willing to lay down office and employment. Many persons who have been questioned about their 20th [proportional fine] have gotten off or have had quick presentation.' He had never seen Banastre's acquittances nor had they been entered in the account books, therefore they were either forged or hearsay. In the end, Banastre had paid £60 as his 'twentieth' liability, instead of £1,500. The committee thereby had lost 'many hundreds of pounds'. Then, using the rapier-courtesies the wealthy employed when fencing with his committee, Dallison damned Howard with late praise: 'by reasons of Lord Howard's constant attendance and presence at that Committee both at Haberdasher's Hall and at Westminster', they had *raised* hundreds of pounds too. The courier testified how Banastre had taunted the committee about Mistress Whorwood being its 'Chairwoman'.[23]

Haberdashers Hall reported to the Commons on 20 June 1651. Members voted that

Mistress Whorwood do pay £600 by her received for processing the order for Sir Robert Banastre's discharge to such use as Parliament shall appoint, and that she stand committed [to prison] until she pay the same. Resolved that the said sum be paid to the Treasury for sick and maimed soldiers.

The Commons Serjeant had the task of arresting her. That month Parliament pressed John Ashburnham for the names of his gold-smuggling accomplices at Oxford, after interrogating Thomas Coke, the Royalist agent. Jane Whorwood was suspected of more than the Banastre case, but the specimen charge exposed her, as it did Lord Howard, 'guilty of bribery'. She escaped lightly. Whatever brief time she spent in prison was not the ten years which Lord Howard was ordered to serve in the Tower; her £600 was a fraction of the £10,000 he was fined. He was also banned from all office, expelled from Parliament and forced to appear before the Commons on his knees. Characteristically, he obtained a medical certificate to avoid the Tower – and lived until 1678.

Twenty years later it was said in another court that

[Brome Whorwood] on his return from beyond the seas [November 1645] did fall out with [Jane] and beat and abused her and for five or six years did forsake her company ... and lived in and about London, far distant from her, and the said Jane being put in prison for her loyalty and service to our late sovereign King Charles [I], Brome Whorwood was desired and entreated for maintenance and refused ... and would not allow her anything.[24]

Returning home was now as necessary and pressing a course as royal service had been in 1643, and Jane had little option, yet her service was not quite forgotten, even in the later hidden years. Anthony Wood, gossip master of Oxford, 'remembered her well, as having often seen her in Oxford. She was red-haired as her son Brome was, and was the most loyal person to King Charles I in his miseries, as any woman in England.'[25]

Notes

1. Hopkins Correspondence, Royal Collection, Inventory No. 1080413, Letter 53, in Jane's handwriting. The salutation has been cut away. Also published inaccurately in Thomas Wagstaffe, *Vindication of King Charles The Martyr*, appendix (1711), see Chapter 8, n. 1. Jack Jones, *The Royal Prisoner* (1965), 122–3, adds that Jane had a pass to Wight on 21 November, but he cites no source. *Mercurius Britannicus*, 5, 13 May, Thomason 71: E.447 [9], and 7, 27 June 1648, Thomason, 71: E.449 [42], described an adventurous life as a 'mad romance', and the Carisbrooke period as 'Avalon ... that late fine romance,

improbable as King Arthur or the Knights of the Round Table': Jane presumably read the news sheets she delivered. Alexander Ross's book, *Mystagogus Poeticus* (1647) ran to six editions; a Scot, he resided at Carisbrooke 1642–5, athough appointed in 1634. A *Helen* Ryder baptised at St Martin-in-the-Fields, August 1612, buried there September 1617, was perhaps related to Jane. Little is known of the Hopkins' of Newport, although *pace* Jones, neither are ever referred to before or during the talks as 'Sir' or 'Lady'. The locations of their home (? *Sun* Inn, ? school house) and of the Newport talks (? town hall, ? grammar school) are also uncertain.

2. *Derby House Letters*, 37, Ireton to Hammond, 22 November, and 38, Cromwell to Hammond, 25 November; John Ashburnham, *Vindication* (1830), 128–9.

3. Bodleian Library, Calendar of the Clarendon State Papers, II, 1649–54, 1185, 27 May 1653; Willliam Sanderson, *Complete History of Life and Reign of King Charles* (1658), 118; HCJ, VI, 108, 2 and 5 January 1649; Cordell Firebrace, *op.cit.*, 181–3.

4. Sir Thomas Herbert to Sir William Dugdale, British Library, Add Mss 42118, 37.

5. William Lilly, *History of Life and Times* (1668, 1774 ed.), 94.

6. Firebrace, *op.cit.*, 184–9, for Parliament's concerns about security at Windsor; Ashburnham, *op.cit.*, 128–9, written before 1671; *The Moderate*, Issue 30, 30 January – 6 February 1649, 290, Thomason 84: E.541 [15].

7. Thomas Howell, *State Trials* (1816), V, 2 Charles II – 13 Charles II, 947–1365, particularly 1198. Bulstrode Whitelock and Thomas Widdrington, 'the country's two most prominent lawyers', absented themselves from the court preparations; Ruth Spalding, *The Improbable Puritan* (1975), 115.

8. Howell, *op.cit.*, 1150, 1200–1.

9. John Oldmixon, *History of England During the Reign of the House of Stuart* (1730), 368, who promptly backtracked, dismissing it as 'so very foolish' a rumour; William Fellowes, *Historical Sketches of Charles I, Cromwell, etc.* (1828), 200; a William Wandesford of Clerkenwell was fined for going to the king's garrison at Oxford, CCC, II, 1260; Hammond's *Humble Address* to Fairfax, 15 January, Wing H606; *Perfect Occurences*, 26 January – 2 February 1649, Thomason 82: E.527 [14].

10. CSP Venetian, XXVII, 1647–52, 246; Brian Fairfax, *Life of 2nd Duke of Buckingham; the Kingdom's Faithful Servant*, Thomason E.541(5), 1738; Clements Markham, *Life of General Lord Fairfax* (1870), 350–1; Sir Thomas Herbert, *Memoirs* (1678), 194; Clement Walker, *History of Independency*, II (1649), 52; Andrew Hopper, *Black Tom* (2007), 214; *Perfect Occurrences*, Issue 110, 826, 2–9 February 1649, Thomason 82: E.527 [17].

11. British Library, Harleian Ms 4705 (*Threnodia Carolina*), f. 47, from Herbert's *Memoirs* in manuscript, shared with Sir William Dugdale and Anthony Wood; Thomas Herbert, *Memoirs*, 122, 150, 176–8, published from the Herbert family manuscript. Also Herbert to Ashmole, Ashmole Ms 317, 31 March

1680, 'dizzy in the head for three months and tired'. Anthony Wood was close to Herbert, reproduced his *Memoirs* (1678), had many of his letters and papers, but never revised his view that Jane Whorwood was the lady of Cannon Row: 'Life of Wood' in *Life and Times of Anthony Wood*, I, xxix (ed. Clark, 1891), referring to his copy of Herbert's account, and his conversations and papers from Herbert, *Athenae Oxonienses*, IV, 15–42 (ed. Bliss, 1820). 'Anthony Wood's authority is not to be made light of': John Ashburnham, *Narrative* (1830), 179. 'Cannon' or 'Channel' Row (today's Canon Row), was a corruption of *Chanoins* (Canons of Westminster) Row, see Montague Coe and Philip Norman, *Survey of London XIII (St Margaret's Westminster, II)*, 239–40 (1930); *Survey of London, XIV (St Margaret's Westminster, III)*, 19, 75, 89 (1931). Cannon Row residents for the period can be named, usually in house order, from army rate lists, poor rate accounts, and relief of Irish Protestant rate lists in Westminster City Archive. The Wheelers lived there from the 1620s; in 1645 Sir Richard Weston of Guildford, Royalist, was their neighbour and Derby House was six doors away. Several houses remained empty, others were occupied by *prominenti* – Walter Frost, secretary to Derby House, Countess Manchester, Lady Katherine Thynne, mother of James Thynne, Black Rod at Oxford, Major George Withers, poet and Parliamentarian, Sir John Trevor MP and William Balfour ex-governor of the Tower. Lady Anne Everard tenanted 'Weldon's house' owned by the Wheelers next door. She described life as 'my little cottage' and death as 'when God shall call me to my feather bed': TNA PROB 11/339, 1672. The estranged wife and widow of Sir Anthony of Much Waltham, Essex, she was grandmother to William Maynard, who married Dorothy Banastre of Passenham. William Wheeler vouched for Everard before the Sequestration Committee in 1643. See also Frederick Sheppard, *Survey of London* (1957), 27, 96–9, on the Wheeler estate. Elizabeth Wheeler was a Cole from Kensington and a sister of Lord Harvey of Kidbroke.

12. Bodleian Library, Ashmole Mss 1141, 28v, and slightly differently worded version British Library, Harleian Mss 4705, f. 65; also Add Mss 42118. The story is also retold in Laurence Echard, *History of England*, II, 639 (1707–18). See Mary Keeler, *The Long Parliament* (1954), 387; Allen Fea, *Memorials* (1905).

13. Stephen Gardiner, *Great Civil War History*, III, 594n, had 'great misgivings' about Herbert and questioned his 'accuracy of detail'; Cordell Firebrace, *Honest Harry* (1932), 51, 191; Thomas Herbert, *Narrative*, British Library, Harleian Mss 4705 and Bodleian Library, Ashmole Ms 1141, Art. II, f. 8b; Norman Mackenzie, *Bulletin of the Institute of Historical Research*, 29 (1956), 32–86, Sir Thomas Herbert of Tintern, Parliamentarian Loyalist.

14. TNA PROB 5, 5275 (5), 114461, May 1684; Philippa Glanville and Tim Wilson kindly shared their thoughts on royal rings; William Pokins' will, 'butler to Madam Master', composed 1696, proved 1698, TNA PROB 11/445; Wheelers' wills, TNA PROB 11/330, 1669, and TNA PROB 11/334,

1670. The Holton ring was with four others, one of them a 'gold seal ring', and 'two small medals of silver' which may have been loyalty medals struck by Thomas Rawlins at Oxford.

15.   See Chapter 1, n.8; Alison Plowden, *Women All on Fire* (1998, 2004 edition), 181. The parallel of Charles's scaffold with Christ's cross dominated Royalist writing. Jeremy Taylor, bishop of Down, produced *The Martyrdom of King Charles, His Conformity Unto Christ* (June 1649), but without a Veronica figure: 'as women beholding Christ's pain wept, many women beholding their sovereign wept bitterly, the ducks fled their pond at St James for Whitehall fluttering about the scaffold, death at the very same hour of day as our Saviour, a barbarous soldier really did spit in his face, our saviour was apprehended at night, so was the king taken out of his bed on the Isle of Wight ...' *op.cit.*, 17–19, 27; see also John Loxley, *Royalism and Poetry in the Civil War* (1997), 169–91.

16.   *The Moderate*, 30, 30 January–5 February 1649, 289–90, Thomason 84: E.541 [4], describes the uneventful crossing of St James's Park in twenty-seven words.

17.   'Mrs Wherwell' [*sic*]: Geoffrey Robertson, *The Tyrannicide Brief* (2005), 204.

18.   HMC Report 70 (1911), Pepys Mss, 300, 29, and 304, 50 among letters confiscated by Parliament on Jersey. Company Court minutes offer no clue about this property.

19.   Ethel B. Sainsbury, *Calendar of the Court Minutes of the East India Company* (1912), III, 1644–9, 145, 317, 320–1, 323, 331, 360; also William Foster, EHR, XIX July 1904, 'Charles I and the East India Company', 456–63; John Nalson, *Collection*, I (1682), 391.

20.   TNA PROB 5, 5275 (6) 114461.

21.   TNA cases in Chancery, C10/32/98, C/10/15/39, C10/19/35 and C9/5/33; Surrey History Centre, Woking, 7230/1/1; James Balfour, *Historical Works*, IV (1824), 27; CCC, IV, 2427; Lady Bowyer's case for sequestration was settled in 1652, CCC, II, 833; HMC 9 Salisbury (Cecil) Mss, XXII, 1612–68 (1971), 430, 445, 453–4, 456–7, show the extent of Diana's borrowing – begging £300 from her son as his 'dying mother', while her horses and coach were at the same time being impounded by a creditor; also a valuation of Lady Dirleton's jewels, including a portrait of the Duke of Holstein set with table cut diamonds, a thirty-four-pearl necklace and a ruby, valued at £1,500 each, and a turquoise engraved with the Dirleton crest. For a harsh pamphlet attack on Diana, see Neville, *News from the Commonwealth of Women*, 5 (January 1650); Maxwell's will, Edinburgh Commissary Court, CC8/8/66, 116–20, composed 26 March 1650, codicils 24 April 1650 and probate 28 July 1652, over two years after his death.

22.   TNA SP 19: 162 for the Banastre case; CCC, III, 1671–3; HCJ, VI, 1650, 448, 30 July; 469, 18 September; 1651; 570, 6 May 1651; 582, 17 May; 590–1, 20 May; 591, 24 June.

23. HCJ,VI, 592, 25 June 1651.

24. Lambeth, Court of Arches, *Whorwood vs Whorwood*, Case 9938, 1672, E 5/29, 10 June 1673. The Court was abolished under the Commonwealth and Jane's original case was heard in Chancery.

25. Anthony Wood, *Life and Times of Anthony Wood*, I, 227 (ed. Clark, 1891).

11

1651–59:
Divorce from Bed and Board

Whore, Jade and Bitch, I had rather kiss Katherine Allen's arse than touch thee.
Brome to Jane Whorwood, 1656

If she were dying and a halfpenny would save her, I would not give a halfpenny.
Brome about Jane Whorwood, 1657

His marriage was inharmonious.
History of Parliament *about Brome*

On 8 May 1651, two days after Parliament began to scrutinise the allegations against Jane and Lord Howard, Countess Dirleton received £500 through her running account with Robert Abbott, the scrivener, from Colonel Sir John Owen, a zealous Royalist who in 1649 had been a prisoner at Windsor, reprieved from execution at the last moment. The money was withdrawn on 24 June, the day before Parliament sentenced Jane to prison pending payment of a £600 fine. The countess's money may have secured her release.[1] Jane was punished leniently in what, despite later propaganda, was a generally conciliatory climate. That summer as she returned to Holton, Charles II evaded Cromwell in Scotland and moved the fighting south of the border.

After the failed 'Engagement' invasion of 1648, William Hamilton had fled back to Scotland, reputedly cursing English Royalists for pressing him into a rash adventure. Enemies at home and the English threat from the south forced him to join Prince Charles at The Hague early in 1649, where Elizabeth may also have joined him. He became second Duke of Hamilton after the execution of his brother James in March. Returning to Scotland with the prince, who was then crowned Charles II of Scotland, Hamilton was excluded briefly from the king's council through the influence of the Covenanters, but after Cromwell's victory at Dunbar port in 1650 (and the destruction of the Maxwell family castle at Dirleton, twelve miles away), the tide swung in favour of the Crown and Hamilton returned to the new king's side. They led an invasion of England in July 1651, repeating the Engagement misadventure of 1648 and with just as little success.

The Scots army of 16,000 made it to Worcester in three weeks. West of Wheatley Bridge, Jane glimpsed her cause momentarily revived, a second Charles Stuart, her brother-in-law at his side, set to recapture symbolic Oxford en route to entering London. Pistols and powder had been smuggled (in barrels marked 'soap') to London, tumults were to be raised in the home counties, and the Isle of Wight was to rise.[2] Sadly, the Stuarts were still out of touch in both their kingdoms. Royalists were war-weary and the outside enemy was bringing an alien religion. To many English the Scots were rogues and this was their fourth incursion in ten years. Charles and Hamilton were welcomed by fewer than 2,000 English reinforcements. In his will, written at The Hague over a year before, Hamilton agonised at depressing and religious length over the grief for his older brother which consumed and drove him, and grief for his late king. The late king's son shared the grief, but sublimed it better.

Despite Cromwell's surgeon treating Hamilton for gangrene at Worcester, the Duke died. Had the size of the Scots force, the English response, and the state of the walls of Worcester and Oxford been different, Charles and Hamilton might have taken Oxford. Merchant friends of the Maxwells, Thomas Adams and Eliab Harvey, were ready to raise London; Christopher Lewknor and Sir Edward Ford were ready to raise Sussex. 'Mr Weston, a papist, and Mr Rogers in Surrey took measure of the affections there.' Young Oglander and Worsley were to lead an uprising on Wight. It was depressingly familiar. Parliament fortified the Oxford magazine in New College, manned Oxford castle and raised a small militia, but the city walls were in extremely poor condition and the Wartime earthworks, overrated even in their day, had already been levelled. Westminster countermanded before the end of August that Oxford be left an open city.

Local Royalists were ready to help Charles into Oxford. The parson-colonel Sir Peter Mewes borrowed £50 from the ex-Bishop of Rochester, and at the king's request 'disbursed it on arms and ammunition which he had lodged in and at a village near Oxford against a time for a surprise of that place'.[3] The village was not named, nor did it rise. Instead, the prisoners from Worcester were herded through Islip and past Holton to London for eventual transportation. Within weeks, General Henry Ireton fell sick on campaign in Ireland and died. After his lying-in-state and funeral, a monumental tomb was erected in the Henry VII Chapel of Westminster Abbey, with effigies of himself and Bridget. Cromwell lost his junior consul and increasingly ruled alone as Lord General, then as Lord Protector.

Jane spent most, if not all of her time at Holton. Brome junior matriculated at St Mary's Hall in 1651, a traditional route for the heir to an estate, and Holton finally reverted to Brome and Jane when Lady Ursula died at the end of 1653. For Brome, Holton's attraction was less its revenue and deer hunting, than Mary Katherine Allen. The affair made Jane's position impossible and Brome's obsession turned home life for the three under the same roof into a continual war which Jane could not win.

Kate, as Brome called her, born in 1626, was the oldest of eight children of a white baker in the parish of St Peter in the East, on Oxford High Street. Her father died in 1642 when she may already have gone into service at Holton Park. Two years later, Lady Whorwood, an obvious white bread customer, lodged next door in All Saints parish, presumably with her grandchildren.[4] Kate was used to looking after younger siblings as well as her mother's bakery. For dame and maid alike, fresh air and the park, despite the risk of flying pickets, were preferable to the typhus, fire and crime on overcrowded garrison streets. At Holton (the date Kate began there is uncertain), after Brome returned from France, Kate asserted herself. Her employment suited both sides – a strong-minded servant was an asset in hard times, even if hostile testimony had her arriving 'as a poor indigent servant with no clothes'. She was legitimately ambitious, a survivor, and rooted for a family who had each received a shilling from their father's will. In 1696 she left an annuity of £10 to her surviving brother, £10 each to cousins, nieces and nephews, and a wealth of jewels, plate, money and cattle.[5]

'From some few years after the marriage Brome Whorwood did take, entertain and keep in his house and ever since had, hath and now doth keep one Katherine Allen for many years past [evidence, 1659].' Kate was half Brome's age, she had his eye and he had her undivided attention. He would also always have the edge on her of status, which he never had on Jane. The relationship was certainly in place by 1651 when Jane returned to Holton; Brome's violence then increased towards his wife, when 'he did beat and abuse her, forsake her company, revile and misuse [her], calling her whore, jade and other opprobrious names', despite their dutiful litter and shared loss of children. Jane was better connected than Brome; her stepfather's wealth had boosted Whorwood finances; her Wartime record and titled parents, not to mention aristocratic sisters, must have made Brome feel inadequate. He had also fled the War. Her affair with Bendish (it had lost him £300) was by the double standard of the day a worse 'sin' than his affair with Kate, even despite his crossing the class divide. In addition, he accused Jane of petty theft. She was probably restless after the hyperactive 1640s, perhaps unhappy with rural domesticity, and was certainly so with their marriage.

The Allen affair lasted the rest of Brome's lifetime. Servants' eyes and ears around rooms built like connecting corridors made illicit (and possibly licit) liaisons difficult to conceal in a manor house. Thin wainscoting, wooden partitions, creaking beds, overcrowding, gaps in floor planks and ceilings, and large keyholes took away privacy. Locked doors aroused suspicion and ribaldry. Servants took sides, and along with neighbours and tenants could provide a loud 'courtroom chorus' of witnesses. Close attachments developed from intimate contact with 'employers trained to be culturally helpless', as when a maid brushed her master's hair. Some servants were confidantes, others spied, and a maid-companion sharing a bed with a wronged wife would be a good listener. Grooms and valets gossiped about a master's coach trips away with the governess. If his mistress had been a former servant her bubble of grandeur could be punctured by pantry revenge. Overheated lovers did the rest, throwing discretion and secrecy to the wind. While Jane neither condoned nor colluded in her husband's affair (which would have nullified any petition for separation), Brome knew her past, called her 'whore' when the bile rose, yet said nothing in court because he lacked the evidence. In the end, the alimony he owed once they parted became the central issue.[6]

The squire of Holton's undisputed adultery with Kate was the cause of his cruelty to Jane, but the cruelty was the basis of her case. Nevertheless, Kate and Brome's adultery was freely cited by her witnesses. 'Between them an unlawful conversation ... many times [they are] with each other at suspected times and places and have carnal knowledge with the body of each other ... they were merry together and cohabited together in other parishes in Oxfordshire', one being Headington where the Whorwoods had Mason's Farm. 'He and Katherine Allen took coach together to Wycombe and London and stayed in the same house together. They retire and be themselves alone for some hours at a time. [He] would keep Kate in spite of any man.' Disdainfully, Jane wrote her off as 'a loose incontinent person'.

Brome's violence was fuelled by drink, for which he was notorious. Allowing for legal clichés, medical and lay witnesses confirmed Jane's 'most cruel and barbarous' injuries. Lady Ursula in her last years knew what went on under her roof, but Jane still afforded her the one alibi by which Ursula could excuse her son's behaviour: 'had she been a better wife ...' The wedding of September 1634 had been inauspicious in every way.

In 1652 Brome barred Jane's Holton friends from the house. The village had its share of post-War malice and class resentment. The park warrener delated Elizabeth Towersey's gentleman husband in 1649 for having given the king a horse (in 1643), and others for lending money to Prince Rupert or for serving under Captain Gardiner (in 1644). When Elizabeth, forty-six, came across from Vent Farm to visit Jane, Brome threatened to 'sit upon her skirts for it' if she went near her. From London Countess Dirleton sent Ann Manwood, her gentlewoman retainer, to monitor Jane's ill-treatment. In front of Lady

Ursula, who had let Manwood into the house, Jane demanded of Brome free-dom in her own home; Brome retorted she could have it 'if Katherine Allen could live with him in the house, and he was abusive'. If mother-in-law was unsympathetic to Jane and afraid of her own son, the countess made up for it with constant support for 'my ill daughter'. Her mother's concern, bordering on interference, may have rattled the Whorwoods, but they could not snub a countess, not even a Scots one. Mother stood by an oldest daughter who had survived smallpox, a father's death, risked her life for the king, endured a dis-astrous marriage and, by 1657, lost three of her four children. Witnesses later agreed that 'Katherine Allen loathed and hated Jane Whorwood', and 'reviled and abused her, with the knowledge of Brome Whorwood, and told her she should go'.

She did go for the first time in 1653, 'flying for the safe good of her life, and seeking relief and alimony in Chancery … after Brome did furiously and barbarously misuse her by beating, striking, kicking and reviling of her, and confining her to a garret or chamber, locking her up and denying her clothes and meat'. Brome hinted that he hoped for her suicide, which would preclude alimony and leave her a posthumous outcast, but it was impossible brinkman-ship for an unbalanced man to provoke her towards suicide, while stopping short of murder. Her absence at least freed him to live with Katherine Allen, but they could not marry while Jane lived. Samuel Pepys faced a similar dilemma with his maid in 1668 and let her go. The debate over remarriage after divorce is a Christian perennial, but in 1653, while bigamy and 'living tally' were human and inevitable, English law still refused remarriage while a spouse lived; separa-tion or annulment, the Protestant reformers' legacy from Rome, remained the only options.[7]

Orthodox Anglicans held to indissolubility or separation, but radical 'puri-fiers [puritans]' like Milton wanted absolute divorce. Mary Milton left her husband in 1642 soon after marrying, but not for fear of her life. Distaste or incompatibility, if that *were* her reason for leaving him, could not excuse desertion. Once marriage was secularised in 1653, at least Chancery and not church courts ruled on separation and alimony. Jane needed a watertight case for alimony, and to be independent of Brome for her personal safety; to escape paying, Brome had to prove that he had done everything to save the marriage. He pleaded poverty, and her culpability, but stayed silent about his wealth, the violence and Kate Allen. In the end, he simply accused Jane of deserting him without cause, and of minor theft.

Jane approached the Court of Chancery for relief. Her mother's friendship with Heneage Finch, Bulstrode Whitelock and Thomas Widdrington may have helped, as it was still rare to fight a marital dispute in public. Judicial separation, *divortium* from bed and board, but not a dissolution of the mar-riage itself, was permitted for adultery or life-threatening cruelty. Brome was guilty of both, but Jane's plea was based on a level of cruelty, extreme, repeated and unjustified. Lesser cruelty, however regrettable, was regarded as corporal chastisement of a wife, permitted as if inflicted on a child or pet. Brome's male superiority was challenged enough by a feisty wife with character; drink did not help, and inadequacy haunted him. His later election to Parliament promised a new start in public life, and Kate Allen was a chance to recreate himself emotionally. Had Jane openly taken a lover, her adultery would have cost her the alimony; her Wartime liaison with Thomas Bendish and perhaps others weakened her case, but she did manage to steal some of the evidence.

Jane's flight, followed by Lady Ursula's death in December 1653, apparently shocked Brome. In January 1654 Uncle Field composed his will leaving £50 and a ring to Brome but nothing to Jane or her children. In August, the day after the old feast of the Assumption of Mary, Brome donated several illuminated manuscripts from grandfather George's study to the Bodleian, including an *Hours of the Virgin Mary* salvaged from the dissolution of Beverley Minster. Rebound and repentance fused.

> He did confess to [Jane] or some of her friends that he had used her ill and he promised to use all love and kindness towards her. She returned to him and did cohabit with him trusting in his promises at his house in Holton for about three years … he undertaking he would use her kindly.

Brome even let go of Kate 'for a while, but he took her back' after Alban Eales had sheltered her in the Rectory.[8] Brome junior and Diana, the surviving Whorwood children, were underage and never featured in court proceedings. Their father's authority over them was absolute, although once of age in 1660, Diana could spend time with Jane in London before marrying in 1677. Her brother's life took a different turn.

In the autumn of 1655, a year after the reconciliation, and as the violence resumed, Brome junior rounded off his education with a European tour. Edward Norreys, son of Sir Francis Norreys MP, of Weston-on-the-Green, accompanied him. Gentry imitated the 'gap year' of the aristocrats' tour, which in 1655 also allowed them to escape and defy the puritan culture at home. Oxford undergraduates, grumbled the Parliamentarian vice-chancellor, did this all the time in 'one long Christmas revelry, the whole year becoming as December'. It also allowed Brome junior to escape the marital war at Holton. Joseph Williamson of Queens College had the ill-paid, thankless task of mentoring and guarding the two twenty-year-olds. Five years later, Williamson would be propelled from obscurity to be under-secretary of state and later Secretary of State to Charles II. In 1655, however, he was not even M.A., and Brome made it abundantly clear who employed him. He sent him money for Brome junior in France, but never on time and never sufficient. The post delayed it, Brome claimed, or Williamson was prodigal. 'You will never find me lacking in my return for kindness' sounded supportive, but Brome junior had to beg money of Oxford dons, including the president of New College, on his father's bond. 'He has not had a farthing to maintain himself, but for me', lamented Williamson, increasingly creditor to *both* Bromes, father and prodigal son.[9]

Brome required Williamson to give his son a watch – 'tell him to use the time well' – but did not pay for it. A writing master and a French tutor had to be hired – 'I show myself a careful father for my son [and] my concern for Mr Norreys is very affectionate' – but the wealthy miser did not pay the fees. Young Brome also had expensive tastes: 'he has taken another house and has his own horses.' Brome junior and Norreys then moved, or rather rampaged with other young gentry, from Paris to Saumur, where English tutors lived off 'tour-ists' in an area less Catholic and less costly than Paris. At Blois they fell in with James Scudamore of Hertfordshire who had just 'diced his way across Europe'. Clashes with French and Scottish young men in town made up the peer education of Norreys and Whorwood as they came of age in a tutor's nightmare. Brome senior wanted his son to see Italy, particularly Rome – a nod to art rather than to recent recusant ancestors – but when plague broke out in Italy, he and Sir Francis decided it was no place for their sons and forbade the journey whether by the Alps or Genoa. Projecting his own discomfort in an Oxfordshire heat wave, Norreys urged salt on his son and warned against strong wine and excessive exercise. He failed to mention women.

Young Norreys fell in love with a lady of Saumur and gambled to impress her. 'We have lost our cloaks. Love cannot be cured by medicine. I have suffered much.' Heartache led to hallucination when he saw his mistress disguised as a pheasant in his garden at dawn on three successive mornings, apparently rebuking him for neglect. Sir Francis wanted him to see Paris, to make up for Rome, especially as German and Dutch were languages 'hardly worth learning'. By January 1657, Brome senior, in London with Kate Allen and 'very ill-conditioned', was 'railing against' tutor Williamson. He wanted his son to return home, but Norreys wanted Edward to make the most of France. Young Whorwood was disgracing himself in Saumur, implicated in a duel, being 'troublesome' to his tutor and landing in jail. Williamson stood bail, but the boy was too influenced by 'much bad company in large *pensions*'. Williamson ran so short of money that an Oxford friend advised: 'Play your cards so that you be not the loser by Mr Whorwood [junior]. Pay yourself in France for there are little hopes of anything here. His father is the same as he was.' Brome senior had other matters on his mind: Kate Allen was pregnant and Jane was about to leave for good.

Major William Whorwood, Brome's younger brother of Oxford garrison days, was involved in the Royalist Penruddock uprising of 1655. He was close to Penruddock, the Marquis of Hertford and Sir Joseph Wagstaffe, his old comrade of the 1648 'tumults'. At Oxford the vice-chancellor raised a militia and arrested suspects. He reported to Thurloe, the intelligence chief, 'there was much riding to and fro in the night in the villages near us, but as yet I cannot learn any certain place of their meeting, so I keep a continual guard. The people [gentry] of the county have met and are backward and cold.' Major Whorwood, Thurloe learned, had visited England in October 1655, after the rebellion collapsed and just as Brome junior was leaving on tour.[10] The officer had been suspect for years. In 1655 he knew his nephew was visiting France. From Paris, where exiles frittered their time waiting for Providence, 'he doth desire his nephew to send him directions how his father may convey letters to him, for he has not where to speak to him'. Whether he met young Brome is not recorded, but the implication was that Brome senior might be tempted into some conspiracy.

Sir Edward Norreys sent frequent affectionate letters to Edward, enclosing private motherly notes from Lady Norreys, but Brome wrote to his son and to Williamson only in his own name, never in Jane's. He demanded a letter a month from Williamson. 'If your power does not work [on Brome junior],' he threatened, 'I will try mine. I am sorry he is such a blockhead.' After twenty months Brome junior returned in June 1657, to what he called 'King Oliver's Dominion', in which Richard Cromwell was Chancellor of Oxford. The twenty-seven foreign coins, found with much English money hoarded at Holton in 1684, may have been his from the tour, if not his father's from Wartime exile. His mother had fled from Holton again, three months before, and Katherine Allen's figure was filling out. He would have heard the saga in gobbets from Edward Stampe, the steward, Alban Eales, the rector, sympathetic servants – and another version from his father.

Alban Eales had taken 'great distaste' at Brome's treatment of Jane after 1654. He refused 'to persuade Jane Whorwood to let Katherine Allen live with [Brome] in the house' and the rector was banned from the park. 'When he had sometime come … he has not been suffered to see, nor did dare to see Jane Whorwood for fear of her husband's anger.' Others were made equally unwelcome. 'Brome did forbid neighbours and tenants to converse or show respect to her or do any favour as some privately did … and he threatened if they did he would sit upon their skirts and turn them out of their livings.' On one occasion 'Brome caught Jane Whorwood going through the park to see Mr Eales' wife in labour, took her against a tree there and hit and kneed her and banged her head'. Two tenants, William Elliott, tailor, and Elizabeth Ball, gentlewoman and widow, who shared a house where Jane 'sometimes went for comfort, were charged not to give any entertainment to Jane Whorwood', Brome threatening 'to thrash Elliott's bones' if he disobeyed. Finally, he evicted both tenants. Katherine Allen, who had already amassed £600, 'gets an allowance, and is a wealthy woman'.

'Contrary to his undertakings [of 1654]', Brome called '[Jane] whore, jade, said she was old and her breath stinketh and did beat, kick, drag her and strike her, and did sometime batter and bruise and wound her, and did curse and threaten to kill her'. Accusations of poor personal hygiene and bad breath were commonplace against the Scots and no amount of Elias Ashmole's prescribed cinnamon, nutmeg, rosemary or sage would have resolved it; Queen Elizabeth's teeth were black and any portrait of Jane would have shown closed lips. Her stomach – IBS and ulcers had other names in the seventeenth century – would be affected by years of dangerous living and domestic fear. The four-year age difference between the couple, negligible to the modern mind, mattered enough then to warrant 'jade' (worn-out nag): 'whore' was too easy.

Whatever Jane may have felt about rural life, she fulfilled her role as lady of the manor. Holton Park had its herbary, or physick garden, from which she supplied medicines for tenants. Jane Ball, gentlewoman of Forest Hill, 'came to get ointment for her husband [George] from Jane Whorwood, which some time before had done some good for her husband, and Brome Whorwood would not permit her to speak to her', but suddenly relented. Jane showed Mistress Ball her bruised breasts, arms and thighs. A pattern was being repeated. 'Jane Ball came down from Jane Whorwood's chamber with the ointment for her husband's dropsy, scurvy and other ailments, and Brome Whorwood met her saying "A pox on Jane Whorwood, he wished she had all those diseases too".' His behaviour went from the uninhibited to the manic, fuelled by drink, aggravated by the stone, sexual frustration and by Kate at his ear.

> He would kiss Katherine Allen but not Jane Whorwood on his return to Holton House from a journey. 'I would rather kiss Katherine Allen's arse than touch thee' he told her. If Jane Whorwood would not let Katherine Allen live with him in the house, he would make her weary of life [and he] took the governance of his house from his wife and gave it to Katherine Allen and commanded his servants to be subject to her. She did govern and order the house and family as if mistress and governess.

In 1659 servants testified that master and governess had 'a base child [1657] whom they christened Thomas', and who was wet-nursed and fostered with Thomas and Audrey Juggins nearby in Forest Hill (a 'Thomas Juggins' was christened there in February 1660). Both had been retainers of Lady Ursula; Elizabeth Pangbourne, née Fish, also the daughter of old retainers, dry-nursed him at Forest Hill. 'It is public fame and knowledge in Holton and surrounding parishes that it is a base child of Brome Whorwood. Katherine Allen doth visit the child with clothing and necessities and Brome Whorwood pays for it.'[11] The boy eventually became Brome's heir when Jane's bloodline ended with her childless daughter, Diana. Tenant villagers gossiped. Brome's misdoings were paraded through the courts for three decades, adding to his growing isolation as an unpleasant and 'disloyal' Whig MP. Having a lawful wife, however bad her breath and however ill she may have been, was his greatest trial, and he was hers. Indignation about his affair lingered. In 1706, twenty-two years after Brome's death, Thomas Hearne called his and Kate's heir 'a fanatical bastard son of the old rogue Brome Whorwood by the famous strumpet Kate Allen'. It was the Tory damning the Whig. Three centuries later, village folktales still told of Brome and Kate.

Countess Dirleton was kept informed by Jane and the countess's own probing envoys like Ann Manwood. On hearing of yet more beatings '[Lady Dirleton] asked [Captain] John Maxwell, gentleman of St Martin-in-the-Fields [James Maxwell's nephew, twenty-six, later a royal equerry] to ride to Holton to see how matters stood. [Jane] had taken to her chamber and bed and the servants dared not come to her or serve her.' Brome admitted the disabled officer ('no use of his right hand')[12] to the house, agreed he had been violent and allowed Maxwell to speak to her – as long as he would try to persuade her to let Kate live with him. 'She can then command anything, otherwise Goddam me, I will break her heart.' More than once Brome drew his sword on Jane, and 'some of his friends reproved him for his violent carriage and furious raging manner'.

Another source of the countess's intelligence was Jane Sharpe, Jane Whorwood's maid and companion, aged about thirty, whom the countess had recruited. Sharpe remembered arriving at Holton from London with Jane sometime in 1656, where 'she found Katherine Allen in Mistress Whorwood's house as major governess of the house [with] command over the servants'. Sharpe was dismissed by Brome after a serious row between Jane and Kate Allen, which she reported back to the countess.

> About a fortnight after[wards] she was desired by Mistress Whorwood's mother to visit Mistress Whorwood to see whether she could be again entertained into her former service. Mr Whorwood bade her begone with all speed and thereupon she did depart out of the house followed by Mr Whorwood who cursed and swore bitterly and saw her to the gate.

Joan Miller, dairymaid, went out of the park one day with Jane's knowledge, and Katherine Allen rebuked her, 'angry she did not ask her permission'. That night Brome met Joan on the moat drawbridge and attacked her with his riding whip. Violence now threatened the servants, and at Easter 1656 Margery Bower confronted Brome with their concern for Jane 'whose arm seems to have been dislocated, consistent with her being dragged by it'. Joan Miller had actually defended Jane when Brome tried to break into her bedroom near where Joan was sleeping in the maid's antechamber at the stair head. Jane was confined to a top-storey tower chamber and denied meat or clothes. When Brome threatened to knock the dairymaid down the spiral stone stairs, she faced up to him insisting 'she was bound in service to do any duty for his wife, as for him', at which he threatened her with a kicking. Cooling off, he approached her later in the laundry asking her 'to inform on Jane Whorwood and he would be a good master to her'. She refused to take sides, saying Jane was 'sad and did no harm'.

On this and another occasion Brome beat Jane 'into a sad and unbearable condition [her] head and face swollen, ears and jaws bruised by his blows and impostumated [swollen] thereby ... she put herself into the hands of a University physician, John Lamphire'. Expelled from New College, Lamphire worked as a local doctor, his infectious good humour famous from garrison days. He may have been doctor to the Whorwoods as Uncle Field Whorwood left him a legacy in 1658. She 'continued under cure at the house of one Stampe or some other house in Oxford for some three weeks', in October 1656. Edward Stampe, a lawyer in Headington, was steward to the Whorwood estates stretching from Holton down to Eastbridge (Magdalen Bridge). His family had held that position since the Bromes employed them as fellow recusants in the 1590s, and his legal advice would have been as appreciated as his kindness. At the same time, Brome 'took Katherine Allen from Holton to Oxford and they carried themselves in a suspicious and scandalous manner, obsessed'.

The serious incident, which Jane Sharpe reported back to the countess in 1656 as the final straw, began with a quarrel between Kate Allen and Jane Whorwood in front of servants in a scullery, the 'Spinery', near the south-west bridge leading from the service wing to the parkland.

> Jane Whorwood charged Katherine Allen with too much familiarity with her husband and told her she had defiled her husband's bed, whereupon Katherine Allen grew very angry and passionate, and in a high and arrogant manner told her to go. Jane with bold expression and being much provoked struck the said Katherine who [ran] up the estate to Brome Whorwood who was in the House in hearing ... He came downstairs to the outside and found Katherine and Jane jostling together and parted them, commanding his wife to go to her Chamber, but she refusing he pulled and hauled her about the entry and passage [screen passage],[13] wherein he found them and told her he would send for his carter to carry her away up if she would not go. He told her he had never had a whore in his house till she, his wife, came. 'I found a whore and therefore found you', meaning his wife, and told the maids not to speak to her.

Jane Sharpe confirmed the 'pulling, hauling and violent thrusting of Jane, her breasts discoloured and black and blue, [Jane Whorwood] saying this was all to please Katherine Allen'. Mistress Whorwood cried out for help, Sharpe remembered, as did Mary Hurles another servant, 'fearing lest Brome Whorwood might do her some great mischief'. Sharpe also recalled lighting a fire 'in her mistress's chamber and airing her linen when Brome Whorwood came into the chamber and swore at her for making up the fire … she replied that it was her Lady's pleasure, whereto Brome told her that it was his pleasure *not* to have it so and [forbade] any fire in her Lady's chamber'. Jane herself testified that her husband had 'broken one part [side] of her head and swore he would break the other'. For some days she existed on 'milk and sometimes an egg'. When she crept downstairs for fresh air from her tower eyrie – in 1684 it had matching green and white bed curtains, valance and counterpane – and walked in the moated garden with her maid, Brome saw her and said: 'Damn you, a plague on you, I thought you had rotted in your nest. How you dissemble! You can walk!' Possibly producing the minuscule Parliamentarian coin from his pocket, he declared: 'If she were dying and a halfpenny would save her, I would not give a halfpenny.'

It was the last straw. Jane finally left home in the spring of 1657, but the *annus horribilis* had only just started. Brome junior was of age, had tested his independence (and his elders) abroad and probably missed his mother on return. With a university friend he visited Winchester College for the annual election of scholars to New College. Afterwards, on 5 September, 'minded to see the Isle of Wight', he hired a boat. 'The vessel, which was leaky, sunk by the time they were half way in their journey [and they] drowned in the seas between England and the Isle of Wight.' Brome may have been tracking his mother's better days, even making for Oglander relatives. A friend wrote to Joseph Williamson, still in France tutoring Edward Norreys and still owed money by the Whorwoods: 'young Mr Whorwood was miserably cast away crossing in a boat with a New College man into the Isle of Wight, about a fortnight since. The father takes it heavily and has sent to search for the body. He will surely see his debts paid.' The body, probably shrouded in animal skins as was customary after a drowning, was buried at Holton on 19 September, but Jane may have been too ill to attend. Sir Francis Norreys wrote to tutor Williamson in November with customary graciousness. 'Thank you for all you have done for Ned [Edward]. I see you will move to Paris with him [from Saumur]. I wish you would come to England with him. The news of [young] Mr Whorwood is sad.' At the former feast of Christmas, 1657, he told Williamson: 'Mr Whorwood will not so much as answer a letter, and his difficulties with his wife increase.' In February 1658 he wrote: 'Mr Whorwood owes me money but disregards his promise to pay.'[14]

Procedurally, Brome could not cross-examine the seventeen witnesses who spoke for Jane in April and May 1659, but they had to convince judges that her life had been in danger. Her extended *familia* of tenants, servants and friends, and Countess Dirleton, rallied. Alban Eales came down from Holton, and Edward Master, later Jane's son-in-law, came from New College with Doctor Lamphire. Countess Dirleton sent Captain Maxwell, Ann Manwood and Jane Sharpe. Holton estate produced William Elliott and Elizabeth Ball, and other local gentry were represented by the Towerseys. Joan Miller, the dairymaid, appeared after standing up to Brome. Mary Hurles, by 1658 employed at Millbank House, Westminster, and Robert Piggott of Eastcheap, who had heard Brome's ranting about Jane, also came into court. Catherine Harris and Margery Bower, who had confronted Brome after the violence of Easter 1656, appeared from below stairs. The witnesses were unanimous, and when some reappeared for her appeal case in 1673, their testimony remained consistent.

Consulting William Lilly was Jane's reflex. She visited the corner house on the Strand on 19 June, two days before she and Brome appeared in person for the judgement of Chancery in 1659, and almost two years after Brome junior died. Diana, now her sole remaining child, was almost of age and may have been in London with her; later she married Edward Master, one of her mother's witnesses. Lilly recorded more freely than he had in Wartime.

> Mrs Whorwood *de marito*. Her husband's [chart] signifies grief at heart, the stone, griping in the bowels, now in the gut, running gout and melancholy. [Despite being] late in recovery, but of no long continuance, yet he will provide well for his daughter, though some advise him otherwise. He will strive to hinder my lady's alimony, by some quirk or trick, but with difficulty, yet when least expected will provide the money. I *viz* the Judge takes my lady's part ... the good lady's own judgement upon the sick part is very well derived.[15]

The court demanded alimony payments from Brome of £300 a year, but for the next twenty-five years he employed every tactic to avoid paying.

At the Restoration, Brome questioned the Protectorate court's partiality and authority.

> After the defendant had paid vast sums of money for her and desiring her to come and live with him at home, she refused so to do but contrary wise petitioned the Lords Commissioners for the Great Seal for alimony and accordingly the defendant was summoned before them. He appeared at a pretended hearing of the cause privately in one of their own houses [and he] was ordered to pay £300 p.a. during their separation and [they] did set forth the defendant's consent thereunto, which he utterly denieth ... He applied to the Lords Commissioner for relief against their sudden and unjust proceedings, but could get none ... [Jane] procured a writ to be left at his house at Holton, for a sequestration [which] went out before he had notice of it ... She did offer the defendant several abuses in land, goods and much hurt, and bloodshed was likely to be shown.[16]

It was his version.

The Countess of Dirleton composed her will in August 1657, shortly after Jane fled Holton, possibly to recover at Guildford Park. Given Diana

Cecil's gambling and compulsive art collecting, Elizabeth Hamilton's twice-forfeited inheritance and Jane's being too ill to act as executrix, the mother's will was businesslike, 'so as after my decease no strife or controversy shall arise amongst my children or any others'. She lavished gifts on friends in Cromwell's circle, on Heneage Finch, a senior judge, on Thomas Widdrington, Speaker of the House and Fairfax's brother-in-law, and on Bulstrode Whitelock. Diana Cecil received £1,000 of which her husband, Charles, was to have nothing, and her significant debts to her mother were cancelled. Elizabeth dowager Duchess Hamilton and Lady Anne Bowyer received £1,700 each. William Weston and Thomas Woodford became trustees of the initial fund of £1,700 for 'my ill daughter Jane Whorwood, for purchase of a rent charge during her life and the benefit thereof towards her support during the life of her immoderate husband who shall have no benefit hereby'. Weston received a 'ring set with diamonds'. For good measure the countess added another £500 for each daughter, smaller legacies for the Hamilton and Cecil grandchildren and for Diana Whorwood; strangely, Brome junior was not mentioned in a will signed two weeks *before* he drowned. Lady Anne acted as executor, given Jane's incapacity. Most disturbing to her daughters, Lady Dirleton made no reference to her husband's famed jewel collection, but Jane at least began life alone with the promise of considerably more support than the silver halfpenny her husband would have denied her.[17]

Notes

1. Guildhall Mss, Abbott Account Book, 1645–52; Clayton Mss, 2931, f. 125, 140; also Ms 2643, f. 1, 99–100; Ms 2843, f. 43, 96, 99, 128, 151, 179, 219 for various customer accounts, Countess Dirleton, Brome, Captain William and Lady Ursula Whorwood (*not* Jane Whorwood, *pace* Linda Levy Peck, *Consuming Splendour* (2005), 257). Between 1651 and 1656 Countess Dirleton transacted much money with Eliab Harvey, East India merchant. For Abbott, see *ODNB* (2004) article, and will 1658, TNA PROB 11/277, 'my good friends, Alderman Langham, Eliab Harvey [senior], John Prestwood'. See Frank Melton, *Sir Robert Clayton and The Origins of English Deposit Banking, 1658–85* (1986), 101, 104. The Abbott/Clayton archive was dispersed by sale but much survives in the Guildhall, LSE, and Bodleian libraries, at Guildford Record Office and at the Surrey History Centre, Woking: Melton, *op.cit.*, 245–51.

2. Thomas Coke (an Ashburnham cousin) had revealed this in the Tower, see HMC, XIII, Portland Mss, 1891, I, 578, 584–5, 589, 'Confessions of Thomas Coke or Cooke', April 1651.

3. Ibid., 584: these confessions were seen as the end 'of all hopes of any rising in England for the king', and as 'a sad and fatal misfortune to the king', Nicholas

Papers, I, Camden Society NS 50, 1886, 224, 20 and 25 April 1651. The road between Islip and Holton is still known locally as 'the Worcester road'.

4. Margaret Toynbee and Peter Young, *Strangers in Oxford*, Appendices 1 and 2 (1973); St Peter's in the East register, transcript, Oxfordshire Archives, Kate's baptism 10 September 1626; her will, TNA PROB 11/439, 1696.

5. Lambeth Palace Archives, *Whorwood vs Whorwood*, Case 3398, 1672, evidence adduced from original testimony, 1659, E5/29, 3, 5; the Holton Inventory 1684 allows rooms to be identified, TNA PROB 5/5275, 114461; Thomas Hearne, *Reliquiae Hearnianae*, 54, entry for 1706 (1735, ed. J. Buchanan-Burn, 1966).

6. Lawrence Stone, *Family Sex and Marriage in England* (1977); *Road to Divorce in England 1530–1987* (1990), 169, 183–228.

7. Lambeth Palace Archives, *op.cit.*, E5/29, 3, 18; Ee 4/f 101 ff. Ann Manwood was the unmarried sister of Sir Thomas Manwood of Bromfield, Essex. She died in 1663 leaving to Lady Carnwath 'my watch which was my Lady Dirleton's', TNA PROB 11/312.

8. Ibid., E5/29, 5, 12, 22, 45; Jane's signed testimony, June 1673, Lambeth Palace Archives, *op.cit.*, Ee 4/f 101 ff; the Brome donations, Bodleian Library, *Catalogue of Western Manuscripts*, 3526.

9. John Owen, *Letters of John Owen*, 82, 83, 95 (ed. P. Toon, 1970); for Brome junior's Grand Tour, see TNA SP 1655–6, CXXVII, 22; CXXVIII, 12–13, 63, 75; 1656–7, CXXIX, 41, 77, 159; CXXX, 56, 140; CXXXI, 1–2; CLIII, 32, 40, 67, 87, 120; CLIV, 36, 71, 82; CLV, 123; 1657–8, CLVI, 191; CLVII, 156; CLVIII, 52; CLXXII–IX, including a notebook of expenses incurred by Norreys and Whorwood; Elsie Duncan-Jones, *Notes and Queries*, CC, 2, 1955, 60–1, 'Sir John Reresby's Quarrel at Saumur', 1656.

10. Nicholas Papers, III, 1655–6, Camden Society, NS 57, 1897, 157–63, where Wagstaffe and James Hyde also feature; John Thurloe, *State Papers*, IV, 1655–6, 87 (1742), anon to Thurloe, 26 October 1655. Major Whorwood was 'fair haired, curled, high nose, hollow eyes, wide mouth, ordinary stature': Thurloe *op.cit.*, VII, 253, coded letter from Brussels, 20 July 1658; Bodleian Library, *Calendar of Clarendon State Papers*, 4, 1657–60, 227, Hyde to Broderick (Hancock), 19 June 1659, 'Will Horwoode, an officer and of good interests in Oxfordshire will, if put in command of the county troop, discharge it well'; Anthony Wood, *Life and Times of Anthony Wood*, II, 519 (ed. Clark, 1891), 'Brome a most ill-natured man'.

11. Holton Church Register, Oxfordshire Archives, Elizabeth Pangbourne, buried April 1694, née Fish, married John Pangbourne 1637, and had daughter Elizabeth in 1638, who witnessed Kate Allen's will in 1695, TNA PROB 11/439.

12. James Magnus, *Account of Thos Scot's arrest by Captain John Maxwell* (1660).

13. TNA PROB 5/5275 (12), 114461, Holton House Inventory: a Spanish table furnished the screen passage leading from the front door to the rear courtyard and separating the great hall from the kitchen wing. Its black and white marble

tiled floor may have been salvaged in 1804 and re-laid in an obscure part of the regency Holton House at Wheatley Park School, tentatively identified there by Nigel Philips in 2007.

14. Anthony Wood, *Life and Times of Anthony Wood*, I, 226–7, September 1657 (ed. Clark, 1891), notes at length Jane Whorwood, who 'was red haired as her son Brome was'; Clare Gittins, *Death, Burial and Interment in Early Modern England* (1984), 48–50, 103–33. SP 1657–8, CLVI, 91, 17 September 1657; SP 1657–8, CLVIII, 52, 17 December 1657; CLXXIX, 83, 24 February 1658; Holton Church Register, OCC Archive.

15. Bodleian Library, Ashmole Ms 436, 106, 19 June, no year, but judgement for her separation was given on 21 June 1659.

16. Clayton Mss, LSE Archive, Box 6, WI–WE 22/4/6, Folder (1659).

17. Countess Dirleton's will: TNA PROB 11/300, composed August 1657, proved 1659.

12

1660–84:
'Poor Mistress Whorwood'

I am likely to perish if Your Majesty's bowels do not turn towards me, so miserable is my present condition.
Jane Whorwood's third and last petition to Charles II, 1681

King Charles II returned to England in May 1660. The calendar was recalibrated from 1649, as if nothing had happened, but simulated amnesia was not a Restoration. The absolute authority of the king was not restored, and the Stuarts had to sit the lesson again in 1688. They had lost a war about consensus, consulting and conscience, and it diminished them. The Crown commanded the army on parade, and the navy on fine medallions, but Parliament sanctioned and financed. Compulsory church attendance was reintroduced, but was harder to enforce than a sacrament test limited to public office. Deposed bishops, like the abbots of 1540, had chosen quiet lives and lost credibility, while non-conformers had tasted freedom. The 2,000 'ministers' expelled, significantly on St Bartholomew's Day 1662, were scapegoats. The spell of the divine right of kings and bishops had been broken.

Revenge was savage, but brief. Charles issued an amnesty in April 1660, ordering severe punishment only of those 'immediately guilty' of his father's death. Twenty-nine defendants, including twenty-four regicides, were tried in the autumn: six were hanged, castrated and disembowelled by the Maxwell house on the site of Charing Cross. One was Thomas Scot, arrested in Liège by Jane's cousin, Captain Maxwell. The very setting sent two signals: an end to the religious fundamentalism which had felled the Cross in 1647, and retribution for the king's murder. The scaffold faced the Banqueting House 300 paces away.

John Milton, who had justified king-killing, was imprisoned briefly and his incriminating books burned; Judge Thomas Hammond and General Henry Ireton had died in 1651, Cromwell in 1658. On no count did Bridget Fleetwood (*olim* Ireton) deserve the simulated public execution of Henry's and her father's corpses, still less the exhuming of her sister, grandmother and one of her own babies. The tomb-monument in Westminster Abbey with her and Henry's effigies was also destroyed. Fairfax was left alone as he had opposed the execution, Bulstrode Whitelock had defended Charles I in the Commons, and William Lilly skated thin ice with accustomed professional verve. A year after his restoration, Charles II confessed himself 'weary of hangings ... but I cannot pardon regicides', so he transported them. Augustine Garland, elected MP for Queenborough when Jane anchored there in 1648, died in a penal colony.

In December Parliament paid back 'debts charged by this Parliament and yet unsatisfied', including £139 to 'Jane Harwood [*sic*]' and £310 to Sir Thomas Adams, but with no further detail. They were not rewarded for service. Jane Lane's £1,000 jewel and pension for rescuing Charles II was self-explanatory. John Maxwell was given £50 for arresting Thomas Scot; 'heroic' Silius Titus received £3,000; and Henry Firebrace received a court appointment for his serving in 'his late Majesty to [his] greatest hazard and expense'. Jane, their indispensable colleague, was completely eclipsed. Dorothy Seymour had two-thirds of her loan to Pindar repaid. The Customs Farm was sold to the surviving farmers, but their huge losses were only partly recouped. Their claim, including interest, simply could not be met, yet without hope of some repayment, confidence in royal tax contracts would plunge. Half the pepper debt of £63,000 was repaid to the East India Company, but without interest. Paul Pindar's executor was still seeking compensation in 1680, Jane his key witness. Pindar's many creditors became just more casualties of the War. The army new-modelled itself again: Major William Whorwood, ex-Oxford garrison, joined New Model Army veterans of Naseby in a regiment with a pardoned regicide as a senior officer. At Holton, Alban Eales became 'Rector' again, led services from the *Book of Common Prayer*, registered christenings not births, and solemnised marriages. In 1665 he was commended by All Souls College to Aldington rectory in Kent as one of the six preacher canons of Canterbury Cathedral, where he died in 1670.[1]

Jane and Brome separated formally in June 1659. He withheld most of the alimony and she fought him, not so 'ill' that she could not employ Parliament, the king and the Sheriff of Oxford for her cause. Her mother, the countess, died in August 1659, just after the separation decree, leaving Jane's trust fund of £2,200 in the hands of her lawyers and with the oversight of her 'noble friends' Whitelock and Widdrington, treasury commissioners. Her lawyer, Thomas Woodford, and Heneage Finch (to be Solicitor General and ennobled a year later at the Restoration), were to 'prevent all suits and controversies, which I by

experience have found troublesome, tedious and wasteful'. Elizabeth Maxwell
Dirleton's assets, however, fell short of her generosity.

Lilly's stars had warned that Brome would withhold the alimony, and when
Jane acted to protect herself Brome called it theft. The £300 bond which she
and Sir Thomas Bendish had agreed with him in 1647, with 'several other
deeds settled by [me] upon my wife I did produce to Thomas Woodford to be
kept [but] Woodford has lately gotten into his hands divers other deeds and
evidences concerning [me and my] estate which ought to be delivered back
to me [which is refused] despite being asked in a friendly manner'.[2] Woodford
retorted that Brome had refused to pay his bills.

Brome accused Jane of embezzlement. In February 1659, when he was still
liable for her debts,

> Jane Whorwood, having taken some causeless distaste against me, withdrawing
> from my company and plentiful material comfort and contentment, repair-
> ing to the City of London and there obscuring herself … became exposed to
> ill-minded people there who knowing me to be a man of considerable estate
> intended to make a prey of me for the pretended necessary support of Jane
> Whorwood.

He accused Robert Walton, merchant tailor, of 'insinuating himself into the
acquaintance of her and pretending great respect and kindness to her and
much forwarding to supply her pretended wants'. Walton, he claimed, sold her
a 'quantity of woollen cloth and drapery wards, ill made and ill woven [which
had] long lain on his hands in shop and warehouse'. Jane charged it *all* to him,
'great quantities of the cloth at excessive rate, to the value of £3–400, for her
private use or for the pretended clothing of her'. The two defrauded him, 'the
cloth was never seen or made use of by [me, Brome Whorwood] and was not
worth above 100 marks [£66] at most'. Jane then sold it back, he claimed, to
Walton for a base price, the difference of £367 being claimed by Walton from
Brome.[3] It was a familiar Ryder-Maxwell scam.

In April 1661 Brome was elected to the 'Pension' or 'Cavalier' Parliament
as MP for Oxford with Richard Croke, recorder of Oxford and Unton
Croke's elder son. Whorwood, the critical Royalist, and Croke, a former
Commonwealth MP, closed a family feud dating back to 1626 when the
Whorwoods accused the Crokes of election corruption. Both represented
land and money in a Parliament which sat until 1679. The Whorwoods had
influence in Oxford city, where cousin Robert was city solicitor, Brome
and his brothers freemen, and Uncle Field a major creditor of the council.[4]
The Restoration honeymoon did not last, and the king's critics, the Country
Party, or 'Whigs' (Scots 'bandits' – once a nickname for Presbyterians), made
themselves felt. They were a loose patriotic, Protestant and conservative group.
Their opponents, the Crown absolutists, or 'Tories' (Irish 'bandits'), were also

patriotic, Protestant and conservative. Brome sat with many who had worked with Jane in her heyday – Ashburnham, Firebrace, Titus, William Wheeler and young William Oglander.

In committee Brome debated regicides' estates, the Great Fire and the rebuilding of London. Commons wrangled with Crown over the succession of the Catholic Prince James, Duke of York, as anti-Catholic feeling fermented. The Dutch fleet sailed openly into the Medway like Drake entering Cadiz. The king needed money and the Navy pay committee, including Whorwood, ordered Pepys to the Bar of the Commons to explain the shortcomings of the fleet. The king's right to bypass Parliament by proroguing or dissolving, and issues of religious tolerance (for Nonconformists, for Catholics too, or for neither), remained unresolved. A gulf opened between Charles II and a sometimes distinctly unloyal Whig 'opposition'.

Jane's sister Elizabeth, dowager second Duchess of Hamilton, inherited Guildford Park on the death of their mother, but died a month later in 1659. Thomas Delmahoy, her second husband, succeeded to her property. Her four daughters had lost their inheritance when their father bequeathed to his executed brother's children; they lost again when their father's property was forfeit after Worcester, and now lost a third time when Delmahoy inherited from their mother. Long before that, in 1638, the £20,000 settled by James Maxwell on Elizabeth's marriage to Hamilton had gone to pay old Hamilton debts, and not to the couple. It was therefore still owed to the widowed duchess or, after her, to her daughters. Maxwell's legendary jewels had also vanished. An *ex gratia* payment by Parliament of £400 a year to the disinherited Hamiltons did not go far. In 1656 the children challenged their mother's and Delmahoy's monopoly over Guildford Park and petitioned Parliament to be allowed to compound for their sequestrated Scots estates. Twenty-seven witnesses in London and Edinburgh answered a schedule of forty-five questions, among them old Sir John Scot of Scotstarvet, Ann Manwood, Captain John Maxwell and Thomas Woodford. The plea was 'against Thomas Delmahoy, whom the Duchess married after [the girls'] father was killed at Worcester, and who endeavours to get possession of an annuity of £500, a legacy of £1000, and some jewels left to the Duchess and her heirs, by her father, James Earl of Dirleton'.

After Countess Dirleton and Duchess Hamilton died in the summer of 1659, Lady Anne Hamilton, daughter of James, the first Duke, became duchess in her own right, wearing black from the day of his execution in 1649 until her death in 1716. She too pressed for the Maxwell jewels, particularly a 'rose with three giant diamonds and a pendant set with heavy pearls'. The Master of the Rolls responded that Maxwell did have 'a great store of rich pearls and jewels, esteemed to be the best in England', which had been either with the countess or Lady Bowyer, but that it had disappeared after Countess Dirleton's death. The countess's brother, Frederick, sought his share; Diana Cranborne fought for ten years for hers; the Goulds, mother and daughter, maids to the late countess, were still claiming in 1675. Lady Bowyer, as her mother's executor, repeated her stock defence – she had embezzled nothing, but had given the Chancery Court goods (unspecified) and securities valued at £30,000 in 1662 to realise the legacy payments: the Master denied that the jewels were among those 'goods'. Delmahoy, whose Guildford Park estate was worth £40,000, offered the Hamilton children the £1,000 bequest and the £500 annuity they claimed, but no jewels. Ann Manwood, the countess's gentlewoman, had 'a watch which was my Lady Dirleton's', and bequeathed to Lady Bowyer 'a gold diamond bodkin and chain' in her will of 1663. Maxwell had several such bodkins from the king's hoard in 1629.[5] It appears he had trained yet another daughter well.

The late duchess's sisters needed money too: Jane received little alimony from Brome; Diana Cranborne's gambling and delusions of station mired her in debt; Anne Bowyer, the practical Martha, underpinned them both, taking seriously her responsibility as executor. She was well provided for by her husband in 1652 with annuities and a manor house, despite his £2,000 fine as a Royalist, and he had been close to her stepfather Maxwell.[6]

Brome's new status at Westminster brought only limited respect. Twice he invoked Member's Privilege when stopped by night constables in 1662; two had to apologise to the House and one was dismissed, for what may have been Brome's own drunken behaviour. Sir Heneage Finch, Solicitor General and University MP, sent a half sovereign through Brome to his son Daniel at Oxford, but warned the boy against ever visiting Holton:

> He will offer you great friendship, for having a fair estate and park near Oxford he will invite you to the recreation of it, which I would not have you to consent, by no means. Receive the offer with civility, but let your tutor refuse you the liberty. He hath undertaken to carry you and the tutor to the tavern, by this you may guess at the man and the reason for my counsel.[7]

Finch, as a friend of Jane's late mother, was guarded. In 1675 Sir Edward Norreys entered the Commons for Banbury, and probably gave Brome a similar wide berth after the experience of two youthful years in France with Brome junior and tutor Joseph Williamson, who also had risen in the world to become under-secretary of state.

Brome at least had a new weapon to use against Jane. In May 1663 he tabled a private member's bill to 'vacate' the alimony awarded to her 'in the late times of Usurpation'. After second reading the bill went to committee, which reported that he had a *prima facie* case. Alimony legislation and decisions under the Commonwealth were not retrospectively validated, because they had simply been announced in 1649 without debate or vote. Within days Jane turned the weapon on him, counter-petitioning for 'Privilege of

Parliament as the wife of an MP and [she] refuses to answer'. She was exploiting a loophole, an old corrupt practice by which households and clients shared Members' Privilege, but the Parliamentary tide was turning against the abuse. The house debated her claim immediately, deciding that 'No wife or servant of any member of this House ought to have Privilege of Parliament allowed against the Husband or the Master'. In 1676 the wives of the Lords were still demanding Privilege.[8]

When 'prorogation followed so suddenly that [Brome's] Bill could not be brought in', Jane petitioned the king to hear the case. Brome agreed to 'be bound by His Majesty's determination' and the king ordered 'both parties, to appear before him at Worcester House, [with] some of the Privy Council and two of his judges'. Watching a similar feuding couple later, Charles muttered, 'better than a Play'. On 15 February 1664 Jane and Brome appeared before the king and councillors, including Archbishop Sheldon, Chancellor Hyde, Princes Rupert and James, and Sir Charles Berkeley. The emotional static of this Privy Council session was more than anything Jane, Kate and Brome could generate between them, and certainly better than many plays. Berkeley had claimed an affair with Prince James's wife Anne, Chancellor Hyde's daughter, and defamed Hyde himself to help the prince end his unhappy marriage; James's mistress, meanwhile, Anne Carnegie, née Hamilton, was Jane Whorwood's niece.

Judgement came three days later. Revenues from Sandwell Park were to be conveyed to trustees 'for payment of £300 p.a. to Mistress Whorwood … Mr Whorwood shall pay £500 in part of arrears already due …£500 more to Mistress Whorwood again on 28th August next, and security [£750] to be given now for the payment of it … Mistress Whorwood [is to] restore the cattle and other things distrained [by the sheriff at her request]'. The income would guarantee her alimony and Chancellor Hyde's cousin, Dr James Hyde, the new principal of Magdalen Hall, Oxford, with Sir William Meyrick, a church court judge, were to be its trustees.

Jane had a moral victory, and yet more prominent trustees, but still Brome did not pay. In June 1665, just before the Court fled the Great Plague, she petitioned the king again, and Charles, 'particularly sensible of the petitioner's sad and distressed condition', referred the case to Chancellor Hyde to enforce the judgements. Brome defied that too, and just before the Great Fire, Jane petitioned the king 'to appoint one more time for hearing her case that she may receive such relief as justice and His Majesty apportion'. Wearily the king agreed, to 'free himself from the further importunities of a matter that hath already been so often before him'. Hearing the couple at Whitehall on 11 August 1666, he accepted that he had omitted the sheriff's distraining costs from his previous judgement; whatever costs Jane had already paid the sheriff were not to be reimbursed her, but Brome was to pay her any outstanding balance, *which she was to pass on*, the sort of transactional loophole a Maxwell daughter would instinctively exploit. Brome's economical version of events came later:

> upon His Majesty's blessed Restoration, the Lord Chancellor [Hyde] took this matter into his hearing several times and although he declared he would never have [given such verdict himself], nor would thereafter do so, he would confirm this illegal one. The late Lord Chancellor, taking a causeless displeasure against this defendant [Brome] caused the king to rehear this case as to costs only, which upon the first hearing was discharged.

On paper in 1659 Jane's income had been respectable: alimony from Brome, and a trust fund from her mother. The alimony failed and her mother's assets evaporated. Trustees Weston and Woodford, died in 1666 and 1671; Whitelocke and Widdrington led lower profile lives after the Restoration, although Widdrington sat in the Commons with Brome. Lord Chancellor Hyde left no mention of Jane in his volumes of *The Rebellion* or in his archive, *The Clarendon Papers,* but he knew of her through his judgements, from his time in Oxford garrison, and from his cousins, Judge Thomas Hyde and Dr James Hyde, physician, who with Sir William Meyrick had all also been at Wartime Oxford. Thomas Hyde had donated over £1,000 to the king through Ashburnham's *Accompt,* and in October 1660 sat in judgement on the regicides at King's Bench. Some unknown sentiment existed between him and Jane, perhaps going back to garrison days: in composing his will in 1661 he set aside 'my India[n] gown to Mistress John [*sic*] Whorwood'; before that he had lent her £150, decreeing that 'my executor is not to expect her debt until she can pay and then I know she will do it of her own accord'.

Thirty years later, that executor, his brother, James Hyde, Regius Professor of Medicine at Oxford and Jane's surviving Sandwell trustee, still would not press for the money, even though the interest was now double the principal. James had been the only Oxford academic to refuse (rather than evade) Parliament's Protestation Oath of 1641; as physician to Charles II in exile, he travelled secretly and frequently to England in the 1650s to raise funds. In his will of 1681 he turned the debt of a sick, bankrupt seventy-year-old into a kindly fiction.

> I give the debt which Mistress Jane Whorwood (wife of Brome of Holton) owes me of about £150 principal which my brother, Dr Thomas Hyde, lent her in her distress and for which I have her bond, to be equally divided amongst my sons. If what is owing to me by bond or mortgage be not all paid and thereby the sum of two thousand pounds to be given to my children will not be raised, my will is that there be a proportional abatement in the portions of all three [sons].

He had known the 'perpetual shabbiness' of exile in Paris and Bruges, and recognised a needy fellow loyalist. The will was witnessed by John Fell, Bishop of Oxford, on whose desk also lay distress calls from Jane and her friends. At Holton, in 1684, where she may have spent her last months with her daughter, a 'calico India gown' along with 'India striped stuff and India satin' was found and inventoried.[9]

Brome's Parliamentary career spanned twenty years, thirty-one speeches and 182 committee attendances. At Oxford in 1665 the Commons sent him to the king to request an audit of army and navy spending: as in 1641, accountability was in the air. Brome was industrious in committee, enquiring into the Duke of York's finances, Sunday observance and enforcing *Common Prayer*; other targets were atheism, profanity and the price of wine. A personal interest in stopping 'artificers and mean persons' poaching his hare and deer extended to 'Quakers and Schismaticks', close cousins to poachers. Brome's sights, however, steadied on the king. He was strident in revenue committees, including during a Hearth Tax enquiry (Holton had eighteen chimneys and Sandwell seven). 'When we have raised the king's supply [of money] we may go home like fools, as we came.'

In 1666 the king postponed Parliament from February to October to prevent impeachment of his supporters. The Commons made a last plea that the Army of the Dutch War be disbanded: 'a standing army is a grievance.' Outrage, fear and the memory of 1648 drove them, but Brome still secured time to reintroduce his bill to reverse the alimony award. The second reading passed it to a committee which included the poet Andrew Marvell. They reconfirmed that Brome had a case and scheduled his hearing for 4 May 1668. Jane counterpetitioned 'hard useage', and James Cecil, her nephew, now Lord Cranborne, helped convey her petition which blocked the bill. She appeared before the Bar of the Commons on 6 May with the files from her Chancery case of 1659. Debate was arranged for Parliament's return from the summer recess, and the House adjourned. When August came the king prorogued Parliament until November, then again until March 1669 when, after a third adjournment, Parliament did not meet until 19 October 1669.

Andrew Marvell was Brome's fellow Whig, but a satirist first. He knew the Whorwood marriage was not a chivalrous episode; he had also been a tutor in Saumur in 1655 when Williamson and Brome junior were there, haunted by the nightmare parent of Holton Park. In *Last Instructions to a Painter*, one of a series of poetic parodies of Waller's panegyric *Instructions to a Painter*, he portrayed heroic MPs fighting the Dutch. Brome's heroism was his St-George-like chivalry towards a sick wife:

> *Forward Temple, Conqueror of Irish cattle, and Solicitor,*
> *…keen Whorwood next, in aid of damsel frail,*
> *That pierced the giant Mordaunt through his mail*

Brome based his claim on anti-Royalist bias in the marital judgement of 1659. 'My wife petitioned the Commissioners of the Great Seal, I being obnoxious to them for my loyalty' (on which count Jane should have been even more 'obnoxious'). 'She procured a decree in my absence that I pay her £300 p.a. from [Sandwell] while we live apart. After the Restoration, for not complying, my estate was sequestered [by the sheriff].' He claimed to have had to pay more sheriff's fees on her behalf than the king had ordered, because 'she and her agents advanced their bills to £1000'. Brome reiterated his 'loyalty both to your father and to yourself', yet his accusation that Jane was inflating the claim and the fees rang true.

The petition went to the king in August, but Jane refused to appear, despite summonses from the Lord Keeper, the Attorney General and the Solicitor General. Charles ordered the Lord Keeper to proceed as if there had been no royal hearing, 'since Mistress Whorwood has declined His Majesty's extra-judicial judgement'. He was weary of 'importunity' when neither party would accept an outcome. Charles had his own marriage problems and it was all quite near the bone. Brome was playing for time and Jane had good advisers still, including Thomas Woodford, James Hyde and surprisingly her nephew Viscount Cranborne, who that year became Earl of Salisbury. The lord keeper, chief justice and chief baron all pressed the king to reconsider, and on 20 August he agreed again to hear the case in person. Both petitioners appeared for an hour in the Red Room at Whitehall at 8 a.m. on 25 August 1669. Four days later, yet again, the original judgement was confirmed against Brome.

In May 1672, as relations between the king and his Whig Parliamentarians became more strained over religion, finance, the standing Army and the royal prerogative, Jane was summoned before the lord keeper to hear a petition from Brome demanding she return to Holton. Reconciliation would annul Brome's alimony liability, and Kate and child now lived away from Holton at Headington (Mason's) Farm. Jane was challenged 'to show why she should not be ordered by [Chancery] to return to him and cohabit, to which ... she offers to appear herself and to show reasons to the contrary'. She appeared in the Court of Arches in 1672–3, rebutted Brome's case and demanded her outstanding alimony. By January 1673, after nearly fourteen years, she had received £2,215, just 45 per cent of her dues. Some of her old witnesses – Captain Maxwell, Mary Hurles and Jane Sharpe among them – came forward again, their testimony unchanged. Brome was so much in the wrong that Lord Chancellor Shaftesbury ordered a down payment of £500, an extra £250 a quarter to cover £1,215 arrears backdated to January 1672, in addition to maintaining for life the £300 annuity awarded Jane by Chancery in 1659. Nor was Brome to invoke Member's Privilege 'to hinder Mistress Whorwood from recovery thereof'. He was not short of money, but one of few country squires to invest (£1,000) in the elite Royal African Company in 1672, along with the great lords of the Cabal and John Locke.

One of Jane's homes in London, where she had 'repaired and obscured herself', was also revealed in court, 'her home or place of usual habitation in Holborn'. Half a century later, in passing, Sir Isaac Newton jotted down another former lodging of hers, in Soho.[10]

Brome lost out on other fronts too. That year, Anthony Wood noted that Whorwood and Alderman William Wright, Oxford's other Whig MP, were 'midwives of the first [sacramental] Transubstantiation Test [to bar Catholics] … How much the gentleman burgess [Whorwood] understands, I can only guess, but I believe his brother, the alderman, cannot pronounce the word.' Wright, he added waspishly, was a keen cockfighter.[11] They were challenging the king's attempt to legislate for toleration. In July 1674 Brome had to reply to an Order of State from Sir Joseph Williamson, Secretary of State, which must have galled given his earlier contempt for tutor Williamson. He also had to 'obey' Williamson's 'command' to 'wait upon' him at Queens College, and afterwards to thank him for allowing him to do so!

Despite his Catholic grandfather, Brome was a commissioner for recusants. 'I am as tender as any man for this gentleman,' he said in debate in 1677 over a Catholic MP, 'but he is fortunate that he has escaped so long and sat here without expulsion.' In November Sir William Temple told Williamson that the Duke of Buckingham, freshly released from the Tower, had visited Oxford after hunting at Woodstock to celebrate. Oxford reciprocated with bells, cheering and outriders. After dining with the council and 'thirty others of great rank and quality', including Brome Whorwood and Sir Timothy Tyrrell of Shotover, 'he left around 7 towards London, proposing to lie at Mr Whorwood's house, four miles from here'. A month later, Diana Whorwood married Edward Master, lay Chancellor to the Exeter diocese and one of Jane's court witnesses, no doubt encouraged by Brome's promise of £5,000 on the birth of a child. The couple remained childless.[12]

Brome's tongue broke rein in May 1678. He voiced the Commons anger at the king's request for Navy funds:

We are now pushed to the point they were [at] in 1641. Everybody knows what is meant. Give money and enslave us again … these last seven years there has been no person to blame but the king. I will obey my king, but had I obeyed as some have done, I had been fitter to be sent for and hanged than have one minute in the House of Commons. I had the ill fortune in what I said in the last Parliament not to be sent to the Tower as a gentleman [here] before me would have had it. We give money now and then, go home and cool our toes. I have talked freely of this to the king. I believe he would hear me now if I went to him …

at which 'many cried out "Go! Go!"' Whorwood was a spirited stalking horse, not just in-House entertainment. Boldly he demanded the lists of those in the Crown's secret pay and service, at which three MPs escorted an unhappy official to Whitehall to retrieve the records.[13]

Brome was one of a cluster of forty-five MPs around Buckingham, and the cabal of Whig grandees who dominated Westminster. Jane's nephew, now the Earl of Salisbury, was among the lords remanded in the Tower in 1677, including Buckingham and Shaftesbury, for opposing the succession of the Catholic Prince James, Duke of York, and for insisting on an election. Parliament had been prorogued for so long, it was *de jure* dissolved. Salisbury deliberately insulted the prince by leaving Hatfield House without provisions or heat for his use on a journey north to escape hostility in London. Brome visited Shaftesbury, and presumably nephew Salisbury, in the Tower that December. Both sides smeared and pamphleteered, the king prorogued and the Whigs impeached. National paranoia peaked in 1678 when Titus Oates 'revealed' a Catholic army ready to pounce on England from the Continent, adding for good measure Jesuit commanders, a plot to kill the king, and a Papal commission, in an evocation of 1588. This time, the king was to be assassinated respectfully, with silver ammunition.

Edmund Verney reported to Sir Ralph: 'Brome Whorwood at Oxford is severe against Papists.'[14] Brome's brother Thomas, a lawyer, also published an anti-Catholic tract warning Charles against absolute rule. Oates lost credibility, but recovered it in 1683 with the news of a conspiracy to kill Charles and James near *The Rye House* inn, Hoddesdon, on their way back to London from hunting. Rumours spread that the Duke of Monmouth, the king's natural son, might head a Whig-Protestant, or even 'republican', rebellion. Alderman Wright had lodged Monmouth in his Oxford house by Canditch (Broad Street) in September 1680, and Brome was as close to Shaftesbury as a modest squire could be.

The king dissolved the Pension Parliament in January 1679; elections followed ten months later, another Parliament met, but it was dissolved in 1680. A third was elected and convened in February 1681. The king summoned it to Oxford, away from hostile London, taking Nell Gwyn and the Life Guards as his escort and entering Oxford to cheering. The same crowd cheered Monmouth and Shaftesbury. Charles proposed a regency protectorate in which William and Mary would oversee the future King James. Brome demanded that the real writers of the royal speech should spell out a cryptic allusion to 'other ways' of tackling the succession problem. Parliament refused the king's regency proposal and when Shaftesbury proposed Monmouth's succession, Charles ranted, dissolved Parliament after only seven days, and had his reasons read from every pulpit. The spectre of war threatened. When Charles sent Shaftesbury back to the Tower in June, even Prince Rupert refused to sign the warrant.

With the dissolving of the Oxford Parliament in March, Brome and Wright lost their seats. The Duke of Buckingham and Lord Lovelace had supported them in the February election, escorted by a torchlight procession across Magdalen Bridge to Carfax. They even stayed with Wright in Canditch. The crowds called for Whorwood, who with Wright had won the election with ease, although his votes had dropped by a quarter over the three elections from 1661. Anthony Wood claimed Whig MPs were out 'purposely to cross the king, raise rebellion and discord in the nation, and to vilify or make cheap the king, court and clergy, in the minds of the commons. Some of the ruder citizens cried out, heated with strong drink, "No University, No Scholars, No clergy, No Bishops".'[15] Typically, Whorwood refused to reimburse Wright his share of their February election expenses.

John Locke had a university post at Oxford and was a friend of James Tyrrell, a fellow academic whose father had land from Charles I in the royal Forest of Shotover. Locke visited Tyrrell both at Oakley and at Shotover, the eastern perimeter of which bounded Holton Park. (Sir Timothy Tyrrell was a legatee of Diana Whorwood Master's will in 1701.)

Oxfordshire Whigs in general, Whorwood and Locke in particular, came under increasing scrutiny. The Assize Court hanged a Whig joiner at Oxford Castle that summer of 1681 for alleged treason, one George Jeffreys acting as prosecuting counsel, and the Christ Church librarian spied on Locke for the Crown. When Oxford elected a Whig town clerk, a furious Lord Norreys 'fell foul' on Brome, calling him 'old knave': Brome rejoined 'young rogue'. His lordship's cane descended on Brome's head, 'with several blows' which 'broke his pate very severely, in the face of the whole crowd'. Whorwood, no longer protected as an MP, told him that if it were not for the disability of old age Norreys 'durst not so deal with him'. Norreys challenged that Brome had 'seconds young enough to revenge his quarrel [by duel], if they thought fit to undertake it, meaning Lord Lovelace, but he [Lovelace] sat very quiet'.[16] Brome, the one-time loose cannon, was ageing and isolated. Perhaps Bishop Fell felt sorry for him when he 'spoiled the sport' by reconciling the two out of court, before suit and counter-suit were to be heard at Oxford Lent Assizes in 1682. Pressure grew upon Locke, Whorwood and other Whigs.

Jane too was into the 'crooked Age' and alone. Diana Cranborne died in the summer of 1675, leaving a will so outdated that her son, Lord Salisbury, had to stand in for the long-dead executor. She left twenty shillings each to the surviving of her thirteen children, neither naming nor numbering them; she ordered a night-time funeral in private and left everything to her servant companion Sarah Gough. She went in style, dreaming of a 'fine home' in London and 'a pretty house with great gardens' at Twickenham, although a stroke had distanced her far from the bride of the Hatfield portrait. 'Having had so loud a summons from heaven,' wrote the Countess of Warwick, disapproving to the point of admiration, 'to prepare her for her dissolution, as being by palsy half dead and yet being so very vain as to play at cards and dice, and dress herself in all the most gay, fine and vain new fashions, was amazing to all who gave great pity for her and amazement at her, knowing she was only so happy as her sottish inconsideration could make her.'[17]

Before Diana's death, Lady Bowyer secured repayment – after a fight – from the East India merchants, led by Sir Nicholas Crispe, of the £4,000 which James Maxwell had deposited with the Company in 1640 against personal liability for the king's pepper debt. Through the Lords and on appeal she also retrieved £4,584 legal costs and accrued interest, but Jane was not listed among the family members who shared a windfall of £1,500 each.[18]

At Christmas 1681, just before her seventieth birthday, her hair now draining of colour, Jane approached the king with some of her old spirit. Perhaps she was feeling the death of James Hyde, her last trustee. 'Your Majesty has been twice graciously pleased to give yourself the trouble to hear the matter in difference [between Brome and me].' Six years previously the Lord Chancellor had referred her case to the Bishop of Oxford, who 'hath ever since put me off so that I am reduced to utmost extremity, even ready to starve, for I am wholly kept without any money to maintain me, both from my husband and from the said Bishop'. Secretary of State Leolin Jenkins reminded Bishop Fell 'about poor Mistress Whorwood', but to uncertain effect. Fell was a kind man, local born, and probably much 'importuned' by Jane as her only remaining trustee of any kind. He left Jane's daughter a Bible in his will of 1686, but his mind was preoccupied with rebuilding his palace at Cuddesdon, his biography of Henry Hammond and, as Wood put it, 'undertaking too many public affairs, few of which he thoroughly effected'.

'I am like to perish,' Jane pleaded, 'if Your Majesty's bowels do not turn towards me. My humble desire is that Your Majesty [command] the Bishop of Oxford ... that I may have a speedy supply, for I have not had one farthing from him for my husband, for these nine months. And what I had for those 7 years before in money or clothes amounts to but £200, whereas my alimony settled was £300 per annum.' It was not a time to bring the Whorwood name to the king's notice and she apologised for Brome's behaviour, particularly as he was then suspected of sedition.

> I beseech Your Majesty to pardon me if I say I am not able to bear my husband's reviling Your Majesty and I hope Your Majesty will graciously pardon this rude paper for I have none to help me, because my husband does so terrify and threaten all those who have formerly assisted me, so miserable is my present condition.

Consistent with the previous thirty years, Jane never cited her service to the Crown, as if governed by an unspoken etiquette. She wrote with the courtly flourish of her Wartime letters, but it was not florid. She was desperate, robbed of 90 per cent of her maintenance, and only her old confidence enabled her 'importunities'.[19]

In June 1683 the Lord Lieutenant of Oxfordshire wrote from Rycote to Secretary Jenkins:

> I have put the militia and its affairs in readiness over the [Whigs] in this county. I went myself to Oxford and sent my brother [Norreys] into the county to disarm such as I thought dangerous, Brome Whorwood [and] Alderman Wright. I did not find any considerable quantity of arms, but took away what I found. I hear that there will be a Whig meeting of Lord Lovelace and others at Burford this week [which Brome may have attended].

Lovelace was arrested in June, Lord Russell in July, and shortly afterwards Russell was executed. John Locke's rooms were searched, after 'several hand-baskets of papers' were seen being taken to his house at Oakley. Brome warned privately – he no longer had a public platform – that the king 'will bring himself to the same pass as his father before him'.[20]

Even in private Brome was not safe. On 4 September 1683, James Eustace of Islip reported hearing Brome criticise the king as they rode together. 'The old king deserved what he had and that this king deserved the same if he had his due and is not fit to govern.' John Hall, a servant at Holton, heard him say much the same, that 'Papists had the king by the nose' and the king was 'a crowned fool governed by knaves and whores'.[21] More ominously, 'This shall not last long for we have one card to play yet, the next new-raised Army officers [replacing] Papist officers [out] to cut our throats.' Brome's natural son, Thomas, had recently been commissioned and Major William was now queen's equerry. 'We'll stop their proceedings. The king is going to govern by an arbitrary power. The best part of my estate is abbey lands and he is bringing us into Popery, but I'll see him [beheaded] before I part with it.' It was wild talk and bogus history: Sandwell Benedictine Priory had been dissolved *by the Pope* in 1626, not by Henry VIII after 1534; not even Mary Tudor had taken back monastic estates from their gentry investors, despite her restoring token monastic communities. Brome's hysterical concern was vented a century and a half after the initial Reformation, a measure of the power of tidal paranoia. Predictably, they arrested him.

Jenkins was informed from Oxford on 6 September that 'Brome Whorwood has always blowed the coals of sedition in Oxford. He is now in custody [Oxford Castle] … Alderman Wright is also bound over to the next Assizes … great encouragement to the loyal here and a fright to all the others.' John Locke fled from Oxford to Amsterdam that day and Brome was ordered to appear with Wright before the Court of King's Bench in London in April 1684.

Jane lost her last sister in 1683. Lady Anne Bowyer, then living in St Margaret's Westminster, left everything to her servant Alice Beaven, also her executrix; Sarah Gough, the servant to whom Diana Cecil had left everything in 1675, witnessed Anne's will.[22] It was the last sisterly snub, with the servants in tow. Two days after Anne's death, her 'natural sister Jane Whorwood' contested the will in the Prerogative Court of Canterbury on the grounds that 'Anne Bowyer was not *compos mentis*', but the Court confirmed the will. Jane's reaction may have been obsessive, but her total exclusion by her sisters was extreme. Understandably, but forlornly, she contested Brome's will too.

George Jeffreys became Lord Chief Justice in September 1683, a 'severe' appointee to frighten Whigs and calm a climate reminiscent of 1642. Whorwood and Wright were charged with 'seditious libel' and 'treasonable words', and Jeffreys would hear their case in April 1684. Anthony Wood, as a Tory might, damned them as 'two clownish and ill natured persons'. The wave of emotion after the *Rye House* Plot was enough to carry away anyone of any age or class; even Richard Cromwell in secluded retirement became suspect. In the great 'pinching frost' of January 1684, when a Frost Fair ran for two months on the Thames ice, Brome felt his failing health and the pressure. He petitioned against being prosecuted 'on malicious accusation by two servants … [for] a royalist and sufferer for the cause 'tis very grievous with one foot in the grave to be blemished with the crime of disloyalty'. The king rejected his plea. Brome came to London with Kate Allen to lodge in Old Palace Yard and to attend the funeral of Major William, who died on 1 April. Brome followed him a fortnight later, aged sixty-nine. 'Brome came here to prepare for his trial and I hear died suddenly from an apoplexy [stroke], but can't hear how he hath settled his estate.' Twelve days later Brome's body was buried at Holton in a funeral organised by Kate. Their son, Thomas, a cavalry officer, would have attended, as would Diana and Edward Master, Kate herself and tenants, but Jane was probably absent. Kate was with Brome when he died and accused Diana, Edward – and Jane for good measure – of 'possessing themselves at Holton House of gold, silver and divers jewels of the deceased while she was at London concerned in providing the conveniences for the interment of Brome Whorwood'.[23]

On 16 April, in the partitioned corner of Westminster Hall which was the Court of King's Bench, Judge Jeffreys demanded sworn evidence of Brome's death. Alderman Wright entered the dock alone and broken, to plead not guilty to 'publishing seditious libels'. Jeffreys, only briefly at Cambridge, asked sarcastically whether Wright's publications were typical of the level of intelligence at Oxford. Wright, a goldsmith, was 'never guilty of learning' or of repartee, and Jeffreys harried him as a 'pitiful and mechanickal [tradesman] rascal pretending to mend the government'. He reminded him explicitly of the strength of judicial rope. Bail was set at an impossible £20,000, of which half was raised. Wright cooled his heels in King's Bench prison for four days and was then freed on the raised half. Back in Oxford, he resigned everything, pleading infirmity – 'my time being not long in this world' (he lived until 1693) – and begging the king for a 'private and retired life'. Charles agreed, not to a pardon, but 'to stop further proceedings for the present'.[24] Brome, as a prominent shire gentleman with a record of vocal opposition in the Commons, would have been less leniently treated had he lived.

Brome willed 'use of all my goods at Holton during their lives' to Diana and her husband Edward. 'From their decease' everything was to pass to his and Kate's son, 'Thomas Brome Whorwood whom I require to be called Whorwood'. He acknowledged several decades with Kate: 'all my goods and everything on the lands at Headington Farm house to my trusty and careful good servant Mary Katherine Allen.' Diana's husband and Kate as executors were to divide 'the rest and chattels between them'. Jane was not mentioned, but before Brome was buried, she challenged the will and Kate's role in it. The Prerogative Court found against her in June declaring Brome to be *compos mentis* and his will valid. Jane may have hoped for the outstanding alimony, or for some last-minute gesture. It was followed by sworn inventories, and suit and countersuit between the Masters and Kate in which each alleged theft by the other(s) of Brome's goods by 'contraction and confederacy'.[25] Kate declared plate and linen from Sandwell, cattle and plate from Headington, and a Bible with two Shakespeare portfolios. Daniel Porter, Oxford pawnbroker, held some silver. The Red Trunk depository of heirlooms and War mementos was still at Queens College. Mary Katherine Allen died in 1697, aged seventy-one, in comfort in a fine house at Tackley.[26]

The contents of Brome's houses at Holton and Headington (Sandwell was tenanted, some of its revenue in trust for Jane) were inventoried. His loose coin, jewels, plate, books, furniture, bonds, credits, rents, cattle, implements and grain in Holton came to £4,735, excluding the personal possessions of Diana and Jane, and the Sandwell and Holton houses and estates. Bodley's librarian catalogued 100 volumes from grandfather George Brome's study.

Jane died aged seventy-two in September 1684, one of an estimated ten per cent of England's population to reach Biblical old age. She may have spent the final summer months at Holton with Diana, who administered her estate worth £40.[27] The boxed emerald and diamond ring in Mr Pokins' custody, the four other rings, the Wartime mementos and 'a box lined in sky blue silk said to belong to Mistress Whorwood' in Kate Allen's old room, did not reappear in any later record. Jane's grave was dug in the chancel of St Bartholomew's, Holton, near that of Brome, and Rector William Master, Diana's brother-in-law, led the funeral on 20 September, two days short of Jane's fiftieth wedding anniversary. Her married lot was to produce Whorwoods and be buried with them. Diana, her remaining family, would have presided as chief mourner in the manor pew. The Passing Bell tolled its knell of six strokes customary for a woman's funeral, perhaps appropriately, this royal agent's only public salute.

It was William Master's third parish funeral since ordination. 'A poor traveller' was buried anonymously between Brome's funeral in April and Jane's burial in September. Katherine Allen would hardly have attended Jane's burial, filtered out by the hierarchy of pews and the harsh exchanges in the weeks after Brome's death. Diana had no children of her own, but Elizabeth Eales, the daughter of Alban Eales, had become her gentlewoman companion since the former rector's death in 1670. Diana and her mother had found support and shelter at Holton Rectory. Born just after the Restoration, the rector's daughter was the nearest Diana came to her own child, or a younger sister.

Undoubtably 'cousin' Thomas came to the funeral. In 1686 he named his first child Jane after his wife, happy in the process to continue the name of his father's abused wife. William Pokins, 'old, weak, but of sound mind' according to his will of 1696, would have been at the funeral, the butler loyal to Jane and her daughter. Doctor Lamphire who had tended Jane's injuries may have come, along with Edward Stampe, the old lawyer who had given her asylum and convalescence. It was bound to be an elderly congregation. Jane's bloodline ended with Diana's death in 1701 and Bowyers from her late aunt, Lady Anne's family, oversaw Diana's will. The Whorwood name and estates passed to 'cousin' Thomas's line. Kate Allen was buried in Holton chancel in 1697.

Few co-conspirators from Wartime were alive to notice Jane's death. Poverty and isolation reduced her to childlike pleading with a king who either did not know, or preferred to forget that his father had once importuned her in a similar isolation. In the summer of her death the great and the good – the second Earl of Clarendon and Archbishop Sancroft – began to enquire about Jane's and others' role in Charles I's final years. By then, Dugdale's sources and memory were suspect or failing, most witnesses were dead, Jane was stilled and no one asked again for many years.[28]

Notes

1. HCJ, VIII, 29 December 1660, 234, 238–43; *Cal Treasury Books 1660–7*, I, 62, 19 September 1660; CSP, 1660–1, 122, 136, Nicholas Crispe petitioning £30,000 'debts of the late king'; William Foster, 'Charles I and The East India Company', *English Historical Review*, XIX, July 1904, 461–2; Canterbury Cathedral Archives DCc/Carta Antiqua z 15; Lambeth Palace Library, VB1/1; Cordell Firebrace, *Honest Harry* (1932), 196–219, on the rewards for loyalists in 1660, admitting that he could find no mention of any recognition for Jane Whorwood.

2. TNA C3/467/115, Brome Whorwood before Chancery, May 1658.

3. TNA C3/467/114, Brome Whorwood before Chancery, February 1659.

4. Anthony Wood, *Life and Times of Anthony Wood*, I, 399 (ed. Clark, 1891; Anthony Wood, *City of Oxford*, III, 54–5 (ed. Clark, 1899); Herbert Salter, *Oxford City Council Acts* (1933), II, 116, 119, 281, 303, 431; Basil Henning, *History of Parliament, Commons 1660–90*, III, 714–16, on Brome Whorwood, and ibid. 768 on William Wright who 'made no recorded speeches'.

5. CSP 1653–4, LXV, 21; CSP 1654, LXVIII, 37; LXIX, 12; CSP 1656, CXXX, 104–7; Elizabeth Hamilton's will, TNA PROB 11/308, proved 1662, six years after composition and three years after her death, due to the disputes; TNA SP 29, XXII, 561, November 1660; Ann Manwood's will, TNA PROB 11/312, 1663; Rosalind Marshall, *The Days of Duchess Anne* (1973), 14–37; Pepys thought Delmahoy, William Hamilton's gentleman of horse, 'a very fine man', and Burnett thought him 'genteel and generous'; British Library, Add Ms 35125, f. 208; Harry Pitman, 'Delmahoy vs Direlton, An Old Chancery Suit', *Scottish History Review*, XXIII, July 1926, 268–74; Delmahoy became MP for Guildford and sold the park in 1681; TNA Chancery case C10/75/48, January 1664, merchants still seeking Maxwell's posthumous liability for the pepper debt.

6. TNA PROB 11/221; Robert Brenner, *Merchants and Revolution* (2003), 71n, 72n, 295, 375n.

7. HCJ, VIII, 389, 19 March 1662; HMC 71, Finch Mss, I, 1913, 208–9.

8. Parliamentary Records, Bray Ms 9, 84–6; TNA SP, 1663, 474, 488; 1664–5, XCII, 64; XCIII; CXXV 29 June; 1666–7, 10, 29; CLXVI, 11 August and related Entry Books are sources for the Whorwood alimony saga, in addition to the case papers in Lambeth Palace Library, Court of Arches Case 9938, *Whorwood vs Whorwood*, particularly the witness evidence in E5/29, and Jane and others' signed evidence in E4/101ff. *The Parliamentary History of England*, ed. William Cobbett, 1808, contains Whorwood's speeches; the House of Commons Journal (HCJ) and Basil Henning, *The History of Parliament, Commons III, 1660–90* (1983), provide chronology, context and biographical detail.

9. Thomas Hyde's will, TNA PROB 11/306, 1661; for the Sandwell estate revenue, Staffordshire Record Office, D 564/S/1/1. The 'gowne' may have been an Indian version of a kimono, a banyan, chaga or dhoti, an open-fronted gown worn by oriental royalty, a unisex wrap or sari, in effect a dressing gown for added warmth. The East India Company imported such garments in bulk; for the Indian cloths at Holton House, see Inventory 1684, TNA PROB/5275, 114461; James Hyde's will, TNA PROB 11/366, 1681.

10. Kenneth Davies, *Royal African Company* (1957), 66. For Jane's residences, see Lambeth Palace Archives, *op.cit.*, A 10, 123, March 1673 for 'her home or her place of usual habitation within the parish of St Andrew Holborn'; Sir Isaac Newton later jotted a note about 'Lady Warwood [*sic*] in King Street, Soho, lived with Mr Hunter [a Scot], friend to Lord Osborne, whose lady can give a character', *verso* jotting, NC4, 510–12, 445v, Mint 000395. Lord Osborne lived in King Square in 1683. Lady Osborne lived at 10–11 Leicester Street in 1717–19, when Newton lived at 35 St Martin's Street. Brome accused Jane of 'obscuring herself in the City of London'.

11. Anthony Wood, *Life and Times of Anthony Wood*, II, 256, 439 (ed. Clark, 1892).

12. Wood, *op.cit.*, 476, 522; Mary Hobson, *Oxford Council Acts, 1665–1701* (1939), 102–5.

13. SO, 7 May 1678, CSP 1678 addenda, 1674–9.

14. Bodleian Library, Claydon House Mss 7, 476, App., 6 October 1679; Thomas Whorwood, *Argumentum ad Hominem ...that Papists may not be saved* (1679).

15. Wood, *Life and Times*, II, 519, 522–3 (ed. Clark, 1892).

16. TNA SP, 1680–1, 417, 421, 4 August 1681.

17. Dirleton Castle was given by the Scots Parliament to Lord Nisbet, although Maxwell had bequeathed it to James, Diana Cranborne's son, who on his father's death in 1660 became Lord Cranborne. Diana Cranborne's will, TNA PROB 11/348, 1675; *Survey of London* (1963), St James Westminster, Part II, 443, 551; HMC Report 7, 738, Lord Ossory to Marquis of Ormonde; Charlotte Fell Smith, *Mary Rich, Countess of Warwick* (1901), 335.

18. On Bowyer and Cranborne vs Crispe, HLJ, XII, 682, 19 April, and 709, 28 May 1675; HL Mss Braye 57, 74–5; CSP 1682, 617.

19. TNA SP, 1682, 421, No. 213.

20. TNA SP, 1683, 431, 89 (I) and 111, 353, 363–4, 370 and July – September 1683; Maurice Cranston, *John Locke* (1957), 199, 228, 466.

21. TNA SP 19: 103, 166–7, also CCC, III 1813; Peter Barwick, *Life of Dr John Barwick* (1724), appendix, 395, also calls her 'wife of Brome Whorwood'.

22. TNA PROB 11/374 and *Sententia*, Lady Anne Bowyer's will.

23. CSP 1683–4, 251; Wood, *Life and Times*, III, 91, 1682–95, 86–94 (ed. Clark, 1894); Bodleian Library, Claydon House Ms, 7, 499, letter from Sir H. Verney, 17 April 1684; *The Newsletter*, 17 April 1684; Wood, *op.cit.*, 93; Holton Church Register, Brome's burial, 24 April 1684, 'about 69'; Anthony Wood, *Fasti*, I, 25, (1721); TNA PROB 28/387/114461, Master vs Allen, 19 April 1684; PROB 5/5275/114461, Master vs Allen; Wood, *op.cit.*, II, 522–3.

24. Wood, *op.cit.*, III, 91, 93–4 (Wright before Judge Jeffreys). No record appears in *State Trials* since no actual trial took place. TNA SP 1684, 438, Nos 58, 76, 8 November 1684; Brome's will, TNA PROB 11/378 (1684).

25. TNA PROB 4/12076 signed by Katherine Allen, August 1684; TNA PROB 28/387/114461, 21 February 1685, Master vs Allen, where both sides refused to accept inventories of Brome's wealth; TNA PROB 4/12076, Inventory of Brome's goods left with Katherine Allen.

26. TNA E 134 2Jas2 Mich 9; C9/115/1, Master vs Katherine Allen and Thomas Allen *alias* Whorwood, October 1686; Kate's will, TNA PROB 11/439 (1697).

27. TNA PROB 6/59, Jana Whorwood, 'late of Sandwell Hall', Letters of Administration to Diana Master, her daughter, November 1684: Inventory valuation £40; Diana Master's will, TNA PROB 11/460 (1701).

28. William Pokins' will, TNA PROB 11/445 (1698); Holton House Inventory of contents, TNA PROB 5/5275 114461 (1684).

Index